The Alchemy of Intuition

Embodied Practices to Access Your Inner Voice

DR. TIFFANY MCBRIDE

Featuring: Caroline Arco • Morgan Costley • Laura Di Franco
Susan L. Ernst • Christine Falcon-Daigle • Teri Freesmeyer
Dustin Graham • Susan C. Jensen • Rachel Kaufman
Marta Kowalska • Jayme Lynn • Vanessa Pacheco
Natalie V. Petersen • Keady Phelan • Dr. Ruth A. Souther
Jennifer K. Sproul • Michele Tatos
Becky Wheeler • Beth Wilson

"You belong here, and your healing journey is honored. That message echoes throughout *The Alchemy of Intuition*. This book celebrates the beautiful, courageous process of remembering who you are—for anyone who has felt different, misplaced, or knew there had to be more than pain. Part mirror, part map, it guides you back to your intuition and inner knowing. This is your book, your community, and your permission to be yourself."

~Leah Johnson, Bestselling Author of *Finding Fantastic Joy*, TEDx Speaker, The Courage to Quit

* * *

"*The Alchemy of Intuition* is a love letter to your own knowing, a soul-whisper calling you to awaken. Through stories threaded with ritual, challenge, magic, and becoming, Tiffany McBride invites you to feel deeply, trust fiercely, and honor the quiet wisdom within. This book is a doorway—into courage, into clarity, and into the tender, untamed power of your intuition remembered. Trust it. Live it. Let it guide you!"

~Julianne Santini, Muse, Mother, and Mystic Guide to the Inner Journey, Bestselling Author of *Love Initiation: Learning the Language of Soul*

* * *

"*The Alchemy of Intuition* is one of those books you feel more than read. It's grounded, embodied, and refreshingly honest about what intuition actually is. Not fluff. Not bypassing. Real lived experience woven through psychology, the body, ancestry, and spiritual practice. Each chapter feels like it comes from someone who has done the work, not just studied it. This book is for intuitive people who want depth without dogma and connection without performance. I walked away feeling more rooted in myself, not more "woo." And that's the kind of alchemy that actually lasts."

~Candice Parisi, Professional Intuitive Counselor

* * *

"This book is like having a room full of wise aunts (and an uncle), openly and honestly sharing their personal vulnerabilities, wisdom, and practices that led them to their most profound truths. They are sharing the most amazing stories of personal transformation—these authors offer truth bombs and give you tools to incorporate into your personal practice.

I had the great opportunity to read this book, and once I started, I devoured it in a day. Yet weeks later, I find myself still reflecting on it and using the prompts, rituals, and magic the authors provided. What a gift! I found it to be a heartfelt guide on connecting with and harnessing intuition for true positive transformation."

~Mary Verzani-Dunlap, Prairie Witch

The Alchemy of Intuition
Embodied Practices to Access Your Inner Voice
©Copyright 2026 Dr. Tiffany McBride
Published by Brave Healer Productions
Cover artwork and design by Dr. Tiffany McBride
Book Interior design and formatting by K.J. Kaschula
Paperback ISBN: 978-1-969999-01-7

eBook ISBN: 978-1-969999-02-4

The Alchemy of Intuition

Embodied Practices to Access Your Inner Voice

DR. TIFFANY MCBRIDE

Featuring: Caroline Arco • Morgan Costley • Laura Di Franco
Susan L. Ernst • Christine Falcon-Daigle • Teri Freesmeyer
Dustin Graham • Susan C. Jensen • Rachel Kaufman
Marta Kowalska • Jayme Lynn • Vanessa Pacheco
Natalie V. Petersen • Keady Phelan • Dr. Ruth A. Souther
Jennifer K. Sproul • Michele Tatos
Becky Wheeler • Beth Wilson

Stay connected for upcoming events, classes, and offerings.
https://www.themysticmuse.org/newsletter

DEDICATION

This book is dedicated to all of my teachers, those who walked beside me in love and those who challenged me in pain. Each of you has been a mirror, reflecting the parts of myself I had forgotten, denied, or disowned. You came into my life in the form of family, lovers, friends, mentors, strangers, and even the spirits who whispered through the veil. Whether through tenderness or heartbreak, you each offered me a lesson that shaped my becoming.

To the ones who lifted me, thank you for reminding me what it feels like to be seen, supported, and celebrated.

To the ones who hurt me, thank you for showing me the boundaries of my own worth and the necessity of forgiveness.

To the silent teachers, the dreams, the losses, the long nights of unknowing, thank you for carving depth into my soul.

Every lesson has been a thread leading me home to myself.

Through your reflections, I learned to listen to the voice within, the one that had been waiting all along beneath the noise, the fear, and the striving. I realized that love is not something to be earned, but something I already am.

This book is for every soul walking their own spiral path toward wholeness, learning, as I have, that even the hardest lessons are sacred.

When you learn to listen to your inner voice, you reclaim your power.

When you trust it, you become the alchemist of your own life.

DISCLAIMER

This book is designed to provide competent, reliable, and educational information on mind, body, and spiritual health and wellness, as well as other related subject matter. However, it is sold with the understanding that the authors and publisher specifically disclaim all responsibility for any liability, loss, or risk, personal or otherwise, incurred as a consequence, directly or indirectly, of the use and application of any of the contents of this publication.

In order to maintain the anonymity of others, the names and identifying characteristics of some people, places, and organizations described in this book have been changed.

This publication contains content that may be potentially triggering or disturbing. Individuals who are sensitive to certain themes are advised to exercise caution while reading.

The opinions, ideas, and recommendations contained in this publication do not necessarily represent those of the publisher. The use of any information provided in this book is solely at your own risk.

Our authors represent cultures worldwide, and as such, there may be differences in language and expressions. As a global publisher, we have made the conscious choice not to edit these nuances, so each chapter is authentic and in its author's words.

Know that the experts here have shared their tools, practices, and knowledge with you with a sincere and generous intent to assist you on your personal journey. Please contact them with any questions you may have about the techniques or information they provided. They will be happy to assist you further and be an ongoing resource for your success!

Foreword
By Rev. Dr. Ahriana Platten

Freedom is my North Star. Not the kind that can be granted or taken away, but the kind that rises from experience and lights the hidden corridors of the soul. True freedom begins in the moment we stop abandoning what we already know. It's found in the breath that expands when we stop shrinking to fit someone else's version of truth.

For as long as I can remember, I've pursued freedom in all its applications. The freedom to think for myself, to feel deeply, and to trust my inner knowing has become the heartbeat of a fully lived life. Too often the world teaches us to override that inner compass. We're trained to seek approval, to temper our instincts, and to assume that someone outside of us holds the map to our future. Over time, and under the influence of a critical world, the sound of our own wisdom fades

The "Alchemy of Intuition" calls that wisdom back to the surface. It's written by people who've faced the world's criticism and dared to listen inward anyway. Their words carry the grounded honesty that only comes from weathering storms and choosing truth over comfort. They listened, they risked, they wrote from the quiet place where Spirit speaks in its real voice.

I wasn't with them in Ireland, but I know the land they walked. A year before their journey, I wandered those same hills and discovered how easily the veil thins there. Ireland breathes memory through stone and water. The land remembers what many of us have forgotten. Those who walk its ancient paths often find that their own voices begin to reflect the voices of the land. Something in the wind invites hope and laughter. Something about the soil inspires stability and peace. The writers who gathered there didn't simply study the landscape. They immersed themselves in it.

Their stories are not polished performances. They're echoes of something ancient. They're reminders of the moment fear loses its dominance and intuition steps to the front. Each story reveals a threshold crossed, a truth reclaimed, a piece of inner authority returning to its rightful throne. Intuition isn't fragile or ethereal. It's direct and steady. It's the pulse of the heart that has waited patiently for us to listen.

Fear has long been used as a tool of control. It tells us that belonging requires silence, that safety lives in conformity, and uncertainty should be feared. Intuition speaks a different language. It invites us to remember that we were born to feel, to sense, to choose. It asks us to stop outsourcing our authority and to honor the indwelling wisdom that needs no external confirmation.

Trust in this alchemy. Pass through the doorway that leads to freedom as a lived reality rather than a concept.

The writers of this collection offer proof that intuition can be embodied and that guidance expresses itself as naturally and reliably as breath fills our lungs. They remind us that inner knowing doesn't always arrive with trumpets. Sometimes it arrives as a soft shift in the chest, a warm recognition, or a sudden sense of alignment.

Reading this book feels a bit like standing in a circle of wise companions who all resonate with the same simple truth: what you need exists within you. These pages invite you to release the belief that you're lost. They show you that wisdom never disappears. It waits. It watches. It rises the moment you turn inward to greet it.

As you move through these chapters, notice what stirs. Notice what softens. Notice the places in you that feel strangely familiar. That sensation is the recognition of your own intuition shaking itself awake.

Let this book accompany you as you return to your inner knowing. Let it encourage you to listen even when you doubt, to trust even when the path is dim, to speak even when your voice trembles. Let it remind you that freedom begins not at the edge of the world but at the edge of your own willingness to believe yourself.

This path is not always gentle. It will ask you to shed illusions and call up courage you may not realize you possess. On the other side of that shedding is something unshakable. There waits the freedom of authenticity. There waits the sovereignty of a soul that no longer bargains with its own truth.

May these words be a mirror, revealing the depth of your wisdom. May they fully awaken the part of you that never stopped knowing. May they guide you back to the deep well of intuition that has always lived inside you.

Trust your inner guidance. It's the voice of your soul.

Rev. Dr. Ahriana Platten

Bestselling Author of *Sacred Menopause: A Woman's Guide to Sovereignty* and *Rites and Rituals: Harnessing the Power of Sacred Ceremony*

Table of Contents

Introduction

Life can be full of unknowns and darkness, often leaving us feeling lost or disconnected from our true selves. Many of us have been brainwashed, indoctrinated, and taught to follow systems established long before us; systems that prioritize conformity over individuality, logic over intuition, and fear over trust. From an early age, we're conditioned to conform to societal expectations, learning to silence our inner voices in favor of external demands.

Yet beneath these layers of conditioning lies an ancient wisdom—an innate knowing that whispers to us in moments of stillness: *Remember who you are!* The challenge isn't only to recognize these influences but to consciously unlearn them, to break free from the narratives imposed upon us, and to embark on a journey of self-discovery and healing.

Embracing the unknown can be daunting, but it's also where transformation begins. In the darkness, we find our light, and in the uncertainty, we uncover our true path. By daring to question, explore, and trust our intuition, we reclaim our power and step into a life of authenticity and purpose, one that isn't dictated by the status quo but shaped by our most profound truths.

* * *

Throughout my life, I've been told how to be and what to be, especially as an independent, educated, and childless woman in the United States. I'm the witchy, unconventional, queer, autistic, ADHD, weirdo type. A rebel with a sweet streak, expressed through my unique style, passion for the Earth and humanity, and a touch of magic and love in everything I do. The messages came from every direction—family, school, religion, and culture—each one shaping me into something that felt safer and more acceptable, but ultimately, not me.

I was a loud rebel as a pre-teen, unapologetically expressing myself, but that fire was easily bullied out of me. My woman-hating stepfather made sure of that, chipping away at my confidence with every degrading word and oppressive rule. At twelve years old, I was uprooted from the city to a small town, across the country, where I didn't fit in, and I was bullied into submission. My vibrant parts were slowly silenced, piece by piece, until I found myself surrendering to the need for survival.

In that desperate need to belong, I became a religious person, not necessarily because I believed, but because it offered me a place to fall in line, be accepted, and quiet the internal war between who I was and who I was told I should be. Christianity became a shield, a way to hide from judgment and the fear of rejection. I buried my weirdness under prayers and rules, convincing myself that if I followed the right path, I could finally be loved and good enough. But deep inside, there was always a quiet voice—a subtle ache—that reminded me I was betraying something sacred within me.

Despite the illusion of acceptance, I couldn't shake the feeling that I lived a life designed by others. This life suffocated the real me. It wasn't until much later that I realized the systems I placed my faith in were never built to nurture my authenticity; they were built to keep me small, quiet, and obedient. The journey back to myself has been messy and painful; unraveling years of conditioning, facing the wounds of my past, and learning to embrace the parts of me that I was taught to reject.

I left the church when I was 26 after spending five years as a pastor's wife and worship song leader. I devoted myself to a life that, on the surface, appeared fulfilling—serving, leading, and following the path I was taught was right. But deep down, I felt a growing emptiness, a quiet knowing that there was so much more beyond the confines of what I was taught. The questions I had buried for years—about myself, the universe, and what truly made my soul come alive—could no longer be ignored. So, I set out to find what truly resonated with me.

Now, I stand at the crossroads of who I was told to be and who I genuinely am, reclaiming my voice, truth, and power. The rebel in me never died; she was waiting for me to be ready to set her free again.

* * *

That rebellion eventually became my best teacher, pushing me to seek understanding, not only of myself but of the human mind.

I majored in psychology, became a licensed clinical therapist, and eventually became a doctor. My pursuit of this path didn't just come from a desire to help others; it was deeply rooted in my own need to understand why I never felt okay, why I always carried a sense of not quite belonging, and why the world around me often felt like it didn't make sense. I searched for answers, healing, and a way to bridge the gap between the external expectations placed upon me and the internal reality I struggled to reconcile.

One of my greatest teachers along this journey was Carl Jung. His work captivated me in a way nothing else had.

Carl Gustav Jung (1875–1961) was a Swiss psychiatrist and psychoanalyst who founded analytical psychology. A pioneering thinker, Jung explored the depths of the unconscious mind, introducing concepts such as archetypes, the collective unconscious, shadow work, and individuation. His work bridged psychology, spirituality, mythology, and alchemy—offering a framework for understanding the human soul's journey toward wholeness.

Jung's exploration of the unconscious mind, archetypes, and the individuation process resonated deeply with my experiences. His understanding of non-ordinary states of consciousness—those realms beyond the waking, rational mind—permitted me to explore the dreams, visions, and synchronicities that followed me throughout my life. His concept of synchronicity—the meaningful coincidences that seem to guide us with an unseen hand—spoke to the strange and magical experiences I could no longer ignore.

Jung's work helped me realize that the subconscious isn't just a shadowy realm of suppressed thoughts and fears; it's a vast landscape of wisdom, creativity, and connection to something greater than ourselves. He taught me that the psyche communicates through symbols, dreams, and patterns, and that healing comes not from suppressing these elements, but from embracing them. This understanding shifted my entire approach, not just to psychology, but to life. It made me realize that healing isn't just about fixing what's "wrong" with us but about integrating all parts of ourselves, even those we've been taught to hide.

One of Jung's most profound contributions to my journey was his concept of psychological alchemy, the transformation of the Self through profound inner work, much like the ancient alchemists who sought to transmute lead into gold. Jung believed that our personal struggles, traumas, and unconscious fears were the raw materials for transformation. Through introspection, shadow work, and a deep relationship with the subconscious, we can transmute our inner "lead" into the "gold" of self-awareness, empowerment, and wholeness. This concept of alchemy resonated with me because it mirrored my own process of healing—taking the painful, fragmented parts of myself and, through self-inquiry and intuition, transforming them into strength and wisdom.

Alchemy, as Jung described it, is an intuitive process. It requires us to trust in the unseen forces at play within our psyche, listen deeply to the symbols and messages that arise, and surrender to the unfolding of our inner journey. It taught me that transformation isn't a linear path but a spiral—the ongoing process of deepening, refining, and becoming.

Through Jung's teachings, I began to view my own journey in a new light. My struggles with identity, my experiences of feeling out of place, and my lifelong questioning of reality weren't signs of brokenness but invitations to more profound self-discovery. I began to realize that the answers I sought weren't outside of me; they were within, waiting to be uncovered through subconscious language, the whispers of intuition, and the courage to step beyond the ordinary into the unknown.

Through Jung, the boundary between science and spirit began to dissolve for me. Psychology became a bridge, a sacred meeting point where the analytical and the mystical could coexist. It was this realization that opened the door to alternative healing.

* * *

I explored practices I once dismissed or viewed skeptically—divination, meditation, plant medicine, energy healing, crystals, essential oils, etc.—each offering glimpses into a different way of being and a deeper connection to myself and the world around me. These modalities helped me begin to peel back the layers of conditioning and see that wellness was more than just physical health; it was about nurturing my mind, body, and spirit as one.

But my first energy Reiki session was the moment that truly changed everything, cracked me wide open, and tapped me into my intuition in a way I never experienced before.

From there, I found myself on a fast track to reopening my psychic abilities, the ones I buried long ago. As a child, I always felt things others didn't, heard whispers from spirits, and sensed energies that made me feel different and, at times, afraid. I lay under my blankets, singing in the dark, hoping the voices and presence would disappear. The fear eventually led me to shut it all down when I was 13, convincing myself that ignoring it was the only way to feel safe and normal.

With each new step into my healing journey, those abilities began to resurface. I started seeing and hearing spirits again, feeling their presence in a way I could no longer deny. Instead of fear, I felt a deep curiosity stirring within me—a profound understanding that these experiences weren't meant to haunt me but to guide me. I was led to a psychic development class, which became a turning point in my life. Through the exercises and teachings, I understood that my abilities weren't something to fear; they were gifts waiting to be reclaimed.

As I delved deeper, meditation became a powerful tool that connected me to something greater than myself. Through stillness and deep listening, I met my spirit guides for the first time; their loving presence had been with me all along, waiting for me to remember them. Everything shifted at that moment. The world I thought I knew expanded beyond anything I had imagined, and I realized that intuition was more than just a feeling; it was a language—a bridge between my soul and the unseen forces guiding my journey.

Spirit guides are benevolent, non-physical beings of light and wisdom who assist us on our soul's journey. They can appear in many forms— ancestors, angels, animal spirits, ascended masters, or archetypal presences that speak through symbols and synchronicities. While their expressions differ across cultures, their essence is universal: they are helpers from the unseen realms who guide, protect, and teach. Connecting with our guides is not about giving away our power—it's about remembering that we are never truly alone and that the universe communicates through intuition, dreams, and the subtle language of the soul.

Listening to my intuition and guides became the foundation of my path. The more I trusted it, the more doors opened, leading me to possibilities I never considered. I no longer sought answers outside myself; I created my own way, embracing the uniqueness of my gifts and learning to walk a path that honored who I was. Since then, I've been forging my own unique journey, guided by the wisdom within and the unseen forces that walk beside me.

* * *

All of these experiences—psychological, spiritual, and energetic—culminated in a deeper understanding of non-ordinary states of consciousness as the true meeting point between healing and embodiment.

For the past decade, I've trained in and utilized modalities of non-ordinary states of consciousness in both my professional practice and my personal healing journey. These aren't abstract spiritual experiences; they're deeply embodied ways of knowing.

Non-ordinary states of consciousness are altered states that expand our awareness beyond the limitations of the everyday thinking mind. These states can be accessed through practices such as meditation, breathwork, trance, dreaming, dance, drumming, or psychedelic experiences. Within them, we enter the symbolic, imaginal realms where intuition, memory, and spirit converge. Shamans, mystics, and healers have long used these states to receive guidance, retrieve lost parts of the soul, and commune with the divine. In modern psychology, they're seen as gateways to deeper healing and integration—where the unconscious can speak, and the sacred becomes experiential.

When we enter these altered states, we shift the brain's ordinary patterns and awaken the body's innate intelligence. In these moments, the body becomes the instrument of intuition; it speaks in sensations, visions, emotions, and images that reveal what the rational mind cannot grasp.

Through this embodied dialogue with the subconscious, I witnessed profound transformation, an unraveling of old patterns, and the emergence of clarity, peace, and purpose. Non-ordinary states invite us to remember that intuition isn't something we think our way toward; it's something we feel and become. This is the essence of the medicine in this book: an invitation to experience intuition not as a fleeting insight but as a living, breathing presence within the body. This compass aligns us with the wisdom of our soul and the consciousness of the earth itself.

* * *

The reason I want to write this book is simple: I want people to be free. I want them to know that they hold sovereignty within themselves, that their power, truth, and healing are already inside them, waiting to be uncovered. Too often, we're conditioned to seek validation and guidance outside of ourselves, taught to silence our inner knowing in favor of societal expectations and fear-based narratives.

However, the truth is that we all possess an innate ability to listen to our intuition, trust ourselves, and navigate life with confidence and authenticity. I want people to stop being afraid. Fear has been a control tool for far too long, keeping us small, compliant, and disconnected from our true essence. The journey to empowerment begins with understanding the difference between fear and intuition and learning which voice to trust and which to release.

* * *

Intuition is the voice of the soul, the knowing that arises without logic or proof. It's the quiet pulse of wisdom that lives beneath the noise of the mind, the whisper that says this way when nothing makes sense. Intuition doesn't argue or explain; it simply knows.

In Jungian psychology, intuition is one of the four primary functions of consciousness, alongside thinking, feeling, and sensation. Where the mind analyzes and the senses perceive, intuition sees through things. It perceives patterns, potential, and meaning. It's the bridge between the conscious and unconscious mind, between human awareness and the divine field that connects all things.

Yet, the most significant barrier to intuition is fear, and the two can feel deceptively similar. Both live in the body. Both speak before logic has time to intervene. But their energetic signatures couldn't be more different.

Fear constricts; intuition expands.
Fear shouts in urgency; intuition whispers in calm certainty.
Fear seeks safety in the familiar; intuition invites us into the unknown.

Fear is a conditioned voice, a product of our survival system and cultural programming. It keeps us looping in "what ifs," tethered to past wounds or imagined futures. Intuition, on the other hand, speaks from timeless awareness. It comes with an unmistakable sense of rightness, even when it leads us into discomfort. The body recognizes this truth as a state of peace.

The nervous system is the body's communication network—an intricate web of nerves, brain pathways, and energy currents that constantly send signals between body and mind. It governs everything from heartbeat and digestion to emotional responses and intuitive impulses. When it functions in balance, our system moves fluidly between states of alertness and rest, helping us feel safe, grounded, and open to guidance.

However, when we experience trauma or prolonged stress, this network becomes dysregulated. The body gets stuck in survival mode—fight, flight, freeze, or fawn—believing danger persists even when it's not. In these states, the body cannot distinguish between a real threat and a memory of one. The heart races, the breath shortens, and the mind tightens around fear. Trauma blurs the signal.

When the nervous system is unbalanced, we often confuse instinct with intuition, reaction with inner knowing. We may believe we're being guided by spirit, when in truth we're responding to unhealed pain. Learning to regulate the nervous system—through breath, movement, stillness, and presence—creates the safety required for intuition to speak clearly. Only when the body feels safe can the soul be heard.

When we regulate the nervous system, we create the physiological foundation for intuition to emerge. In that space of calm coherence, we shift from reactivity to receptivity. The body becomes the sacred instrument through which intuition speaks its language: subtle, peaceful, and clear.

* * *

Healing trauma and calming the body aren't separate from spirituality; they're the doorway to it. Every time we choose to breathe through fear, pause before reacting, or listen inward rather than outward, we reclaim our sovereignty. This is the alchemy of Self, transforming the lead of fear into the gold of trust.

To Carl Jung, alchemy was far more than an ancient attempt to turn lead into gold; it was a psychological process that mirrored the evolution of the human soul. The alchemists' furnaces and crucibles were symbols of our inner transformation. They represented the opus—the great work—the lifelong journey of turning the dense, unconscious material of our psyche—our shadow, pain, and fear—into the radiant gold of self-awareness and integration.

For Jung, psychological alchemy was about the union of opposites: spirit and matter, light and shadow, the masculine and the feminine, the conscious and the unconscious. Transformation occurs when we're willing to face our darkness, not to destroy it, but to transmute it. Every trial, heartbreak, and initiation becomes raw material for growth. In this way, alchemy isn't just a metaphor; it's a map of how the human soul evolves through fire.

Jung identified four primary stages in this inner alchemical process, each representing a phase of human transformation:

- **Nigredo (Blackening):** The stage of death, dissolution, and disorientation. Here, the old Self begins to break apart. It's the dark night of the soul, where everything false must fall away.

- **Albedo (Whitening):** The purification. Through awareness and healing, clarity begins to return. We start to see the truth beneath illusion and wash away what no longer serves.

- **Citrinitas (Yellowing):** The dawning of illumination. Insight, wisdom, and intuitive awareness emerge. The soul begins to remember its own light.

- **Rubedo (Reddening):** The final integration, the union of opposites, where spirit and matter, intuition and action, merge into wholeness. We embody the gold we've been seeking.

These four stages are not linear but cyclical, a spiral of becoming that repeats throughout life. They echo the same movement we make when awakening intuition: descending into the shadow, purifying through truth, illuminating through awareness, and rising as the embodied Self.

* * *

When Laura asked, "But why is it the alchemy of intuition?" my answer was simple: because you must face your own alchemy to hear your inner voice truly.

Intuition isn't just a gift, it's an initiation. You cannot access its full power without first walking through the fire of transformation.

To hear the inner voice, you must first dissolve the noise: the inherited beliefs, family conditioning, societal programming, and internalized shame that keep you disconnected from your truth. This is **Nigredo,** the dark night of the soul, the breaking down.

Then comes **Albedo,** the purification, where you begin to see what is yours and what was never yours to carry.

Citrinitas brings illumination, the golden dawn of clarity, where intuition becomes alive within you.

Finally, **Rubedo,** the integration, where your inner voice and outer life become one and the same.

This is why it is called *The Alchemy of Intuition.*

Because to live intuitively, one must be willing to die to everything false.

To remember your inner voice, you must let the fire refine you until only truth remains.

When we surrender to that process, we emerge not as followers of external authority, but as sovereign beings, each of us our own philosopher's stone, our own source of wisdom.

The alchemy of intuition is not an abstract philosophy; it's a living, embodied practice. Through non-ordinary states of consciousness, breathwork, energy healing, somatic movement, and ritual, we awaken the intelligence that has always lived within the body. These practices regulate the nervous system, dissolve fear, and open the subtle channels through which intuition flows.

In these altered yet grounded states, we remember: intuition isn't a thought; it's a vibration, a felt sense, a living truth. The more we learn to anchor our spiritual experiences in the body, the more integrated, peaceful, and powerful our intuition becomes.

This book is a map, a mirror, and an initiation. It will guide you through the alchemical stages of awakening, from fear to freedom, from fragmentation to wholeness, from silence to the song of your soul.

It's time to rise, break free from the limitations imposed upon us, and become the fullest expression of who we truly are.

This is your invitation to remember.

This is *The Alchemy of Intuition: Embodied Practices to Access Your Inner Voice.*

Prologue: The Alchemy of Ireland
A Pilgrimage of Death, Purification, and Rebirth

PREFACE - THE CALL BENEATH THE PYRAMIDS

It began on my fortieth birthday, standing in the golden dust of Egypt.

Laura Di Franco and I were there on another sacred journey, tracing the roots of ancient wisdom, when a quiet voice rose between us, *Ireland.* It wasn't a thought or a plan yet, but a calling. A pulse. A knowing. We both felt it: the next great book and pilgrimage would lead us to the Emerald Isle, to a land older than memory and alive with magic.

Two years later, that whisper became a promise.

Alongside my dear friend and co-weaver, Becky Wheeler, we began planning what would become an alchemical voyage—not just for writers, but for seekers, healers, and visionaries ready to meet themselves in the mirror of the land. Every detail was shaped with intention and ritual. This was not a retreat; it was a living initiation.

In March of 2025, I came to Ireland with Becky to walk the route we had mapped in spirit. I went as a pilgrim to listen before leading. Ireland met me in her raw beauty, fierce winds, ancient stones, and the kind of silence that speaks. What I encountered there was a personal alchemy: death and rebirth woven through song, symbol, and synchronicity. The land itself became my teacher.

That journey transformed me. It burned away the final remnants of who I had been and showed me how to hold space for others to walk their own initiatory fires. When the time came to lead our circle of co-authors, I understood the path we would travel together, not simply across sacred sites, but through the inner landscapes of death, purification, illumination, and integration.

What unfolded in Ireland was more than a pilgrimage; it was the embodiment of *The Alchemy of Intuition*. Each site became a stage of transformation, each ritual a key unlocking something ancient within us.

This prologue isn't just a record of where we went; it's an invitation into the same current of change. Whether your feet have touched Irish soil or not, the alchemy lives in you, too. As you read, breathe with the land, listen between the lines, and let the mystery move through you.

May this journey awaken the voice within you that remembers: you are the land dreaming itself into being.

DAY 1 - OPENING CIRCLE

We arrived in Ireland under a gray-green sky, the kind of light that feels alive, soft, porous, holy. The air carried the scent of rain and peat smoke, and somewhere beyond the hills a rook called, low and throaty, as if announcing our arrival. The journey that lived in my heart for two years was finally breathing through.

Even for those who couldn't be here in body, the connection was palpable. We felt all who were part of this work—writers, healers, seekers—woven invisibly into the same field of intention.

We gathered for our opening circle, exhaling the long travel, inhaling the land's presence. One inhale to arrive. One exhale to release. Intentions filled the air as each person shared the moment they knew it was a yes for this journey. It was beautiful to witness our individual stories weaving into one living tapestry.

I shared my own story of stepping into the stones of Beltany Stone Circle months earlier, when Becky and I came to map this pilgrimage. The path felt like a portal; trees bending into a tunnel, shadows and light shifting like thresholds. When I entered the circle, a song rose out of me, not planned, but given. I sang to the land, to the ancestors, and to all who would one day be a part of this book.

Sisters of the light,
Brother of the stone,
Sisters of the light,
Brother of the stone,
Come home, Come home

I felt them, unseen beings, standing alongside me. When the song ended, the land placed a single crow feather in my path: a blessing, a sign, a confirmation of the medicine I was meant to carry.

Now, sitting here again with a circle of seekers from around the world, I invited everyone into a guided meditation—a vision walk through Beltany Stone Circle—where each person could meet the ancestors of Ireland in their own way and receive a gift from the unseen realms. One by one, eyes closed, each pilgrim journeyed inward and returned with something luminous—a word, a symbol, a felt knowing—to carry in the heart as we began this collective work.

This was our beginning.

From here, the journey would take us through death and fire, through breath and water, through the many ways the soul remembers itself whole.

Before we closed that night, I offered a little wisdom from the rooks, black-feathered corvids, cousins of the crow, who live in vast communities across Ireland.

"Rooks remind us that harmony is not sameness; it is movement together while honoring difference. As they thrive in connection, so do we, weaving our unique voices into a shared song."

"This," I told the circle, "Is the essence of our work: a rookery of storytellers rising together."

Now we turn toward the first stage of alchemy—death, the sacred dissolution, the letting go that makes way for transformation. Soon, we will travel south to Deerstone Lodge in the Wicklow Mountains and to Glendalough, where the veil thins and endings meet beginnings.

Even across oceans, you are part of this story.

The land knows your name. The ancestors know your name.

You are woven into the magic unfolding in Ireland.

A LITTLE HISTORY OF BELTANY STONE CIRCLE

Beltany Stone Circle rests on Tops Hill outside Raphoe, County Donegal. It's one of Ireland's largest and most significant stone circles, dating back to around 1400–800 BCE in the late Bronze Age. The circle once held over eighty stones (about sixty-five remain), each standing like an ancient sentinel keeping watch over millennia.

"Beltany" comes from *Beltane,* the Celtic fire festival marking the beginning of summer, a celebration of fertility, renewal, and the turning of the seasonal wheel. Many believe the site was aligned to the Beltane sunrise, when dawn light pierces the circle in a sacred pattern. For thousands of years, Beltany Stone Circle likely served as a gathering place for ritual, initiation, and ancestral communion, a threshold between worlds.

Local lore tells us the stones are alive with memory, guardians of wisdom who remember every ceremony, prayer, and song ever offered here. To stand within their circle is to feel the pulse of time, to sense the hum of something ancient and benevolent whispering still to those willing to listen.

* * *

GUIDED MEDITATION,
THE JOURNEY TO BELTANY STONE CIRCLE

Close your eyes.

Take a deep breath in, and let it out slowly.

Feel your body soften into the Earth beneath you.

With each breath, imagine becoming lighter, ready to step into another time, another place.

See yourself at the foot of a winding path. The air is cool, alive with possibility.

Before you, the trees rise tall and ancient, their branches arching overhead like a cathedral.

As you walk, the trees lean closer, shaping a tunnel of shadow and light. It feels like stepping into the unknown, the beginning of a story, the opening scene of a mystery.

Breathe into that. You are safe. You are guided. You are meant to be here.

Step by step, the path carries you upward. The earth is soft beneath your feet. Wind stirs the leaves with whispers that might be words. Perhaps you hear the wings of a rook in the distance. You are not alone. The ancestors walk with you.

Then, the trees part. You emerge into a clearing, and the stones of Beltany rise from the Earth, tall, weathered, powerful, guardians of time and memory.

Slowly, you walk toward the center. Notice how the stones seem to watch you, as if recognizing you. Turn in a slow circle once or twice, opening your senses and letting energy swirl around you. Feel the circle gather you in, wrapping you in protection and belonging.

Begin to walk the circumference. One by one, acknowledge the stones, keepers of wisdom, witnesses to countless ceremonies and lives. Feel your footsteps join the story; your breath joins the breath of all who came before.

When you are ready, begin one final round. With each step, feel the ancestors beside you, gentle yet strong. Something at your feet glimmers, shines, or simply calls to you.

Bend down and pick it up.

A gift, left just for you by those who love you beyond time. Perhaps it's an object, a symbol, a word, or a felt energy. You know it belongs to you. Hold it to your heart. Feel its meaning settle into your being. This is yours to carry forward, a reminder that you are never alone, always guided, always remembered.

Return to the center with your gift. Let its energy ripple through your body, filling you with strength, love, and a sense of belonging. Feel the blessing of the land, the ancestors, the elements, and the stones that surround you.

Take a deep breath. Bow in gratitude to the circle.

Wiggle your fingers and toes, and when you are ready, open your eyes and carry your gift into the world.

* * *

DAY 2 - GLENDALOUGH

Morning broke gently over Dublin. As we loaded the bus and began our drive south, the mist that wrapped the city started to lift, revealing rays of soft gold spilling over the rooftops. The air felt alive, as if the world itself were exhaling.

The farther we drove, the more the landscape opened, rolling hills giving way to the wild, generous expanse of the Wicklow Mountains. Fields glowed with sunlight. Sheep dotted the slopes like small white cotton balls. Laughter moved through the bus as we watched the countryside unfold, its beauty stretching our hearts wide open.

It felt as though Ireland herself welcomed us, inviting us to breathe deeper, expand before we descended.

By midday, we reached Glendalough, the valley of the two lakes. Founded by St. Kevin in the sixth century, this ancient monastic site still holds the hush of devotion. Stone tombs, towers, and remains rise from emerald grass, weathered yet enduring, reminders that even sacred structures crumble, but spirit remains.

Between the Upper and Lower Lakes, thresholds open. Here, endings meet beginnings.

Death is not an end but a doorway.

THE TEACHING OF DEATH

We gathered in a circle as the wind moved through the valley, and I spoke of the first stage of alchemy, Nigredo, the blackening, the sacred dissolution. Everything dies: people, stories, seasons, identities.

We spoke of the Death card in tarot: the skeleton astride a horse, a rising sun behind him, a reminder that every ending carries the seed of a beginning. Death is not destruction for the sake of pain; it's the divine breaking down of what no longer serves, so that what is truer can live.

As the words settled, silence descended, a living, breathing silence that demanded reverence.

WALKING THE RUINS

We moved through the ancient stones in silence, each of us carrying one question like a sacred plea:

"What is ready to die in me so I can step into a new life?"

The cemetery and the ruins spoke in their own way, wind through moss, wings overhead, whispers beneath the breath. Every archway felt like a portal, every stone a mirror. The land was teaching us through beauty and decay: nothing is truly gone, only transformed.

THE ROOK'S SACRIFICE

Long before this pilgrimage, death had already found me.

Months earlier, on our Ireland pilgrimage, I received my first initiation into this mystery on a road near Loughcrew. Becky and I drove through the countryside, sunlight spilling over green hills. Everything felt aligned, simple, perfect. And then it happened.

A crow hopped into the lane. The car ahead struck her. Feathers rose like smoke in the air. Heart pounding, I gasped and shuddered. Becky pulled over, lifted the crow from the road, and we laid her beside a tree;

circled her with branches, wept, and honored her. In my bones I knew: this was a sacrifice, a messenger, a teacher of alchemy.

Through tears, I whispered, "I died back there." It wasn't only about the crow; it was about what needed to die within me so something new could live.

That day on the roadside became the first initiation. When I stood before the Upper Lake months later with my co-authors, I understood why the crow had died, so I could learn how to live differently.

CEREMONY AT THE UPPER LAKE

Carrying that medicine, we created a nest and altar at the Upper Lake—moss, feathers, branches, mushrooms, apples, stones, and one of my broken crow statues at the center. It stood as a mirror and a symbol of death.

Each pilgrim stepped forward in turn, drew a card, and named what they were "dying to:" old patterns, stories, and identities dissolving into the mist. The circle was quiet, except for breath and water, the soft rhythm of surrender.

The mountains watched. The lake reflected back our release. Everything that died became part of the landscape's breath.

THE FIRE OF TRANSMUTATION

As night descended, we gathered around the fire, one of humanity's oldest portals of transformation. Each person wrote a word, a wound, or a part of themselves ready to release on a small wooden stick.

We sang "Sacred Fire," our voices rising into the cool air as flames devoured what no longer served. Fire consumes, and it purifies. It is death's loving counterpart, fierce yet merciful.

And then, without effort, the fire became joy.

We feasted on a beautiful meal, prepared with food rich in color and prayer. We surprised one of our co-authors with a birthday cake; her laughter filled the barn. A local musician strummed Irish and classic rock songs and joked that he needed more American girls in his life, "You're fun!"

We danced under the low beams until the air pulsed with music and laughter.

Grief and celebration coexisted as one.

This is the alchemy of death: to let go, to grieve, and then to remember that life is a celebration. Death does not erase joy; it refines it.

Together, we flowed through endings and beginnings, fire and laughter, through it all.

A LITTLE HISTORY OF GLENDALOUGH

Glendalough, *Gleann Dá Loch,* "the valley of the two lakes," lies cradled within the Wicklow Mountains, about an hour south of Dublin. Its story begins in the sixth century with St. Kevin, a hermit-monk who sought solitude and prayer in the forested valley.

Over time, his retreat drew followers, and a great monastic settlement grew around him, a place of study, pilgrimage, and spiritual initiation that would flourish for more than six hundred years.

The site became one of medieval Ireland's most important centers of learning and devotion, often called the "monastic city." Its round tower, stone churches, and scattered crosses still stand amid moss and mist, keeping watch over the sacred valley. Pilgrims once came here to bathe in the two lakes, believing their waters healed body and soul.

Yet Glendalough's holiness is older still. Long before St. Kevin, these lands were revered by pre-Christian peoples as a thin place, a threshold where the veil between worlds softens. The lakes were seen as portals of death and rebirth, their mirrored waters symbolizing the passage between the physical and the spiritual.

Even now, when wind sweeps through the ruins and ripples the surface of the Upper Lake, it feels as though the ancient prayers of monks and druids alike still linger in the air. Glendalough remains what it has always been: a sanctuary of endings and beginnings. This valley teaches the soul how to die, live, and begin again.

* * *

A RITUAL FOR YOU—THE FIRE OF RELEASE

Light a candle or sit near a flame.

Ask yourself: *What is ready to die in me so I can step into a new life?*

Write the story, belief, or pattern on a small piece of paper.

Burn it safely (or bury it).

Whisper:

"What I release becomes medicine for my path."

Place your hand over your heart and breathe deeply.

Feel the warmth of transformation.

Know that your release ripples into the land, and that the ancestors hold you, too.

* * *

DAY 3 - BREATH, DEATH, AND RENEWAL

The morning light spilled softly through the windows of Deerstone, our eco-lodge nestled among the rolling green of County Wicklow. The air smelled of rain and woodsmoke, and everything seemed to hum with quiet anticipation.

We gathered in a circle, still tender from the death ceremony at Glendalough the night before. There was a hush that only followed profound transformation, that sacred silence where something old has died but the new has not yet fully arrived.

It was here that we began to write again, not just with pens but with breath. Laura Di Franco guided us inward, reminding us that the story of death is never complete without the story of renewal. The words came slowly, like morning mist lifting from the hills, revealing what was ready to live again.

After lunch, we entered a Shamanic Breathwork journey. Outside, rooks called from the trees, their voices rough, ancient, as if keeping time for our descent. Mats lined the wooden floor. Blankets wrapped around us. The drum and the rooks' croaking began, slow and steady, echoing the rhythm of the Earth itself.

The circles' breath deepened, in through the nose, out through the mouth, a tide of life force washing through the body. At first, it was resistance: tightness in the chest, the mind trying to hold on. Then came surrender.

Tears, laughter, visions, silence—each breath seemed to pull another thread of the past loose, each exhale an offering to the fire of transformation. This is the threshold work, dying and being reborn in the same breath.

When the journey ended, we lay in stillness. Someone wept softly. Another smiled through tears. The room smelled of lavender and salt and humanity.

We grounded ourselves with warm Irish shepherd's pie and tea, eating and chattering, honoring what had been released. Later, as dusk settled over the hills, we gathered once more around the fire.

The flames crackled as we entered another ceremony of purification, the element of fire meeting the breath, preparing us for the next leg of our pilgrimage: the sacred waters of the River Boyne and the ancient tombs of Newgrange and Knowth.

I remember watching the sparks rise into the dark sky, thinking of all we carry and all we must let go of to live.

A LITTLE HISTORY OF SHAMANIC BREATHWORK

Shamanic Breathwork® was developed by Linda Star Wolf, founder of Venus Rising Association for Transformation, a lineage dedicated to the healing power of altered states of consciousness. Rooted in ancient shamanic wisdom and guided by Jungian psychology, this practice uses rhythmic, connected breathing combined with music, movement, and focused intention to open the doorway between the conscious and unconscious mind.

Unlike traditional talk therapy, Shamanic Breathwork invites participants to journey inward, to access the wisdom of the soul, meet their shadow, and awaken the inner healer within. The breath becomes a bridge: oxygen feeding body and spirit, rhythm awakening memory and vision. Through this process, repressed emotions and buried stories surface, offering the opportunity for profound release, forgiveness, and transformation.

Each session is unique, a sacred voyage that mirrors the alchemical process of death and rebirth.

Old patterns dissolve; new insight and empowerment emerge. The breath carries us through the stages of alchemy: descent, purification, illumination, and integration, just as the elements of nature do.

For me, this modality has been one of the most powerful tools in both my personal and professional practice. It mirrors the very heartbeat of my work, transforming pain into power, fear into freedom, and separation into connection. The breath is life itself, and through it, we return home to who we truly are.

* * *

A SIMPLE BREATHWORK RITUAL FOR LETTING GO

Sit comfortably, one hand on your heart and one on your belly.

Take three deep breaths, in through the nose, out through the mouth with a gentle sigh.

With each inhale, draw in new life force, the seed of what is being born.

With each exhale, release what is ready to die, old stories, grief, fear.

Continue for five to ten minutes. Let the breath move the emotions; let them flow.

When you are done, place both hands over your heart and whisper:

"I let go of what no longer serves. I am open to the rebirth of what is true for me."

Remember: breath, fire, water, and words are all teachers of alchemy.

Each release makes space for what waits to be born.

Let the breath carry you.

Let your heart stay open to the mystery.

* * *

DAY 4 - NEWGRANGE, KNOWTH, AND THE RIVER BOYNE

Morning broke with soft mist curling above the fields as we gathered for a nourishing breakfast, warm porridge, fresh bread, honey, and laughter. Our hearts were lighter after the previous day's ceremony. The rain had passed, leaving the land washed clean and glistening. We set out toward the sacred valley of the Boyne, home to Newgrange, Knowth, and the River Boyne, sites that hold the ancient memory of light's return.

THE TOMBS OF VISION - KNOWTH

At Knowth, we entered passage tombs older than the Egyptian pyramids and Stonehenge, dating back over five thousand years. The mounds are ringed with more than 200 carved stones, the largest collection of megalithic art in all of Europe. Spirals, zigzags, and concentric circles ripple across rock like coded messages from another realm.

Inside, time bends. The air feels thick with presence, as if the ancients still breathe within the walls. Some scholars believe these carvings were born from trance states, the vision-language of shamans and seers translating what they saw behind the veil into stone. Standing there, we could almost feel the rhythm of those ceremonies, the heartbeat of the Earth beneath our feet, the pulse of human longing to remember its source.

Knowth holds both grief and memory, a reminder that every burial also seeds renewal. Here, death is not an ending but a threshold to the next beginning.

A LITTLE HISTORY OF KNOWTH

Knowth is one of the three great passage tombs of the Brú na Bóinne complex in County Meath, constructed around 3200 BCE. Two great mounds and eighteen smaller satellite tombs spread across the landscape like ancient constellations in earth form. Its carvings, over 200 in total, make up nearly half of all megalithic art discovered in Western Europe.

Archaeologists believe the builders tracked solar and lunar movements, using the mounds as cosmic calendars and ceremonial chambers for the dead. Yet myth tells another story, that these stones were not simply burial sites but places of initiation, where the living communed with ancestors through sound, rhythm, and altered states. To walk here is to enter a living memory, a temple of both death and rebirth, where vision was carved into eternity.

THE LIGHT RETURNS - NEWGRANGE

At Newgrange, we stepped into another world—a spiraling passage that leads to a stone chamber perfectly aligned with the Winter Solstice sunrise. Each year, on the darkest morning, a single beam of light enters the roof-box. It travels down the passage, illuminating the tomb's inner sanctum for just seventeen minutes.

To stand there was to witness the promise of renewal itself, darkness pierced by light. A sign inside the visitor center read: *There is always rebirth, and in the darkest of places, there is light.* I smiled, a mirror of our own alchemical path. After the death and dissolution of the days before, this was the first flicker of purification.

Outside, I visited a great rookery, watching them whirl and caw, those wise black birds, kin to crow and raven, messengers adding their voices to the day's teachings. Their cries echoed over the Boyne Valley, as if the ancestors themselves were singing of rebirth.

A LITTLE HISTORY OF NEWGRANGE

Newgrange, also part of the Brú na Bóinne complex, was constructed around 3200 BCE, making it older than Stonehenge or the pyramids of Giza. The mound spans nearly an acre and is encircled by a ring of massive stones etched with spirals and solar symbols. It served as both tomb and temple, marking the cycles of death and rebirth through solar alignment.

The Winter Solstice alignment symbolizes the eternal truth woven into human consciousness: that light will always return. For the ancient peoples of Ireland, this was not just astronomy but ceremony—a sacred conversation between Earth, the sun, and spirit. Newgrange remains one of the world's most powerful sanctuaries of renewal.

And above it all, the rooks keep watch.

These wise black birds live in large, raucous rookeries across Ireland's countryside. Their calls echo like a living chorus of ancestors, carrying messages between the seen and unseen. In Celtic and European folklore, rooks are guardians of sacred places and protectors of threshold spaces, such as burial mounds, stone circles, and ancient groves.

Rook medicine teaches the power of community, communication, and collective transformation. They remind us that harmony is not sameness; it's moving together while honoring differences. To encounter a rook is to be reminded that we're never truly alone; we move with both our human kin and the unseen ones at our side.

Their flight across the Boyne Valley is more than a coincidence; it is a benediction. A reminder that rebirth isn't only individual but communal, that every voice, every song, and every story adds to the mysterious chorus carrying us all through the significant transitions of life.

THE GODDESS RIVER, BOANN

Our final pilgrimage of the day was to the River Boyne, the living current that winds through the Boyne Valley. Myth tells us Boann was once a mortal woman, a poet and priestess, who dared to approach the Well of Wisdom, a sacred spring guarded by nine hazel trees whose nuts contained the world's knowledge.

Though she was warned not to circle the well, Boann's longing for truth was greater than her fear. As she walked around it, the waters rose and burst forth, creating the river that still bears her name. Though her body was dissolved, her spirit became immortal, a goddess of transformation and courage.

Standing by her waters, we offered flowers and whispered our prayers. Then we cleansed in her river, washing away what no longer served us—grief, doubt, remnants of the old self. Rain fell softly as if the heavens wept with us, a baptism of renewal. Later, in the sauna, we continued the purification by sweating, releasing, and surrendering.

A LITTLE HISTORY OF THE RIVER BOYNE

The River Boyne, named for the goddess Boann (*Bo Find*, "the White Cow"), flows 70 miles from Kildare to the Irish Sea. In Celtic mythology, Boann is the daughter of Delbáeth and wife of Nechtan, guardian of the Well of Segais, the Well of Wisdom. When she defied taboo and walked around the well counter-clockwise, its sacred waters rose and transformed into the river that bears her name.

Boann's myth is one of courage, curiosity, and sacrifice, the refusal to remain confined by fear or law when truth calls. She is the embodiment of the Divine Feminine Alchemy, the willingness to risk destruction for the sake of awakening. Her river still flows through the heart of Ireland, carrying the eternal current of transformation.

As this day closed, the land itself became our teacher: the visionary carvings of Knowth, the solstice light of Newgrange, the wild courage of Boann, each a reminder that

Death is never the end.
There is always purification.
There is always rebirth.

* * *

WATER RITUAL FOR RELEASE

Fill a bowl, cup, or bath with clean water.

Hold your hands above it and breathe. Whisper:

"Like Boann, I release what no longer serves me.

May the waters carry it away. I am open to wisdom, light, and rebirth."

Wash your face or arms, imagining heaviness carried downstream.

When finished, pour the water outside or down the drain with gratitude, returning it to the Earth.

* * *

DAY 5 - CACAO CEREMONY AND ECSTATIC DANCE

This day flowed in its own timing; nothing was on schedule, everything in surrender.

A lesson in slowing down, softening, and trusting the unfolding.

Laura Di Franco guided another potent workshop to shape our stories, a time to tend what the journey had begun to awaken.

The sound of pens scratching, tea being poured, and wind whispering through the trees—it was the music of creation. Laura guided us through reflections on voice, truth, and transformation, reminding us that every story we write is also a spell we cast.

"To create," she said, "is to remember we are co-weavers with the divine."

I watched as faces softened, shoulders relaxed, and words flowed. What had been buried under fear and self-doubt began to emerge, raw, honest, glowing.

CACAO AND ECSTATIC DANCE CEREMONY

In the afternoon, we entered a cacao and ecstatic dance ceremony, honoring the Peruvian lineage and the keepers of this sacred plant medicine.

We gathered in a circle to work with Peruvian cacao. Together, we stirred it with intention, singing into the cacao, letting our voices carry spells of release and renewal.

We drank together, inhaling its rich, earthy scent while a goddess song, sung for thousands of years, washed over us.

And then we rose.

We danced.

One by one, bodies began to sway, then spin, then soar, dancing with wild abandon, letting the Earth pull at our feet while the sky pulled at our arms. It was breathtaking: luminous souls moving freely, connecting with the land, the ancestors, and their inner goddess selves, weaving alchemy into every step.

We released and expressed, unashamed, unbound, free, entering an altered state where heart, mind, and soul could be purified.

At one point, I closed my eyes and felt the pulse of hundreds— ancestors, friends, and unseen guides—moving with us. The energy surged through the floor like electricity. For a moment, we were one heartbeat, one breath, one flame.

When the music slowed, we rested in stillness, the kind that hums with aliveness.

Breath heavy, skin glistening, hearts wide open.

We ended with soft singing, voices blending into a lullaby of gratitude.

The air shimmered. The land seemed to listen.

We closed with a decadent three-course dinner, candlelight flickering, glasses clinking, laughter rising.

Stories flowed like water, weaving us closer with every bite and smile. Around that table, we weren't just writers; we were a rookery forming, a circle of souls sharing nourishment, joy, and community.

The perfect end to a day of release and renewal.

A LITTLE HISTORY OF CACAO AND ECSTATIC DANCE

Cacao, Theobroma, meaning "food of the gods," has been revered by the Mayan and Aztec peoples for over 4,000 years as a sacred plant teacher. It was used in a ceremony to connect with the divine, open the heart, and foster harmony among community members.

Unlike processed chocolate, ceremonial cacao retains its natural theobromine, a gentle stimulant that enhances blood flow and emotional clarity. When prepared with intention, it becomes vibrational medicine for love, creativity, and presence.

In modern ceremony, cacao bridges the ancient and the new. It's not a hallucinogen but a heart opener, helping us feel more deeply, love more freely, and remember that joy itself is holy.

Ecstatic dance, too, is ancient. Long before words, humans prayed through movement. From the Dionysian rites of Greece to the whirling dervishes of Sufism, dance has always been a way to commune with spirit. In our time, it reemerges as a form of shamanic healing, no choreography, no judgment, just movement guided by the soul.

Together, cacao and dance form a potent alchemy, Earth's sweetness meeting the fire of embodiment.

Through them, we remember that joy is not frivolous; it's sacred medicine.

A LITTLE HISTORY OF KILLEEN CASTLE AND THE OLD CHURCH

Killeen Castle, near Dunsany in County Meath, was initially built in the twelfth century by Hugh de Lacy, one of Ireland's Norman lords. Over 800 years old, the castle has been rebuilt, expanded, and transformed many times, now a grand estate and golf course blending modern luxury with medieval roots.

Throughout its long history, Killeen Castle served as a stronghold of the Plunkett family, who later became the Earls of Fingall. The estate has witnessed Ireland's evolving story—from the Norman conquest to Gaelic resilience to modern renewal.

Adjacent to the castle stands the old Killeen Church, sometimes mistakenly called Killeen Abbey. Built around 1425, this Gothic-style church served as the castle's private chapel and spiritual heart. Though now in ruins, it remains a national monument, its pointed arches and carved stones still echoing with prayers from centuries past.

* * *

AT-HOME RITUAL: CACAO / TEA + DANCE

If you don't have ceremonial cacao, use tea, coffee, or warm water. Intention is everything.

Prepare Your Cup: Boil water slowly, with presence. As you stir, whisper: "I release. . ."

Bless the Drink: Hold the cup, breathe, imagine prayers infusing the liquid. Hum or sing if you wish.

Sip with Intention: Slow sips. Taste fully. Inhale steam. Imagine warmth carrying release out and filling you with light.

Dance: Put on a heart-stirring song. Start gently, grow freer. Feet offer the old to earth; arms call in joy. Let breath be the drum; let heart lead.

Close: Place your hands over your heart and thank yourself and the divine within.

* * *

DAY 6 - FAIRY FIELDS

We rode to Pat Noone's fairy fields, rolling green pastures alive with wind and whisper. Curious animals grazed nearby, and the land itself seemed to hum with ancient stories.

Pat greeted us with warmth and humor, sharing tales of the fairies and sacred stones that have been resting there for over 5,000 years. We listened like children at a fireside, spellbound by his stories of portals and unseen realms.

One by one, each of us stepped into the fairy portal, honoring the unseen ones. The air shimmered. Laughter mixed with reverence.

Back in March, I glimpsed a past life here, a vision of tending the land as a guardian of the threshold. This time, as I stood within the circle, a soft breeze carried a gentle whisper through the grass:

Thank you for helping others believe in magic again.

Pat welcomed us to picnic on his land, a feast of bread, fruit, and laughter shared beneath a sky heavy with silver clouds.

We closed the day with a candle ceremony, cleansing head, heart, and soul, with a bit of help from our fairy friends. Flame flickered, wind swirled, and something unseen seemed to join us in the dance.

On the bus home, clarity sparked like sunlight through rain. Purification is working. Perspectives are opening.

Alchemy is wild like that: when you let go and follow the flow, magic shows up every time.

FAIRY MAGIC

In Ireland, the fairies, the Aos Sí, are said to live within mounds, hills, and sacred stones. For thousands of years, people have honored them as guardians of the Earth, keepers of magic, and messengers between worlds.

Folklore warns: never disrespect a fairy tree or stone, to do so invites misfortune.

But honor them, and they bring blessings, healing, and protection.

The fairies remind us that magic is not superstition, it's a relationship. The land is alive, and when we listen, it speaks.

The fairies are more than folklore.

They are symbols of the unseen, of the living mystery that still breathes within the land and within us.

When we honor them, we honor the parts of ourselves that long to believe, to wonder, and to stay connected to the invisible threads of spirit.

May your head be clear, your heart open, and your soul renewed as you carry this magic forward.

A LITTLE HISTORY OF THE FAIRIES AND PAT NOONE'S FAIRY FIELDS

In Irish mythology, the fairies, or Aos Sí (pronounced *ees shee*), are not the tiny, winged creatures of modern tales but an ancient, powerful race, descendants of the Tuatha Dé Danann, the shining tribe of the goddess Danu.

When the Milesians, the ancestors of modern Irish people, arrived in Ireland, the Tuatha Dé Danann withdrew into the mounds, hills, and sacred stones, becoming the *people of the mounds*. There they remain, unseen yet ever-present, guarding the land's magic and maintaining harmony between the worlds.

For millennia, the Irish have honored these beings with deep respect. Fairy forts, lone hawthorn trees, and stone rings are still left untouched by farmers who know better than to disturb the dwellings of the Good People.

To make offerings of milk, bread, or flowers was to keep the peace with the spirits who protect the fertility of the soil and the well-being of the people.

This reverence continues at Pat Noone's Fairy Fields in County Galway, where the land itself vibrates with old energy. Pat, a local farmer, healer, and modern-day mystic, tends to ancient stones and portals said to be over 5,000 years old. He welcomes visitors to experience the fairies' presence firsthand, sharing stories passed down through generations about healing wells, fairy pathways, and elemental guardians that still move through his fields.

Pat often teaches that "the fairies are guardians of balance, caretakers of land and spirit." They remind us that every action has a ripple and that magic belongs to those who approach the land with love. His fields are not tourist sites; they're living sanctuaries, places where folklore and faith meet in the green heart of Ireland.

To walk there is to feel time soften, as though the veil between worlds thins, and the ancient ones lean close, curious and kind.

* * *

CANDLE CLEANSING RITUAL

Light a simple candle.

Close your eyes and take three deep breaths.

Imagine mossy stones, wildflowers, and a gentle breeze moving through your hair.

Hold the candle and whisper:

"I call upon the spirit of the fair folk, guardians of Earth and magic. Thank you for guiding and protecting me."

Pass your hands slowly (safely) over the flame, over your head, heart, and belly, clearing anything heavy or stagnant.

Place your hands over your heart and say:

"With head, heart, and soul cleansed, I walk forward in magic and trust."

Blow out the candle, knowing that your intention carries into the unseen.

* * *

DAY 7 - BECTIVE ABBEY AND ROCKFIELD HOUSE

Today had its own rhythm, strange, slow, and full of lessons. Nothing went according to plan, and yet everything unfolded perfectly in its own time.

We began at Bective Abbey, where ivy and light intertwined through crumbling cloisters. The air felt ancient, sacred, a meeting of shadow and grace. I could almost hear the chants of monks carried on the wind, the whispers of devotion still clinging to stone. It was as if time itself had paused to remind us: *Not everything sacred runs on schedule.*

By afternoon, we arrived at Rockfield House, a vision straight out of *Downton Abbey.* The grand estate stretched wide beneath the gray-blue sky, all velvet drapes, spiral staircases, and sprawling green lawns. The authors were giddy, laughing like children exploring a castle. Their joy was contagious. The land felt alive with possibility again, the next stage of our alchemy stirring.

As evening fell, we gathered in a circle for the fall equinox and Virgo new moon solar eclipse, a cosmic convergence of dark and light, death and renewal. Outside, wind whispered through the trees; inside, candles flickered and hearts opened. We spoke intentions aloud, to balance what was dissolving and to welcome what was being born.

We rest beneath Rockfield's high ceilings and starry skies, preparing for dawn's ascent up Loughcrew, where the sun will pierce the ancient cairns and awaken the light within us all.

A LITTLE HISTORY OF BECTIVE ABBEY AND ROCKFIELD HOUSE

BECTIVE ABBEY

Bective Abbey was founded in 1147 by Murchad O'Mael-Sheachlainn, King of Meath, as a Cistercian monastery and a "daughter house" of Mellifont Abbey. Its Latin name, *Abbatia de Beatitudine,* meaning "Blessedness of God," speaks to its spiritual aspiration.

Unlike many Cistercian sites, Bective was located not in remote wilderness, but on fertile lands along the River Boyne, giving it both spiritual depth and pragmatic strength as a productive monastic community. Over time, it grew in influence; its abbots held significant standing, even sitting as spiritual lords in parliament.

During its medieval peak, Bective was remodeled and expanded, especially in the 13th–15th centuries, with additions of fortified walls, cloisters, and monastic ranges. But its fortunes declined during the Dissolution of the Monasteries under Henry VIII in the 1530s, at which point its lands and structures were gradually converted into a fortified manor and passed through various private hands.

Today, Bective stands as evocative ruins: the cloister archways, the chapter house, the carved stonework, the fragments of aisles and walls, each telling stories of devotion, decline, adaptation, and memory. Its presence looms on the banks of the Boyne, silent yet speaking.

ROCKFIELD HOUSE

Rockfield House, located just outside Kells in County Meath, dates to the late 18th century and was built by the Rothwell family.

Over time, improvements in the mid-19th century made the Rothwells major landowners in the region.

In the 20th and 21st centuries, the house changed hands several times and underwent restoration. The current estate retains its historic character: large rooms, dramatic staircases, parkland and gardens, and modern amenities blended within the old walls.

Rockfield sits on about 68 acres of mature gardens and grounds, with a lineage of social gatherings, retreats, and elegant interiors, a living house of ceremony and hospitality.

DAY 8 - LOUGHCREW

This day was one of the most potent days.

We journeyed to one of my favorite places in all of Ireland, Loughcrew.

Everyone piled sleepily onto the bus at 5:15 a.m., bundled in layers, breath misting in the cold air. The drive was quiet, reverent. As dawn began to stretch its fingers across the horizon, we climbed the steep, grassy mound together, wind biting our faces, hearts pounding with anticipation.

Reaching the top just as the first rays of sunlight broke through felt like stepping into another world. The sky blazed gold and rose, and the land shimmered with dew, alive, ancient, waiting.

We came to take part in an Equinox ceremony, a pagan rite honoring the balance of light and dark, day and night, life and death. The Hag of Loughcrew, the Cailleach, presides here, the great crone goddess, keeper of endings and beginnings, midwife of winter's descent. Legend says she scattered the great stones of Loughcrew from her apron as she strode across the land, shaping the cairns that still crown the hills.

At the precise moment of balance, the Fall Equinox, the rising sun streams into Cairn T, illuminating carvings etched more than 5,000 years ago: spirals, suns, and mysterious symbols of cosmic order. This is how our ancestors marked the turning of the year, preparing for the descent into darkness, reflection, and renewal.

To stand there, watching the sun rise and the light enter the tomb, was breathtaking, a golden river flowing into the heart of stone. For a moment, it felt as if the Earth herself exhaled, and every soul gathered there breathed in unison.

It was also freezing.

We didn't linger long once the sun rose, but we carried its warmth, its inner fire, back down the hill with us.

TEA CEREMONY AND THE BREATH OF THE PLANTS

Back at Rockfield House, the day continued in a softer rhythm. Our local friend Daryl and his partner welcomed us into a tea and breathwork ceremony, a space of stillness and plant wisdom after the storm of wind and light.

The tea was brewed from herbs Daryl had hand-gathered at Ireland's sacred sites, Scots Pine needles, hawthorn berries and bark, elderflower, meadow sweet, each leaf infused with story and spirit. As we drank, we were invited to meditate with the plants, to feel them move through our bodies like memory.

Each sip felt like communion with the land itself, the essence of Ireland moving through us. It reminded me how much I long to return to my own practice of working with teas, infusions, and herbal medicine.

Then Daryl guided us into a gentle breathwork journey—not the fiery release of days before, but a quiet inward turning. The breath deepened, slowed, and softened, each inhale opening space for peace, each exhale melting away tension. It was simple, pure, profound, a descent into stillness.

When it ended, the room was hushed. Hearts steady. Faces serene.

We finished lunch, then I found a patch of sunlight near the window, pen in hand, heart full, writing these words to you.

Here comes the great awakening, the rise of consciousness.

Hello, inner sun.

A LITTLE HISTORY OF LOUGHCREW AND THE CAILLEACH

Loughcrew Cairns, known in Irish as *Sliabh na Caillí*, "the Hills of the Witch," form one of Ireland's most ancient ceremonial complexes, dating back to 3200 BCE. The site comprises more than thirty passage tombs scattered across the rolling hills of County Meath, aligned to the Equinox sunrise.

According to myth, the Cailleach Bhearra, or "Veiled One," created the cairns by dropping stones from her apron as she leapt across the landscape. Each stone mound became a resting place of initiation and remembrance, a bridge between the seen and unseen.

The carvings inside Cairn T are among the finest in Ireland: spirals, circles, and sun symbols carved into stone nearly 5,000 years ago. Twice a year, on the Spring and Fall Equinox, the rising sun pierces the inner chamber, lighting the carvings in golden flame, a reminder that even in darkness, light always returns.

Loughcrew remains a living temple, where myth, astronomy, and spirit converge, a place where the bones of the earth remember the stars.

* * *

PLANT-SPIRIT TEA BLESSING

Purpose: To attune to the wisdom of the plants and your own inner knowing.

You'll need:

One herb that feels right (fresh or dried)

Boiling water, mug, and quiet space

Steps:

1. Place your herb in the cup. As you pour the hot water, say: "Spirit of [plant name], teach me your medicine."

2. Cover the cup and let it steep while you breathe deeply, hands over your heart.

3. When ready, sip slowly, eyes closed, and feel the plant's energy moving through you.

4. Ask silently: What do you wish to show me? Notice any sensation, image, or word that arises.

5. End with gratitude, returning any leftover tea to the Earth.

* * *

DAY 9 - CLIFFS OF MOHER

This day was pure magic in Ireland.

The sun blessed us with a rare golden glow and a perfect 60 degrees as we boarded the bus for the long, winding journey south to the Cliffs of Moher. Initially, this stop wasn't even on our itinerary. Still, after visiting in March 2025, I knew I had to bring everyone here. The cliffs are one of those sacred thresholds where the veil between worlds feels thin, where wind, sea, and sky meet in wild conversation.

When they finally came into view, it was like beholding a cathedral sculpted by time itself, stone and mist rising into eternity. Waves crashed far below, gulls wheeled overhead, and for a long moment, none of us spoke. We simply stood there, silent, humbled, breathing in the majesty of it all.

On the way back, wanting the whole Irish experience, we ducked into a cozy pub, laughter and loud music spilling from the inside. The food was hearty, the pints perfectly poured, and our laughter echoed louder than the music.

We were a joyful, loud rookery that night, full of stories, songs, and the kind of connection only Ireland can conjure.

A LITTLE HISTORY OF THE CLIFFS OF MOHER

Rising over 700 feet above the Atlantic Ocean, the Cliffs of Moher stretch for more than five miles along Ireland's rugged western coast in County Clare. Their name comes from the old Gaelic *Mothar,* meaning "ruined fort," referring to a promontory fort that once stood on Hag's Head, the southernmost point of the cliffs.

These ancient sea cliffs were formed over 320 million years ago, sculpted by wind, water, and time into towering walls of sandstone, shale, and limestone, striations that hold the memory of the Earth's own evolution. From their heights, one can see the Aran Islands, Galway Bay, and even the Twelve Bens mountains of Connemara on a clear day.

In Irish folklore, the cliffs are said to be guarded by Mal, a sea witch who fell in love with the hero Cú Chulainn. When he rejected her, she chased him across the coast until she leapt to her death from Hag's Head, turning to stone as she fell, her spirit still said to linger in the waves and winds.

Standing at the edge, the Atlantic wind in your hair, you can feel why the cliffs have long been a place of both awe and initiation. They remind us of our own smallness and strength, that even as we stand before vastness, we are part of it.

DAY 10 - HILL OF TARA

On our last full day, we stood upon the Hill of Tara, the ancient seat of the High Kings and home to the Stone of Destiny, *Lia Fáil.* Here, legend says, the rightful ruler would stand upon the stone, and it would roar in recognition of their sovereignty.

We gathered in a circle beneath a vast blue sky, the wind carrying whispers of our ancestors.

Each person stepped forward to the stone, speaking one truth they were ready to claim, their own sovereignty, their authentic becoming.

This was the final stage of alchemy, the reddening, the transformation, the moment when all the death, purification, and awakening merged into radiant wholeness.

Voices trembled, then grew strong. Tears fell. Laughter broke through. Each declaration rose like a spell into the wind:

"I claim my voice."
"I am ready to live my truth."
"I trust my magic."

After the ceremony, joy took over. We dressed in costume, flowing fabrics, gowns, crowns, scarves, and furs, and gave life to our truths through poetry, song, dance, and storytelling. The room overflowed with laughter, tears, and love as each person became the embodiment of their alchemy.

Later that evening, we gathered for our farewell dinner, candlelight flickering, glasses clinking, hearts full and tender. We exchanged gifts, laughter, and stories, celebrating another birthday.

It felt divinely orchestrated that our journey had both begun and ended with a birth. In the language of alchemy, it was the perfect circle: the death of who we were when we arrived, and the rebirth of who we had become.

Birthdays are more than moments of aging; they are symbols of transformation. Each candle is a reminder of the light we carry after walking through the dark. Each toast is a celebration of the many selves we have shed and reclaimed along the way. There was a sweetness in that realization, that endings and beginnings are never separate, only mirrors of one another.

It had been ten days of pure magic, laughter, ceremony, and transformation. A journey from darkness to light, from death to sovereignty. As we prepared to return home, a new chapter began, literally and symbolically. Ireland has given so much; we now carry her magic into our writing, our hearts, and our lives.

A LITTLE HISTORY OF THE HILL OF TARA AND THE STONE OF DESTINY

The Hill of Tara, or *Teamhair na Rí,* "Sanctuary of the Kings," lies in the heart of County Meath, the ancient spiritual center of Ireland. For over 5,000 years, it has been a sacred site of kingship, ceremony, and myth.

Tara was once believed to be the dwelling place of the gods, a threshold between worlds where the High Kings of Ireland were crowned. Its ceremonial mounds and earthworks, including the Mound of the Hostages, Rath na Ríogh (Fort of the Kings), and Teach Cormaic (Cormac's House), align with the movements of the sun and stars, marking equinoxes and solstices with precision that still astonishes scholars.

At its summit stands the Lia Fáil, or Stone of Destiny, a tall, phallic granite pillar said to roar when touched by the rightful king. In ancient times, sovereignty was seen as a sacred marriage between the ruler and the land itself. To lead, one had to be chosen not only by people, but by the goddess of the Earth, a union of power and humility, responsibility and devotion.

Myth tells that the Tuatha Dé Danann, the shining ones, brought the Stone of Destiny from the mystical isles of the north, along with the sword, spear, and cauldron, the four treasures of their wisdom tradition.

To stand upon Tara today is to feel that legacy beneath your feet, a vibration of sovereignty that transcends politics and title. It's the sovereignty of soul: the moment you remember you are your own ruler, guided by spirit and anchored in truth.

* * *

RITUAL FOR YOU—THE STONE OF DESTINY

Find a stone that calls to you, from a riverbank, forest, or your own backyard.

Hold it in your hand and whisper one truth you are ready to live:

"I step into my sovereignty by. . ."

Place the stone somewhere visible, on an altar, desk, or windowsill, as a reminder of your power and your path.

Each time you see or touch it, let it anchor you back into the truth you claimed.

* * *

FINAL BLESSING AND SUMMARY

From the first breath of our opening circle at Beltany Stone Circle to the moment of sovereignty upon the Hill of Tara, this pilgrimage has carried us through every stage of alchemy: death, purification, illumination, and rebirth.

We have walked through mist and sunlight, through grief and laughter.

We have released our stories by firelight, been cleansed by the waters of Boann, anointed by Irish rain, and serenaded by the call of rooks across the hills.

We have breathed ourselves back to life, through words, through song, through the rhythm of the land.

Along the way, writing became more than a craft; it became medicine.

Each page, each prompt, each reflection, a crucible where grief turned to wisdom, and memory to light.

Ireland held us like an old song: stone and wind, myth and spell, fairies and ancestors all humming in the background of our becoming.

Now, as we return to our homes and our daily lives, we do so changed, clearer, braver, more true.

We carry within us a rookery of voices, rising together in chorus, each distinct, yet part of the same great story the earth is telling through us.

I hope you will enjoy these beautiful stories.

With much love,

Dr. Tiffany McBride,

Medicine Crow Woman

The Intuitive Story Behind the Cover Design

Before I ever set foot on Irish soil, the symbols for *The Alchemy of Intuition* had already spoken to me. For over a year, the key kept appearing, in dreams, in meditations, in unexpected places. Sometimes it showed up in art, other times in real life, glimmering like a secret reminder. I didn't yet know its meaning, only that it called me to pay attention.

In early 2025, I finally sketched the key, sensing it might belong somewhere within this project, though I wasn't sure where. Then, in March 2025, I traveled to Ireland, a pilgrimage that cracked open my creative and spiritual vision. Everywhere I went, symbols emerged: stone circles, rivers, spirals, feathers, and the rook, that dark-winged messenger of mystery. In Celtic tradition, the rook is a carrier of truth between worlds, a guardian of story and sovereignty.

After returning home, I attended a Crow Warriorship workshop, where I received a clear vision for the cover design. The rook appeared again, holding the same powerful stillness I felt in Ireland. I saw how the book should look—the sacred geometry, the symbolism, the way the energy needed to move. I created it exactly as I saw it, following my intuition.

But as an artist and a human, I still questioned myself. *Is it too mystical? Too personal? Could this truly be **the one?***

A few months later, I got my answer.

In the summer of 2025, I visited my friend Nancy, a medicine woman in Colorado. The moment I stepped into her home, I looked through the doorway to her back patio, and there it was: a sculpture of a giant crow made entirely of wire.

"Is that real?" I asked, startled.
She smiled. "No, it's made by a local artist."

That evening, we shared dinner and conversation, and I played a few songs on my ukulele. When I finished, Nancy looked deeply moved. She left the room suddenly and returned with something hidden in her palm. "Hold out your hand," she said. Into my palm, she placed a key. "When you were singing, I just saw this key and knew it was for you."

I gasped, half laughing, half crying. "You have *no idea* what this means."

We stepped outside to the wired crow. In its beak was a turquoise crystal. I placed the key gently on its lower beak, and for a moment, time stood still. My friend Natalie, standing nearby, understood immediately that this was the living reflection of the book's spirit.

When I showed Nancy the design on my phone, she was stunned. "Did you just make this?"

"No," I said softly. "I made it months ago. This is confirmation, this is the cover."

When I went back home, I placed the key on my Ireland altar beside another key I received earlier at the Crow Warriorship gathering. Only then did I notice the tiny engraving: Ephesians 6:19.

That verse reads: "Pray also for me, that whenever I speak, words may be given me so that I will fearlessly make known the mystery of the Spirit."

It was the missing piece, the living message of this book. *The Alchemy of Intuition* is about listening to that same inner spirit, allowing divine words and truth to move through us, and speaking them into the world even when it feels risky.

The turquoise crystal, the key, and the wired crow each carried this message home: that our voices are sacred instruments, our intuition the doorway, and our words are the keys that unlock the mysteries of love, healing, and transformation.

That day, I no longer doubted the design.

About the Artist
Cover Design by Dr. Tiffany McBride

Founder of Holistic Vibrations LLC and The Mystic Muse, Tiffany is a visionary artist, author, and designer who weaves myth, psychology, and mysticism into visual storytelling. Her creative process is intuitive, guided by dreams, symbols, and intuition, transforming inner experiences into imagery that speaks directly to the soul.

Through *The Mystic Muse,* Tiffany offers book design and creative direction to independent authors and small publishing houses because she sincerely believes that every voice can heal, awaken, and inspire.

Chapter 1

Rising from the Dead
Healing Ancestral Wounds Through Ceremony

DR. TIFFANY MCBRIDE, LCPC, DSPS, RMT, ORDM

My Story

"I'm going to kill myself! I'm going to kill myself, and it's all because of you!" I screamed into her face as I held her to the floor.

Then, as suddenly as the dream began, I woke up. My chest was heavy with the echo of those words.

The violent dream shattered the silence I kept for decades. That raw scream—the one directed at my mother in the dream—was the truth trying to claw its way out. It wasn't about the present moment; it was about the primal, desperate rage frozen inside me since childhood. I've always been familiar with death and the never-ending cycle of wanting to die. It's followed me around since I was a child.

After the initial shock wore off, I reached for my phone, needing to ground the terrifying imagery in reality. I called a friend.

"I just had an alarming dream about my mother," I managed, my voice still rough.

"Oh, dang, do you want to share it with me?" Natalie asked.

I told her the entire scene: the trial, the accusation, and the crushing feeling of being pre-judged.

"In it, I was being accused of things I hadn't done, pulled into a trial I never consented to. A 'test' of my worth hung over me, but before the results were even known, the damage had already been done. Faces surrounded me, a jury of strangers and ghosts, who had already convicted me. Their judgment was sharp and unrelenting; their minds were changed about me before the truth could surface."

I paused, remembering the physical pain in my chest. "It no longer mattered what the test revealed. It was too late. They had already decided who I was, and that decision ripped something sacred from my chest. I felt my whole life collapse, as if the meaning of everything had been built on a fragile thread tied to the world's acceptance. Without that fragile acceptance, I was nothing. I had no purpose, no breath, no reason to keep going."

Then I got to the climax: "And then, my mother appeared. My fury turned toward her, like a storm that had been waiting its whole life to break. Rage and despair spilled from me as I screamed at her, my voice raw, my body trembling with grief. I had her on the floor, yelling that I was going to kill myself, that it was her fault. Her fault that I had come to this place. Her fault, I could no longer bear to live in a world without meaning. The words tore out of me over and over: 'I'm going to kill myself; I'm going to kill myself, it's because of you.'"

Natalie's silence was heavy. "Wow, what do you think it means?"

The clarity that followed the scream was the strongest answer I ever received.

"I think to break the curse, I need to forgive my mother."

"What curse and forgive her for what?"

Since I was a child, I've been obsessed with death, in a morbid way, yes, but also as a constant companion, a quiet teacher lingering at the edges of my life. Even as a toddler, I sensed presences that others couldn't see:

shadowy figures standing in the doorway of my bedroom, misty children crouched on the floor, playing silently with my toys. They weren't of the living, yet they were more present to me than many of the adults in my world.

My childhood was steeped in sadness, a tangle of broken-home syndrome, an emotionally absent father, a codependent and mentally ill mother, and step-parents who seemed plucked straight from the villains in the movies. I understood the story of Cinderella far too young, recognizing my own reflection in its themes of neglect and cruelty by the time I was eight. Poverty, instability, and abuse weren't abstract ideas; they were my everyday reality.

My stepfather was the abuser. My stepmother was the alcoholic who eventually drank herself into an early grave. And in the quiet aftermath of screaming matches, slammed doors, and nights when no one came to tuck me in, it was the invisible silhouettes, those ghostly companions of my childhood, that became my friends. They were my only solace in the night, my witnesses, and my confidants when the world of the living felt too sharp, dangerous, or absent to hold me.

As I moved into adolescence, the shadows inside my home grew darker still. At thirteen, the ghosts were no longer just the ones I saw at night; they were also the ghosts of safety, innocence, and belonging, all slipping away.

"This is so hard to talk about," I whisper, even now, when I try to tell the story of that 7th-grade year.

My stepfather's words were shards of glass, each one slicing into me, leaving a fresh wound. *Stupid. Lazy. Crazy.* The labels echoed in my head, branding me with his contempt. His hands, heavy and unpredictable, were a constant threat, a reminder of his power. He delighted in breaking us down, forcing us into months of silent confinement, "lessons" in obedience that chipped away at our souls.

School offered no sanctuary. The whispers slithered down the hallways after me, insidious and relentless. *Freak. Evil. Witch.* The words, laced with venom, clung to me like a shroud. Rumors, twisted and amplified, painted me as a monster. Shoves and snickers punctuated the whispers, a constant barrage of low-level assaults.

The threats escalated, death threats scrawled on my locker, whispered in my ear, anonymous notes slipped into my books. The boys were the worst. Their words were laced with sexual innuendo, their hands constantly grazing and poking at me, leaving me feeling dirty and violated. My former friends—the ones I thought I could trust—had joined the others, their silence a deafening betrayal.

My mother, who seemed to be my only refuge at the time, sided with my stepfather.

"Mom, I didn't do anything!" I pleaded.

She crossed her arms, her voice cold and certain. "I talked to your stepfather, and he said you probably did."

My chest caved in. Behind her, he stepped closer until his breath was in my face. "You're a mean person," he hissed. "People don't like you. You deserve what's coming to you."

I froze, wishing I could disappear. This was the moment when the never-ending cycle of feeling betrayed, abandoned, unprotected, and alone began.

The rope tightened around my throat. A physical manifestation of the noose I felt tightening around my life. The pills in my stomach felt heavy, a leaden promise of oblivion.

The world swam before my eyes, the taunts and the pain blurring into a single, unbearable hum. Just as the darkness threatened to swallow me whole, a voice, clear, strong, and utterly certain, pierced through the despair:

No. This is not your end. You were born for more than this.

I gasped, the rope falling away like a discarded snake. Tears streamed down, mixing with the fear and a dawning sense of disbelief. I didn't know where the voice came from, but in the deepest part of me, I knew it had pulled me back from the edge.

I stumbled into the mirror. I saw a stranger staring back. My face was a map of brokenness: tiny red dots, petechial hemorrhages, marking the places where blood vessels had burst from the pressure, a grim, undeniable record of how close I'd come to the end.

"No one noticed. No one knew. I walked around school the next day as a zombie. Ever since that day, I have never really felt alive, constantly fighting for my life and always wanting to die."

"Oh my god. I can't imagine what that must feel like."

"I've spent decades trying to feel alive, trying to be 'okay.' I've done the therapy, the self-help, the meditation, I've built a whole life that, on paper, should feel stable and healed. But there is always more!"

"Yeah, tell me about it," Natalie nudged.

"It's hard to explain. My lifelong fight to feel alive wasn't just about not wanting to die. It was a battle against this core belief that I wasn't *worthy* of being alive. That's the real curse, the worth wound."

"The worth wound; that's powerful."

"Yeah. I've spent decades trying to trust myself, to love myself, to claim my own magic, my intuition, the ability to see and hear things others can't," I sighed. "But from the beginning, people told me it was wrong. My stepfather, my peers, they called it crazy, evil, freakish. So I learned to hide it."

"That's so painful. And the dream you told me about, the one where you screamed at your mom, does it connect to that?"

"It does. That scream wasn't just rage. It was my soul pointing to the source of the worth wound, the moment my mother sided with my abuser. That was the moment I learned that my life, my reality, my feelings didn't matter. After that, I started trusting strangers and ghosts over my own inner voice."

"It's heartbreaking how deep those messages go."

"Yeah. And it's not just me, that's the thing. Generational trauma doesn't only pass down pain; it passes down *patterns*. We inherit not just our ancestors' wounds but also their survival strategies, silence, self-erasure, hypervigilance, always deferring to outside authority instead of trusting ourselves."

"So it's like the silence becomes its own curse."

"Exactly. This is how a curse works, not as magic in the fairy-tale sense, but as a living pattern. One generation feels unsafe to speak, the next doesn't trust its perceptions, and the next may not even recognize its intuition at all. It's a slow erasure of self, moving like a shadow through a family line."

"So how do you stop it?" Natalie inquired.

"By doing more than just surviving. By becoming witnesses, truth-tellers. We name what was hidden, speak what was silenced, and reclaim the parts of ourselves that were called unworthy or dangerous. That's how I think you break a curse, not by punishing your ancestors, but by freeing yourself from the patterns they couldn't heal."

A few weeks later, I led a group to Ireland, a land steeped in myth and ancestral memory, determined to use the ancient practice of alchemy to transmute the past. We began with death, the Nigredo, the stage of blackening and dissolution.

I believed I'd already faced death in my life, but the Irish mist and the weight of the land forced me into a deeper layer. The air itself felt older, heavy with stories that predated language. Wind moved like a keening across the hills. Rain slicked the stone walls of ruins that once held monks, warriors, and poets; lichen crawled across their faces like veins of time. Rooks circled overhead.

Here, death wasn't about dying; it was about the death of the false self, the self-built on the world's fragile acceptance. Every step I took across bog and stone felt like walking on a threshold between worlds. The smell of peat and salt carried something familiar, like the scent of walking to grade school in the backwoods of Washington. The ground beneath me pulsed with memory: famine graves, songs lost to colonization, the bones of my own lineage.

Everything came flooding back—the rumors, the accusations, the betrayal, the gaslighting—but this time I felt how I internalized those voices, how I turned them inward. Ghosts didn't just haunt me; I hosted them.

The physical landscape mirrored my internal state. I stood among the ruins of monastic stones, and at the same time, among the ruins of my own worth. Mists curled around me like ancestral breath. The stones beneath my palms were cold but steady, whispering of endurance. It was as if the land itself held up a mirror and said:

Here are your ghosts. Here are your ruins. This is where the alchemy begins.

The climax of the journey was the Stone of Destiny, the Lia Fáil. Rising from the Hill of Tara like a sentinel, it was more than a relic; it was a living symbol of authentic sovereignty, a touchstone for those who were ready to claim their soul's throne.

As I approached the stone, the worth wound screamed its final, desperate words:

You are a fake. You are crazy. Your magic is a lie. You don't deserve this.

This wasn't just an echo of childhood; it was the family curse itself, the intergenerational trauma speaking its last, desperate word.

But the voice of intuition, the same one that commanded me to live years ago, rose louder. Not a whisper this time, but a roar that filled the mist and the marrow of my bones:

You are an ancient druid. Believe in your magic and power. You are here to rebirth others back into their authentic truth. Your life is worthy. Your magic is the truth. You are the source of love.

I didn't forgive my mother in that instant.

I forgave myself for believing the curse.

For years, I confused forgiveness with absolution, as if to forgive her meant erasing the truth of what happened, pretending her silence hadn't carved its way into my bones.

But that day, forgiveness wasn't about her at all. It was about me finally laying down the burden I had carried since childhood—the belief that her inability to love me the way I needed meant I was unlovable.

I saw then that she, too, had inherited the wound. She was raised inside the same shadows of abandonment and unrequited love; taught to shrink, to please, to silence the voice that might have saved her. What she passed down wasn't just pain; it was fear. A fear older than either of us, rooted in generations of women who learned that survival required disappearance.

So when I forgave myself, I wasn't letting her off the hook.

I unhooked myself from the lineage of shame and fear.

In that moment, something inside me softened, not toward her, but toward the little girl in me who spent decades trying to earn what was already hers: worth, belonging, love.

Forgiveness became a homecoming. Not a bridge to my mother, but a return to myself.

I placed my palms on the cold stone. A single vision flashed: a luminous cord stretching from my belly into the Earth, woven with the pain of generations, my mother's silence, my grandmother's shame, the ache of women who loved too hard and were never seen.

It pulsed, alive, braided from threads of shame, appeasement, and unrequited love. It kept me bound for lifetimes.

A question came, not in words, but as a knowing: *Are you ready to release what was never yours to carry?*

I was afraid. To cut that cord felt like dying. But I knew that to keep it meant never living.

"Yes," I whispered. "Yes."

Heat flooded my hands. The stone flickered from black to red to gold. The cord loosened and dissolved into light.

I release the pain of love that does not return to me.

I release the voices that called me unworthy.

I call back my love, my power, my worth, and my name.

I return to myself what was stolen and lift from myself what was never mine to carry.

From the roots of my ancestors to the wings of my descendants,

I break the cord of shame and silence.

I stand sovereign, whole, and seen.

The contract is broken. The curse is ended.

Now I'm blessed with the gifts of my ancestors, the strength of my fathers, the mystic gifts of my great aunt, the musician in my grandfather, the singer in my grandmother, the writer in my mother, and the artist in my own becoming.

Their voices live in mine. Their dreams breathe through me. And at last, I'm free to create, not from their pain, but from their power.

The Medicine

To hear your inner voice, you must first learn to recognize which voices are not yours.

From birth, we're shaped by the chorus of our ancestors, our family systems, our culture, and the collective wounds passed down through generations.

These voices teach us how to survive, but survival isn't the same as truth. Some of the voices we inherited whisper love and resilience; others echo shame, silence, or self-doubt. Over time, they become so entangled with our own that we mistake conditioning for intuition.

True intuition lives beneath the noise. It's the quiet pulse that remains when all the borrowed stories fall away. To hear it again, we must release what no longer belongs to us.

This ritual is a sacred act of reclamation—a cord-cutting ceremony to release inherited patterns and return your voice to its natural frequency.

You will need:

- A candle or small fire

- A length of string or ribbon (to represent the ancestral cord)

- Paper and pen

- A bowl or fireproof container

1. **Begin in stillness.**
   Close your eyes and breathe deeply. Feel the invisible cords connecting you to your lineage—threads of love, pain, protection, and silence. Whisper gratitude for all that has been carried forward.

2. **Write two lists.**
   On one side of the paper, name what you wish to *keep* from your ancestors: their strength, creativity, faith, courage, wisdom, humor, or song.

   On the other, name what you choose to *release:* their fear, shame, addiction, self-doubt, silence, or unworthiness.

3. **Hold the cord.**
   Imagine it stretching through generations, mother to daughter, father to son, lineage to lineage. Feel its weight, its love, its grief.

4. **Speak aloud:**
   "I honor the ones who came before.
   I keep the medicine that strengthens me,
   and I release the pain that is not mine to carry.
   I cut the cords of fear and silence,
   and return to the truth of my own voice."

5. **Cut the cord.**
   With intention, snip or tear the string. Breathe. Feel the space that opens.

6. **Offer it to the fire.**
   Let the smoke carry your release. Watch the flames transmute the old stories into light.

Sit in the stillness that follows, the sacred quiet where your true voice begins to speak again.

Dr. Tiffany McBride, (she/her, they/them)

Dr. Tiffany McBride is a Doctor of Shamanic Psycho-Spiritual Studies, a licensed clinical psychotherapist, a creative life coach, a trauma recovery guide, an energy master and teacher, a birth and death doula, an ordained shamanic minister, an expressive musician, an artist, and a seven-time bestselling author.

As founder of Holistic Vibrations, LLC, Tiffany bridges psychology and mysticism, utilizing integrative remedies and altered states of consciousness to help people heal trauma, navigate addiction, explore women's and LGBTQIA+ issues, and reconnect with their intuition.

With over two decades of experience, Tiffany embodies the union of science and spirit, weaving ancient wisdom with modern therapeutic methods to guide others toward wholeness and self-discovery. Their life's work reflects a deep commitment to compassion, service, and transformation.

Looking ahead, Tiffany envisions expanding her reach through global courses, retreats, and workshops, empowering others to embark on their own healing journeys. Through her blend of clinical expertise, intuitive insight, and creative expression, she inspires others to reclaim their power, voice, and authentic selves.

Outside of her healing work, Tiffany loves to write, make candles, create art, sing, play ukulele and guitar, dance, spend time in nature, attend concerts, and connect with the community.

If You Are Struggling:

Healing can awaken deep emotions. You are not alone. If you ever feel hopeless or in crisis, please reach out for help:

- **988 Suicide & Crisis Lifeline (U.S.),** Call or text **988** or visit 988lifeline.org

- **Trans Lifeline:** 877-565-8860 (U.S.) | 877-330-6366 (Canada)
- **The Trevor Project:** 1-866-488-7386 or text **START** to 678-678
- **International help:** findahelpline.com

Help is available. You are worthy of care, love, and healing.

To learn more about Dr. Tiffany's work, visit the "About the Author" page.

CONNECT WITH DR. TIFFANY:

Websites: https://www.tiffany-mcbride.org

https://www.themysticmuse.org

Instagram: https://www.instagram.com/witchycrowwmn83

Facebook: https://www.facebook.com/profile.php?id=61552573784401

https://www.facebook.com/profile.php?id=61576753293948

Chapter 2

Remember Your Roots
Deepening Relationships with Plant Medicine
CHRISTINE FALCON-DAIGLE, MFA, RYT-200

My Story

"Where I come from in Kenya, we have a saying," Mohammed said, "A home without a grandmother is like land without a well."

"Oh, I love that!" Mom piped up. We had just arrived in Wales from Ireland, on the final leg of our three-week trip, which began in Scotland. The rhythmic sound of the windshield wipers soothed me as we enjoyed a lively conversation over the hour-long ride through the darkness to our hotel.

"How do you say it in your native tongue?" I asked. I could tell from his eyes in the rearview that my question made him smile.

He spoke a beautiful language completely unfamiliar to me, then in English added, "There's no exact translation. In Swahili, we have many different words for water."

Still, we understood the meaning: *Without the wisdom of a female elder in the home, a house is lacking in something fundamental and life-giving.*

A few days earlier, we participated in a powerful breathwork session in Ireland that included a plant medicine component. The young, native Irish couple who led it reminded me of the land itself: gentle and light-filled with deep, ancient roots.

Daryl and Cía passed out delicate porcelain tea cups with different floral motifs.

"These belonged to my mother," Daryl said to our group—all women, spanning five decades in age—already deeply bonded by a week spent exploring our lives through Carl Jung's Four Stages of Alchemy.

We sat in a circle on the floor—yoga mats spread out atop a plush wool rug with an ornate and colorful design. Our session took place upstairs, on the second floor of our final home for the author's journey: a three-story, centuries-old mansion, complete with resident peacocks, hidden doors, and no less than a few ghosts.

"Before I serve you the tea," Daryl said, "I want to tell you about the tea."

He shared the names and descriptions of each plant, its medicinal powers, and the place where he'd harvested them.

"We have hawthorn berries from Lough Cru; hawthorn leaf and flower from the Hill of Tara; also, elderflower from the Hill of Tara; Scots pine needles from the forest that I lived in for nine months; and meadowsweet from the bank of the River Boyne."

As he named each sacred site, I could picture it in my mind. *I know that place. We've been there!*

Daryl's deep, resonant voice had a lyrical quality to it, and his words fell over us like a spell or an incantation. It was enchanting and stirred my soul to feel the reverence in his voice as he spoke about each place. He had a relationship with the land from which he sourced the various ingredients for our tea.

Our delicate tea cups were filled, one by one, from Daryl's thermos.

"Now, I invite you to connect with the spirit of the plant, and ask it to come into your body," Daryl suggested. "Hawthorn is a heart opener," he said, and I imagined it to act like other heart openers I ingested, like cacao. I took a sip and held it in my mouth for a long moment before swallowing.

In this manner of connecting with the tea, I was instantly transported back in time, some thirty years.

I am in California. My Uncle Brad is still alive, and he is serving me stinging nettle tea on the floor of his Spanish-style stucco home in San Mateo, where we sit on a rug in front of a roaring fireplace. "Take a minute to smell it before you drink it," he instructs me, "connect with the spirit of the nettle plant."

As we drank our tea in silence, I felt the uncanny presence of my uncle, here with us in Ireland.

With no interest in marriage or children, he had been spiritually adopted by the Lakota Sioux Tribe on the Rosebud Reservation in South Dakota, where he split his time until he died of cancer at 49. He had instructed me in much the same way Daryl did, to recognize and honor the spirit of plants, and to ask their spirit to enter and aid me. I smiled fondly at the memory.

After we drank our tea, Daryl had us lie down. He led us through a powerful breathwork session, during which he played multiple instruments against a background of recorded music, including a didgeridoo from Australia.

I had done breathwork before, and for some reason, I didn't expect to go very deep. Boy, was I wrong!

While I focused on a single continuous breath, I felt a powerful, energetic connection to my father's mother—a grandmother I had never met but always felt an inexplicable pull toward. The connection was so powerful, it felt almost physical, as if I held her hand across the veil. Holding my other hand, I sensed someone else: the spirit of my daughter. The transmission from past to future ran through me like a current as I breathed. This collapsing of time and space is hard to explain in words. It was pure *feeling*.

When the session was over, Daryl gently called us back to the present moment. As we began to stir and sit up, he invited us to share.

"If and when you feel called, I will hand you the talking piece. It's made from the branch of a hazel tree."

I gasped. *Hazel was my grandmother's name!*

I reached out and accepted the stick from Daryl. Clutching it with both hands, I relayed what happened to me to the best of my ability, aware that nothing I said could capture the felt sense of it.

I explained how the spirit of my paternal grandmother, whose name was Hazel, came to me. "She *had* to have been Irish! My father—who always believed he was solely Danish—has more Irish DNA, it turns out, than Mom!"

"Hazel Edith was a shadowy figure in our family. She was one of a large number of siblings whose mother died in childbirth when Edith, as she was called, was only two. A few years later, she and her younger sister were put in foster care when their father was arrested for bootlegging and jailed. The other, older children were separated and adopted out. . ." I choked back tears, imagining their fear.

"Edith and her younger sister Irene were raised by an elderly couple, who took them in as teenagers, essentially adopting the two girls. These were the grandparents who raised my father, while his parents were gone, during the war years," I said, awash in compassion for the unimaginable loss of their entire family.

Everyone nodded and waited patiently for me to finish. "This has been so profoundly healing for me to connect with my paternal grandmother on the land of our ancestors—something I hadn't even realized I was longing for."

I lifted up the talking stick. "To hold this hazel branch in my hand, and to feel a real connection that stretches back not just to her, but to her mother, and her mother's mother in an arctic land imbued with light. . ." I trailed off, overcome by emotion. I took a deep breath, "It's helped me understand in a visceral way for the first time exactly whose granddaughter I am." I was flooded with emotion and gratitude.

When I was complete, I passed the stick to the next person. When everyone finished sharing, Daryl asked if anyone would like to say anything else.

Mom raised her hand. "Did our tea have nettle in it? My brother Brad used to make stinging nettle tea, and it reminded me of that."

"It's interesting you would ask that," Daryl replied. "I usually do put nettle in the tea, but I didn't have any; however, as I was speaking my words over it, I called in the spirit of the nettle." I felt chills all over my body and laughed to myself.

Of course you did.

A realization that I had many years before hit home: *It's all connected—life.* The first time I really understood this, consciously, was after a vivid dream, some fifteen years earlier, living in Bolinas.

"IT'S ALL ENERGY!" A powerful woman's voice jolted me awake.

Under a mountain of blankets, I was still and solid as a redwood. My pounding heart seemed to shake the entire bed. No one else was home. I strained to hear the voice again, listening for any sound of movement.

Who—or what—was that?!

I was on an enormous suspension bridge in my dream, covered in thick, tangled jungle vines. I clearly saw the way the emerald green serpentine plants coiled around and climbed up the cables, like Scarlet Runner beans in the garden.

It was after that dream that I enrolled in and completed a two-year horticultural therapy course. It's as if the woman whose voice I heard *woke me up* and urged me to learn all I could about how the plant kingdom could benefit humanity, and then share it with others.

Through my study of plants and healing, I was led to the wisdom keepers in certain indigenous traditions in the Americas. In ceremony and with expert guides from these lineages, I cultivated my own relationships with certain entheogenic plants.

Used by ancient people for thousands of years in ceremonies and rituals, and to connect with the divine, entheogens may have played a role at Newgrange, something we learned about while visiting the Neolithic passage tomb in Ireland.

Constructed in 3100 BC, Newgrange is one of the oldest manmade structures in the world—older than the pyramids in Egypt and Stonehenge.

The session with Daryl and Cía touched on my deep respect for the mystery and magic in the natural world, and an inner knowing that our planet isn't just a mere rock floating in space, here for us to take from without giving back; nor are we separate from her. She's a living, conscious being, the source of all life on Earth. We belong to her, and we must live in right relationship—that is, with respect and reciprocity. It also ignited a desire to help others connect to their ancestral roots through the natural world around them.

My time in Scotland, Ireland, and Wales with my mom is an experience that I know will continue to grow and expand over the years to come. A journey like ours plants many seeds. Those seeds will germinate and—when conditions are just right—birth new expressions of life into being.

The Medicine

Plants and humans have evolved together for millennia. Of course, we would have deep, ancient relationships with them.

"Even your great-grandmother Isabel Lopez brought mint from Mazatlán to San Francisco to remind her of home," Mom told me, after the ceremony with Daryl in Ireland.

In the 1988 documentary series *The Power of Myth* with Bill Moyers, Joseph Campbell described how Americans were cut off from our roots—not just our mythologies and rites of initiation, both of which are deeply tied to the natural world, but from Mother Nature (i.e., our ancestral homelands) herself. He believed this was a cause for so much of our nation's suffering and *disease*.

Intuitively, I know this is true. I hadn't known *how* true until I returned to some of my ancestral homelands. We're all indigenous (i.e., native) to land somewhere. Some of us have multiple ancestral homelands. For example, I have DNA from both Native American and European ancestors. My ancestors are both the colonized and the colonizers who oppressed them.

Whether by choice or by force, many of us come from lands far away. As humans, we must adapt and learn to *grow where we're planted.* But there is something to be said for *digging in the dirt* of the place our people—or peoples—originated.

Plants are kin; they root us to the earth. They link us to place and are as much our relatives as our human families. They can help us deepen our relationships with the world around us, our ancestral homelands, and our family lineage.

KNOW YOUR ROOTS
A somatic exercise for *remembering your roots*

Most of us are familiar with the traditional family tree, where the lines extend upwards. This exercise involves drawing yourself as a tree, and then the family roots, extending down, underground. Imagine diagramming a sentence.

1. Begin with yourself. In the upper third of a poster board, draw yourself as a tree. Then draw a line to indicate the Earth. This is the intersection of personal identity (the land you inhabit now, along with its culture) and all of your ancestors, along with their various lands and cultures.

2. Now for the roots: list each of your (biological) parents; below them, each of their parents; then, your grandparents. Continue with this, as far back as you can. The complex web of interconnection mirrors all the genetic and epigenetic information that lives in you today.

If you don't know this information, that's a great place to begin your research! Talk to your family members—our elders are living libraries.

FURTHER POINTS OF INQUIRY

Research and write about each one of these essential roots in your lineage.

What do you know about them? If not the land where you currently reside, what land did they come from? Why did they leave? What were some of the plants and the customary ways people used them in that land/region?

Be as specific as possible. This is the fertile soil that feeds and nourishes you, the living human tree.

Epigenetics, the study of how our genes are expressed (which is not fixed), has shown that trauma is passed down at least 7, if not 14, generations. And it's not just our ancestors' trauma and disease but their resilience as well.

HONORING FIRST PEOPLES

One additional thought to consider is the identity of the original inhabitants of the place you now call home. Research First Peoples in your region. Who were they? What language did they speak? Find ways to acknowledge and honor them and their descendants.

JOURNAL PROMPTS:

- What were your ancestors' sources of strength? How did they survive the hard times?

- What were the stories, practices, belief systems, and structures that helped them survive?

- Did they come from a harsh climate or a warm tropical one? Was it an arid or water-sparse region? Did they save seeds? Did they preserve food?

- How did they store information and resources? What were their written and oral traditions?

- What or who helped them survive?

- What was their cosmological and/or spiritual belief system?

All people, when you go far back enough, worshipped the Earth. They lived with a sense of the sacred in their daily lives. Paganism is just an adaptation of shamanism, a belief system that recognizes the divine in everything.

Anima mundi is a Latin phrase meaning "world soul" or "soul of the world." It represents a concept of an animating principle or vital force that connects and animates all living and non-living things in the universe, suggesting an intrinsic link between everything in nature. This idea has ancient philosophical roots, including in the work of Plato, and has been explored by thinkers throughout history.

This wasn't taboo or considered nonsense. This was a commonly accepted way of being.

It wasn't until the split with science that matter became divorced from spirit. The root of the word *matter* actually has the same root as *mother*. It was at this same time that the Earth, and all wild processes associated with her, were vilified and deified as "dirty", even "evil." She was maligned, right along with all things associated with the feminine, such as dreams, emotions, intuition, plant medicine, and magic.

You can see how important understanding the root of everything is, whether it's the etymology of a word, the epigenetics of your family tree, or the actual root structure of a plant. Roots give us information, resources, and deepen our connections to ourselves, each other, and the world around us.

FREE RESOURCES

If you'd like to learn more about horticultural therapy, check out Smithsonian Gardens' YouTube channel:

https://www.youtube.com/watch?v=EtqkVWwELvY

Or listen to singing plants in Damanhur, in Italy!

https://www.youtube.com/watch?v=aZaokNmQ4eY

RECOMMENDED READING

Last Child in the Woods: Saving Our Children from Nature Deficit Disorder by Richard Louv* (*Keynote speaker at the 2025 AHTA Conference)

The Hidden Life of Trees: What They Feel, How They Communicate by Peter Wohlleben

Your Brain on Nature: The Science of Nature's Influence on Your Health, Happiness, and Vitality by Eva M. Selhub, MD, and Alan C. Logan, ND

Braiding Sweetgrass: Indigenous Wisdom, Scientific Knowledge, and the Teachings of Plants by Robin Wall Kimmerer

Seeds of Hope: Wisdom and Wonder from the World of Plants by Jane Goodall

Christine Falcon-Daigle is the CEO of Transformanity Collective and a member of the American Horticultural Therapy Association. She holds a Master of Fine Arts in Writing and Consciousness from California Institute of Integral Studies and a Bachelor of Arts in Psychology, with a minor in English Literature from Dominican University. An award-winning poet and best-selling author, she's Associate Producer of the multi-award-winning documentary *The Last Stand: Ancient Redwoods and the Bottomline,* which aired nationally on PBS. Her unpublished manuscript, *This Is What I Know,* received an Honorable Mention in the William Faulkner Wisdom Writing Competition in 2007. A certified women's circle facilitator with Global Sisterhood, she's led monthly women's circles in Marin County since 2022, and in 2024, launched her transformational coaching practice. Certified in The Miracle Way™, a new model of leadership, she currently helps manage the Hoffman Institute Retreat Center in Northern California. She has completed courses in labyrinth construction, horticultural therapy, sacred storytelling, and Collective Trauma Integration Process (CTIP). As a Baptiste Power of Yoga instructor, Christine trained with master yogis Sherri Baptiste and Michele Hebert, and studied *pranayama* with Richard Miller, founder of iRest. She has supported local and international yoga retreats since 2010. In 2024, Christine founded Transformanity Collective, LLC, offering daylong in-person retreats in collaboration with other healing arts professionals. In 2024, she became a founding board member and officer of Big Mesa Healing Sanctuary, a 501(c)(3) based in Marin County, California, and is committed to nature-based healing in community. Christine's online course "How to Start a Healing Writing Circle" is available through the Brave Healer Transformation School. In partnership with Compassion in Action and Solidad Correctional Facility (SCF), it's now available to inmates for free.

CONNECT WITH CHRISTINE:

Website: http://www.christinefalcondaigle.com/

LinkedIn:
https://www.linkedin.com/in/christine-falcon-daigle-0000a1113

Substack: Through a Crack in the Pavers
https://substack.com/@christinefalcondaigle?

Brave Healer Transformation School: "How to Start a Healing Writing Circle"
https://bravehealertransformationschool.com/How-To-Start-a-Healing-Writing-Group-order

Facebook: https://www.facebook.com/christine.falcone.332/

Instagram: https://www.instagram.com/cfalconmoon/

https://www.instagram.com/transformanity/

Chapter 3

Unshakeable Confidence
The Somatic Path to Embodied Heart-Centered Leadership
KEADY PHELAN, DCC, ACC

My Story

No fear.

This is a first, Keady.

I stopped walking.

When was the last time you walked alone at night without looking over your shoulder or quickening your pace? Never!

No clenched jaw. No racing heartbeat. No looping thoughts of all the dangers I imagined, but I couldn't see.

As I walked through the garden at Killeen Castle, County Meath, Ireland, near our lodgings, wrapped in warm layers, the cool night mist on my forehead, nose, and cheeks, I looked up into the starlit sky and paused, a moment of gratitude to the night. My body relaxed, my heart rate slowed, and a big smile took hold.

I'd been in Ireland for about a week on a writing retreat led by our lead author, with our publisher, and eleven other women, all of us crafting our own unique chapters for this book. We walked our own paths of transformation, exploring the four stages of alchemy—death, purification, the rise of consciousness, and transformation—and through this journey, accessed our intuition, shared insights and learnings, and our voices, being seen and held in community.

And here, in this dark garden, I realized I transformed something I carried my entire life.

Fear.

Not the kind that keeps you alert and safe from actual danger. The kind that lives deep inside, coiled tight, ready to strike at the slightest provocation. The kind born of shame, rooted in self-judgment and self-doubt.

For most of my life, my body stored negative experiences like a vault—a raised voice, mocking tone, someone else's disappointment in me. Each moment embedded itself in my nervous system, creating automatic threat responses I had a hard time controlling.

And I finally discovered a through line: hearing my name called.

"Keady."

That single word could send my heart racing, throat closing, and palms sweating. It meant I was in trouble. I did something wrong. I was bad.

It took me decades to understand why.

THE SCHOOLYARD CHANT

"Keady!"

My 4th-grade teacher called my name as I walked into the classroom.

"You're late, again. Go to your desk."

That morning, I walked toward my classmates, all lined up waiting for our teacher to open the door.

I heard it.

One voice. Then another. Then all of them, in unison, in singsong rhythm.

"Love and kisses, Keady. Love and kisses, Keady."

They chanted the last line of a love letter I gave to a boy I had a crush on—something I'd seen in an *After School Special,* a popular 1970s kids' TV show.

Their voices started quietly, building as I got closer. Heat rose from my toes to my head. I trembled with each chant.

I turned and ran, tears streaming down my face as their roars of laughter faded behind me—humiliated and crushed by their pleasure in my pain.

As I rode my bike home, I rehearsed what I'd tell my mom.

"I feel sick."

She pressed the back of her hand to my forehead.

"You don't have a fever. Go back to school," she reprimanded.

All I wanted was for her to hug me and say, "Okay, honey. Go back to bed. You'll feel better soon," words I never heard.

I was afraid to tell her what I did, how everyone made fun of me.

So I rode back to school. I walked the walk of shame through the classroom door, past their whispers, to my seat, head down. I wished I could disappear.

Why does this keep happening to me? Why is everyone so mean to me?

I experienced many similar scenes like this growing up—being picked on, feeling embarrassed, ashamed, and afraid.

These moments taught me to be small, to hide my true self, to shove it all down. I learned that the real me—who just wanted to feel loved, be included, and experience joy—was too much, too wrong.

Every time someone called my name with urgency or frustration, my system prepared for an attack, threat, or danger.

My name became a warning bell. By the time I reached middle school, even hearing 'Keady!' in kindness could trigger panic.

THE FIELD, MY ONLY OUTLET

"Keady! Control yourself!"

My soccer coach's voice cut across the field.

I was twelve years old, playing center midfield, and I just fouled a player a little too hard, a little too late, and got a warning.

Grrr! My frustration howled deep within me.

Off the field, my emotions had nowhere to go. I never dared express how I really felt, fearing punishment or ridicule.

But the field was the only place I could let my emotions fly, all the anger and hurt—untethered, sometimes unwelcome, and it felt so good.

It was my only reference for managing emotions, other than the inner voice that kept me in line—*be good, don't make waves, and do what you're told.*

I lived this way for decades. The soccer field eventually led me to college, then a corporate leadership career. I learned to channel my intensity into achievement—climbing the ladder, proving my worth, perfecting the art of looking calm and confident while my inner world screamed otherwise.

THE CURIOUS SKEPTIC AND THE FIRST RELEASE

I worked with an executive coach to be more confident, less defensive, and more succinct and decisive.

"Keady, I think working with a somatic experiencing practitioner (SEP) will be great for you." When my coach suggested this, I was skeptical until I yawned my way into freedom.

My SEP's office was calming and comfortable. She didn't ask me to lie on a table or close my eyes, at least not right away. We sat and faced each other.

She asked me some questions and then paused me as I told her about my difficult day.

"What are you noticing in your body?" she asked.

I scan head to toe as instructed.

"My throat feels tight."

I had no idea I felt that way until she asked me.

"Good," she said gently. "Just notice. Don't try to change it."

We sat in silence, and I felt ridiculous.

What am I supposed to be noticing?

"Stay with it. You're doing great. Just breathe into the tightness."

I took in some nice deep breaths, and before I could think, my jaw opened wide.

I yawned—a deep, full-body yawn that seemed to come from my belly.

"Ahhhh, that feels good."

"Ahhhh," she mirrored me loudly.

My eyes widened, caught off guard by her response.

"What?" I laughed.

She smiled. "Your nervous system just discharged some energy. That's what a yawn is—a release."

I sat there, stunned. For the first time in my life, something moved through me without me having to fight it, stuff it down, or run it off on a soccer field.

This is different.

- My curious skeptic transformed into a true believer in this work.

- I learned how to regulate my nervous system.

- How to recognize my old, conditioned threat responses.

- How to pause, breathe, and move the energy through and out of my body.

These became stepping stones on my path to feeling free to be me and to being truly confident internally.

THE FALL

A few years into working with my SEP, I hiked in Yosemite Upper Falls with my best friends to celebrate our 50th birthdays. It was a perfect, warm, sunny day. After a two-hour hike up, we sat in the cool water and laughed until our sides hurt.

We took a shortcut over the rocks instead of retracing our steps on the main trail. My friends, Michele and Pam, navigated easily. I followed Michele, my backpack loose and uneven as I gripped my walking stick.

I eyed the jump between two rocks.

Easy. I can do this in two steps.

I jumped and completely missed.

My ankle jammed the top of the uneven rock as I flew over, and my other leg dragged behind. I landed hard, dazed, sunglasses cracked against my face, blood dripping, warm down my cheek.

What the—?

Without thinking, I slowly scanned my body the way I practiced with Mary. *Neck—okay. Spine—okay.* I wiggled my fingers, my toes. Everything worked. I breathed deeply, got up slowly, and went back to where I started.

"Michele!" I yelled, trying to keep my voice steady.

"I need you."

I heard her call back.

"What's up, sweetie?"

She squatted with me.

Her face flashed concern before settling into calm.

"You're okay. It doesn't look that bad." Her tone reassured me.

Pam appeared right beside us, concerned and loving. Together, they helped me navigate back to the trail, where a nurse happened to be passing by. He checked me, and there was no sign of concussion.

My ankle and face throbbed as we began our descent. Michele held my arm. Pam took the lead. Both encouraged me the whole way. Going at my pace, I stayed present and breathed into each painful step. Michele and Pam kept saying how amazed they were at how calm I was. I felt calm.

THE LOOP

For days, I couldn't stop replaying the fall. It woke me up at night—the moment. *Crash!* How I flew past and landed face down. Over and over, my mind relived it, and I couldn't stop it.

I told Mary everything in our next session—the fall, my somatic response, the scene on repeat.

She led me somatically back through the experience, and paused me when my body activated. Tears flowed, and my body shook as it released the energy. Once I finished and my nervous system settled, she asked:

"How would you have done it differently?"

I saw it clearly.

"I hand over my backpack and drop my walking stick."

I continued.

"I sit down and carefully move from one rock to the other until I emerge on the other side, unscathed, to my friends' bright, smiling faces."

I saw myself doing exactly that, over and over. I slowly breathed into this new memory through the rest of the session.

Now, this is what I remember. The loop stopped. My nervous system has released the fall and created a new experience, a new pathway integrated.

I SEE THE PATTERN

In the kitchen one evening, I chopped vegetables when my husband called from upstairs.

"Keady, I have a question."

My heart started to pound.

Here it comes. How did I mess up? What did I forget?

But this time, I saw the story.

I placed my hand on my chest and felt the rapid thump-thump-thump.

I took a breath. Then another.

"Yeah?" I called back, my voice steady. "What's up?"

"I can't find my cell phone. Can you call it for me?"

That was it? His phone?

I burst into laughter—not at him, but at myself, at the old pattern that held me hostage for so long. My name being called was a threat signal my whole life.

But not anymore.

That's when I knew it, the thread that was there all along.

My name has been the trigger.

MASTERING MOVING ENERGY THROUGH

I'm now in a year-long coaching mastery program, expanding my skills and helping my clients experience deep and lasting change by awakening transformation from within. The work is intense and vulnerable. It's asking me to step into full visibility as a coach and leader.

And old fears keep showing up.

You're not enough. You're going to fail.

The other day, I prepared for a potential client call. As I reviewed my coaching offer and pricing, butterflies swarmed my belly, and my throat tightened.

I didn't override the sensations with a pep talk. I closed my eyes, silently breathed into the sensations, and inquired within.

Is there a story here?

Yes. The old story that I'm not worthy, that I'm asking for too much. The same story I've been telling myself since I was a child.

I let the story be there—acknowledged it—and then I set it aside, not pushing it away, just not letting it lead.

I sat with it all, and the sensations shifted. Within moments, the contraction lightened and then dissipated altogether.

I opened my eyes, looked around my office, and saw the light coming through the window. I heard birds singing outside and felt my feet on the floor.

From this spacious place, I got on the call—clear, calm, confident, and fully present and in service to the person across from me.

This is what somatic awareness has given me: the ability to move energy through my body quickly—not by force, but by awareness, allowing, and accepting.

And by pausing the inner story that keeps the emotion and energy stuck.

IRELAND: THE GIFT OF FULL CIRCLE

Arriving in Ireland, I didn't know how profoundly the experience would affirm my transformation.

One morning, as I stepped onto the bus, one of the other authors—a woman I was beginning to know—smiled warmly at me.

"Keady," she exclaimed, with the Irish pronunciation—*Kee-dee.*

My heart opened. A smile spread across my face—wide, unguarded, genuine.

"Hi." I smiled back.

I felt seen and welcomed, not threatened.

For the first time in my life, hearing my name felt like a warm embrace.

On our final day, we visited the Hill of Tara, one of Ireland's most sacred sites. While the group browsed the shops, I felt pulled toward two donkeys grazing near the entrance to the ancient hill.

We saw them earlier that morning and greeted them briefly. But this time felt different. Something in me knew I needed to be with them.

I approached the younger donkey slowly, showing him the back of my hand in greeting. He lowered his head—*an invitation.* I gently scratched his forehead, my touch soft and present.

After a moment, he lifted his head and turned it to the left.

Okay. You're done. I see you.

I didn't push or try to get more connection. I simply honored his boundary.

But then he looked back at me and closed his eyes. I placed my left palm on his neck—just resting there, connecting, feeling this beautiful animal's warmth under my hand.

My breathing slowed and deepened. A calm washed over me.

Suddenly, the donkey's muzzle pulled back, he showed his teeth, and yawned—a huge, full-body yawn! Then another.

Then a full body shake, a sign of release.

Tears streamed down my cheeks.

I sensed the donkey felt safe enough with me to release something, to discharge what he held, because my nervous system was calm, regulated, and present.

My hand still resting on his neck, I tearfully whispered, "Thank you."

My entire life, I unconsciously projected my internal chaos onto others—my tension, fear, and need to control. People and animals could feel it, even when I tried to hide it.

Through my somatic practices, I learned to create a different field, one of presence, safety, and regulation.

THE PATH TO EMBODIED HEART-CENTERED LEADERSHIP

My somatic journey—from a little girl frozen by the sound of her name to a woman who can walk alone at night in a foreign land without fear—taught me something essential about leadership.

Unshakeable confidence isn't obtained in the mind; it comes through the body and a connected heart.

When your nervous system is dysregulated—stuck in fight, flight, freeze, or fawn—your access to clear thinking, heart-centered presence, and wise action is severely limited. You operate from survival, not from choice.

But when you learn to pause the story, and allow your emotions and physical sensations, something profound opens up—your mind quiets, your heart connects, and your body grounds.

And from this balanced place—this integrated wholeness—you can access your intuition, inner voice, and authentic leadership.

This is what I mean by embodied heart-centered leadership. It's not about being perfect or never getting triggered. It's about having the somatic awareness and tools to return to presence, regulate yourself, and create a field of safety and possibility for yourself and others.

The medicine I share here is one of the foundational tools of my journey and of my coaching container. It's simple and takes practice. It requires you to slow down, turn inward, and befriend the sensations in your body rather than resist or override them.

This is an invitation to begin your own somatic path—to discover what becomes possible when you learn to move energy through your body, release what's been stuck, and respond from a place of presence rather than protection.

The Medicine

It takes 90 seconds to feel an emotion—tight shoulders, knot in your throat—before it moves through your body. If it stays longer than 90 seconds, you're in a story about what the emotion means, keeping it stuck in the body.

This gentle exploration guides you to notice, allow, accept, and move energy through the body.

Try these five essentials for this practice:

1. **Choose a mild trigger.** Start with a 3-5/10 intensity. Bring the situation to your mind.

2. **Be with the sensation.** Close your eyes. Notice where you feel energy in your body (contraction). Drop your attention directly into the sensation (knot, tightness)? Is there a shape/color/image/ movement?

3. **Allow and accept it.** Breathe into the sensation, welcoming it exactly as it is with love and compassion. Greeting it somatically. Without a story. All sensation.

4. **Complete.** Feel your nervous system settle (lessens, yawns).

5. **Then. Ground and reflect.** Feel your feet. Look around the room and jot down a few notes about what you experienced.

SAFETY AND PACE:

Practice inside your window of tolerance. If you feel overwhelmed (anxious, frozen, spaced out), pause. Open your eyes, feel your feet, name five things you see.

This work isn't about fixing yourself—you're not broken. We're simply creating new options and partnering with the body's wisdom, at your pace.

AN INVITATION TO DIVE DEEPER:

You have everything within you already to have unshakeable confidence. Somatic exploration supports you to experience this more fully. If you want to dive deeper and experience the guided somatic exploration, click here: https://keadyphelan.com/somatic-guide

Keady Phelan has practiced somatic exploration as both coach and client for 10+ years. This deep, embodied work transformed not only her own life but also shaped her entire approach to leadership and personal growth. Driven by a profound purpose to awaken transformation from within, Keady brings a multi-level approach to women leaders and entrepreneurs ready to lead with embodied presence, confidence, and authenticity.

With 25+ years as a corporate leader, Keady understands firsthand the unique pressures, patterns, and possibilities that women in leadership face. She made her own courageous transition from corporate leadership to living her purpose as a women's transformational leadership coach—a journey she shares in her chapter, "Nudges from the Universe: Transforming Shame into Self-Compassion and Self-Acceptance," in Brave Healer Productions' book, *Find Your Voice, Save Your Life*. She's a certified leadership and Enneagram coach and is currently Mastery Method trained through the Institute for Coaching Mastery, pursuing her certification. The Mastery Method is central to her coaching practice, allowing her to work with clients on multiple levels—somatic, emotional, mental, behavioral, and unconscious. This work integrates nervous system awareness, unconscious reprogramming, and embodied transformation to create profound and lasting change. From this new ground, you emerge as a present, grounded, confident leader—one who is inspired by heart and fully expressed in purpose.

Keady draws inspiration from nature, writing music, spending time with family and friends, and wants nothing more than to create a world where each person has a kinder, gentler relationship with themselves and others.

CONNECT WITH KEADY:

Website: https://www.keadyphelan.com

Contact Keady: https://keadyphelan.com/contact

Instagram: https://www.instagram.com/kdpcoaching_keadyphelan/

Chapter 4

Connecting to Source
The Intuitive Healing of Holy Fire III Reiki

DR. RUTH A. SOUTHER, CRMT, BH, SH, FF

My Story

"I. Can't. Breathe."

As I walked through the lounge area of the Marlin Hotel in Dublin, I noticed a woman fanning herself.

"What's wrong? Can I help you?"

"I. Can't. Breathe," she gasped again.

My hands immediately became hot as Reiki ignited with the higher vibrational Source from which all healing medicine flows. Some call it divine, heavenly, universal, cosmic—all are correct and can be used interchangeably. It's essential to note that this energy flows through me, yet it doesn't engage my life force.

"May I touch you?"

She nodded.

I placed one hand on her chest and the other behind her shoulder. "Take a deep breath. In through the nose, and out through the mouth."

I illustrated the breathing technique, as my palms pulsed with heat. I could feel her heart pounding beneath my fingers.

"What's your name?"

"Sahine."

"Keep taking slow, deep breaths, Sahine."

She nodded again as she tried to follow my directions. After five minutes, she began to calm down.

"The. . .the hotel. . .caused this."

Her heart fluttered, and the panicked gulps of air started again.

"I'm sure they'll take care of it. For now, inhale. Exhale. Again."

The energy I offered began to take hold. Or rather, Sahine allowed it to connect and bring her to a state where she requested we go to the lobby.

"Can you stand?"

"I think so."

With my arm around her for support, we made our way to the reception desk. I was still pulsing Reiki, now through my whole body into hers.

"I feel better," Sahine panted as I helped her lower herself into a chair near the front desk.

"Where are you from?" I wanted to engage her in talk, which would help center and ground her.

"India."

"Wow, that's a long way from Dublin. Did you travel alone?"

"Yes, for the first time. I'm all alone." Her words trailed off.

I felt her breath ease and her body relax. Too relaxed. Unconscious, she fell to the side and started to slide out of the chair.

"Help," I shouted. "Someone, please help."

Immediately, two people rushed over in alarm. While the young man helped stabilize her, the woman called emergency services.

"An ambulance is on the way," she told us.

Sahine was pale and limp. My concern intensified as the heat from my hands increased.

"We've got her," the man told me. "You don't have to stay."

"I want to. I don't feel right leaving her."

Sahine needed me. I was certain of that. Whatever happened with the hotel, I was the last face she saw before she passed out. I wanted her to see me when she opened her eyes.

Within a few minutes, her lashes flickered. A moment later, she was wide awake and screaming at the hotel's assistant manager.

"This is your fault! This hotel gave me a seizure—I want a refund. I'll sue you."

At this point, I stepped back. The Reiki stream ended, and my hands cooled. I had no idea what was going on until she shouted, "The shower wouldn't drain, no one brought fresh towels, or cleaned my room. No one is taking care of me."

I was struck by that last phrase.

No one is taking care of me.

A desperate cry from a sad and lonely woman.

I wanted to know more about her life and why she traveled alone. My thoughts went wild as I made up a story: a recently divorced woman testing out her "freedom" and having the courage to travel alone. Of course, I didn't really know why she was here.

The assistant manager later told me, "Sahine was taken by ambulance to the hospital."

"I hope she's okay." I felt connected to Sahine even though I'd just met her.

"It happened last night, too. She came around quickly, then."

Why would she do something so dangerous, particularly when traveling?

Sahine returned to the hotel the next morning and checked out for her flight home to London. I was relieved to know she wasn't going all the way to India.

I wished her a safe journey.

Every time I thought of her, my hands became hot from the energy source. I directed it to her long distance and hoped she would accept the tiny bit of support as she traveled.

PRE-REIKI TRAINING

In the mid-90s, I belonged to a group of women who formed an energy circle. We had no guidance other than our intuition and two individuals who were body workers (massage and physical therapists). We met once a week, and anyone who needed a boost would lie in the center, allowing us to lay hands on her.

It was great practice for what was to come.

Jen was hysterical. Her seventeen-year-old friend broke his neck in a diving accident. She begged us to help, and with the young man's mother's approval, we agreed to give it a try.

We gathered in the dimly lit, sterile, medicinal-scented hospital room with the hissing and beeping machines that kept him alive. He was in an induced coma in the hopes that the swelling would recede, and the doctors could see what they were up against.

We held hands around his bed, joining with each other before placing our palms on his silent, sheet-clad form. There was an immediate jolt. It felt like he was no longer present.

Had he decided to abandon his body?

"What do we do?" I whispered.

"We send him energy, and he can use it any way he wants. If that means he uses it to pass, that is his decision," Katie responded.

We all nodded and sank into the momentum of our connection.

Fast forward thirty years. I overheard a woman who had recently joined one of my classes talking about her son. He had broken his neck in a diving accident.

I felt a chill spin up my spine.

Pam lifted one hand. "The reason I joined this class is to learn more about healing. Right after the accident, a group of women came in and did some kind of powerful mojo for my son. I had to leave the room because the energy was so strong. Even the nurses felt it as they walked by and wondered what was going on in there."

"Oh my god," I gasped. "I was with that group of women."

"No," Pam leaped to her feet. "Really?"

She hugged me with tears in her eyes. "Thank you, thank you, thank you. I believe you all saved him."

"How is he?"

Pam smiled. "Although he has quadriplegia, he just got married, has a job, and is happy. He has a little use of one hand, which helps."

I was so happy to hear he had survived and was doing well. Our little group couldn't take credit for his recovery, other than perhaps giving him the strength to return to his body and prepare for the difficulties ahead.

Another pre-Reiki event that drew me closer to understanding how energy worked was when a long-time friend needed sinus surgery. She'd been losing spinal fluid through her nose, and a patch was required to stop the leak. To do that, the surgeon had to cut open her skull and go from the inside to make the patch stay in place.

The five of us, including the one undergoing surgery, held hands and formed a strong, energetic circle before her procedure. Halfway through the long surgery, all four of us had throbbing headaches. Fifteen minutes later, the headaches simultaneously stopped for all of us.

Turns out our friend woke up when they sawed through her skull.

Yep, that's when we all suffered right along with her. It stopped when the surgeon noticed, and the anesthesia was upped. As soon as our friend was in her room, we broke that circle pronto.

Those early days were powerful and taught me a lot about healing circles. But I knew something was missing. After each session, I suffered from headaches, nausea, and exhaustion.

POST-REIKI TRAINING

A close friend told me, "I'm a Reiki Master, and you're advanced enough to receive a Reiki Attunement."

Bada Bing Bada Boom. Without further ado, she placed the Usui symbols in my psyche. I felt nothing—no change—and still no understanding of how it all works.

Several years later, I became good friends with a Reiki Master who taught classes. Finally, the energy practice fell into place. I learned how to let Source flow through me but not use my personal energy. I left a session rejuvenated, as Reiki supported both my client and me.

"I think you should teach a class with me," Elliott announced.

"I don't think I'd be good at teaching Reiki."

"Why? You teach all kinds of things and do a great job."

"I don't know," I admitted, yet I wanted to even though I was nervous.

Elliott gently guided me through three days of classes, including Master Reiki, which gave me the confidence to continue teaching.

Soon after, William Lee Rand (www.reiki.org) downloaded the Holy Fire modality. HF seemed counterintuitive because there were no physical attunements, only *placements* and *ignitions* (downloading the Master Holy Fire III Symbol). Students connect directly to Source through specific meditations.

Holy Fire Reiki Masters teach techniques, illustrate the many ways to use Reiki, encourage confidence, instruct on how to channel (allow the energy to flow from Source rather than using your personal vitality), and how to work with specific client issues. There's much more to it in the three-day training, but this gives the overview.

The point is to not deplete your stamina when working with healing vibrations. Through Reiki training, I could support Sahine with ease and no judgment, without depleting my own natural resources. I simply allowed Source to guide me.

Reiki: A Japanese relaxation method (Usui) with hands-on (or hands-near) practice that helps the nervous system settle and invites the body's own healing responses. Sessions are fully clothed, consent-based, and feel like quiet, guided rest.

Holy Fire® III: A new form of Reiki introduced three years ago by the International Center for Reiki Training and William Lee Rand. It is both powerful and gentle, providing purification, healing, empowerment, and guidance. The energy is noticeably more refined and comes from a higher level of consciousness.

Note: Reiki complements—but doesn't replace—medical care.

Source: William Lee Rand's description for the larger current flowing through (not from) the practitioner. Call it universal life energy, Spirit, the Divine, Nature—use what fits your worldview. Website: Reiki.org.

The Medicine

Although I cannot provide the actual symbols (even though they're easily found online), they're sacred to Reiki and shouldn't be used unless training has been completed. However, I can offer a step-by-step approach to help you avoid feeling unwell after working with energy.

- First, clear any negativity through a short chakra-clearing (7 energy points in your body) meditation.

- Imagine white light flowing from your crown (top of your head) all the way through your 3rd eye (forehead) to your throat, moving down to your heart, then to your solar plexus (abdomen), to your sacral (belly), and out through your root chakra (between your legs).

- Let this light run through you until you feel clear and clean.

- Ground yourself by connecting to the Earth. Imagine roots extending from the soles of your feet down into the rich soil and pulling up a solid foundation to work from.

- Your energy is now unencumbered and contained within you.

- There are several techniques for drawing directly from the Source.

    1. Imagine you are standing behind a rainbow waterfall. Sniff the air. It's filled with the fresh scent of a gentle rain as the droplets touch your skin. It is the taste of divine energy.

    2. Reach through the waterfall. Allow your fingers and palms to absorb the energy and direct it toward the person, place, or thing you want to offer healing to.

    3. In your mind, say, *may this energy be used for its highest good, and if not received by the individual, may it be offered to Earth.*

    4. Allow yourself to receive energy at the same time. The Source sends it out and also returns it to the practitioner.

    5. When your session is complete, offer gratitude and release the connection.

- Imagine a beam of light cascading from the heavens. Most often, it's golden or white light that appears; however, the light can be any color you desire.

    1. Step into the light and let it flow through your body.

2. Feel it igniting your cells, preparing you for your work.

3. The light offers you restorative, soothing vitality.

4. Accept this gift as you become the catalyst for healing others.

5. Allow the energy to emanate from your fingers and palms and direct it to your intended goal.

6. In your mind, say, *may this energy be used for its highest good, and if not received by the individual, may it be offered to Earth.*

7. When your session is complete, offer gratitude and release the connection.

- Open your crown chakra and invite in the divine Source.

  1. This is often described as a tickling or prickling sensation on your scalp.

  2. Allow Source to fill your body through the chakra points.

  3. Feel it as it permeates the cells in your body, and notice the surge of strength, courage, and calm, confident relationship you've created with Source.

  4. You may use this connection solely for your own healing, rather than offering it to others.

  5. If you are planning a session, it is much like the above: let the energy flow from your hands toward and into the person you are working with.

  6. In your mind, say, may this energy be used for its highest good, and if not received by the individual, may it be offered to Earth.

  7. When your session is complete, offer gratitude and release the connection.

- Always check in with the individual. How are they feeling? Did they have any visions or thoughts that arose during the session?

- Check in with yourself. If you feel depleted, you've drawn on your personal energy rather than the divine Source. You should feel rejuvenated and energized, rather than tired and mentally foggy. Review how to separate yourself from personal stamina and link with Source.

Dr. Ruth A. Souther has practiced in the metaphysical and natural arts for 35 years. She is a Master Shamanic Facilitator with Aahara Spiritual Community in Springfield, Illinois, a Master Reiki practitioner, hypnotherapist, ritualist, and minister. She co-facilitates Alchemy: A New Earth Priestess Mystery School with Stephanie Urbina Jones and Terran Woodliff.

She wrote *The Heart of Tarot* (an intuitive guide to the cards), *Vega's Path: The Elemental Priestess,* and three novels: *Death of Innocence, Surrender of Ego,* and *Rise of Rebellion.* The fourth, *Obsession of Love,* is forthcoming. She is often the 'Writing Wrangler' for collective anthologies, including those through The Edge authors' group. She has contributed to many Brave Healer books, including the *Shaman Heart* series from Freedom Folk and Soul.

She is an Initiated Priestess through Diana's Grove and has taught with the Reclaiming Collective of San Francisco at Missouri and Texas Witch Camps. She has studied Tarot and Astrology since 1990, teaches many classes in both subjects, and provides readings in person and online.

Ruth created Vega's Path Priestess Process, which has been ongoing since 2012. She is a facilitating member of The Edge of Perception and The Sanctuary of Formative Spirituality, a non-profit spiritual organization. She is a contributing author and board member/Chief Editor of Crystal Heart Imprints. This independent co-operative press supports and guides authors in their creative projects.

Ruth lives in Central Illinois with her husband and two dogs, happily navigating life and always doing her best to offer compassion and care to anyone in need.

CONNECT WITH RUTH:

Email: ruthsouther52@gmail.com or perceptiveedge@gmail.com

Website: https://www.vegaspath.com/

Facebook: https://www.facebook.com/ruth.tipswordbryantsouther

Chapter 5

Find Your Soul-Self
Healing the People Pleaser Problem

SUSAN L. ERNST

Even in loss and change, your soul-self walks with you.
If you dare to listen, her voice will lead you home.
~ Susan L. Ernst

My Story

For much of my life, I carried a habit I mistook for kindness: people-pleasing.

I said yes when I wanted to say no. I shaped my choices around what I thought others needed or expected of me. On the surface, it looked generous. Inside, it drained me more than I realized.

THE MOVE

"Is she breathing?" I asked, peering down at the olive-green canvas carrier at our feet, its brown straps cinched tightly at the top. I could barely see inside the mesh panels.

"I'm not sure. Can't really see her face from here," Alissa replied, sitting back in her seat with a slightly stern look. Then she smiled patiently, patting my arm. "Hope so."

"Lis, seriously—she doesn't seem to be moving." I strained against my seat belt, but it wouldn't budge.

"Mom, she's probably asleep. Remember? I gave her one of the pills the vet prescribed." She turned toward me, her eyes reflecting her inner thoughts.

"Oh, right." I rubbed my forehead with both hands, willing my monkey brain to settle.

What the heck! How can she be that calm? If Kitty wakes up, she's going to howl and scare everyone to death!

My cat developed an interesting habit. She howls loudly whenever she is upset or wants something. The vet says it's because she's deaf. *One nervous old lady and an old, deaf cat flying across the country—what could possibly go wrong?*

"Good morning, ladies and gentlemen. Welcome aboard United Flight 321 with service to Washington, D.C.. . ." The flight attendant's voice droned through the cabin as I fixed my gaze on the carrier under the seat.

"And please pay no attention to the crazy lady in the back who won't take her eyes off her suspicious-looking carry-on bag," I muttered to myself.

The engines roared to life. As the plane taxied from the gate, I gripped the armrests, knuckles white, eyes glued to the carrier, waiting for the inevitable catastrophe.

Cut me a little slack! I'm moving across the entire country with my cat!

"Oh my God, Lis—what if she pukes?" I whispered, glancing nervously at the passengers across the aisle. None of them gave the bag at my feet a second thought.

Alissa exhaled loudly, her eyes shifting from the window back to me. "I wish the vet had given me a pill for you."

We both laughed.

The anxiety was real. What I didn't realize then was that this flight marked more than just a move. After more than seventy-five years in California, I was beginning an adventure that would transform me in ways I couldn't yet imagine.

The potential for embarrassment and my constant worry over how others might react kept my stress level soaring on the plane. In my mind, it was a Space Mountain horror ride—white-knuckling the bars, pressing my head back against the seat so my neck wouldn't snap, eyes squeezed shut, wishing I was short enough that they never let me on in the first place.

On the other hand, Kitty's first cross-country flight was a "nothing-burger," as my daughter would say. She slept contentedly the entire way.

Leaving California meant leaving my home, cherished friends, and the places that shaped me. Excited? Of course. But grief, too, and it was real, the loneliness sharp. Yet beneath it all was a quiet resolve—a faith that somehow, in time, I'd find my footing again.

You will finally be living near both of your daughters and their partners, as well as your grandchildren. This is an answered prayer, I reminded myself, craning my neck for one last glimpse of my beloved San Francisco Bay.

The logistics alone were overwhelming—selling my home, saying goodbye to neighbors, and deciding what to keep and what to let go. Then came the challenge of re-establishing my real estate appraisal practice on the other side of the country. Every decision carried extra weight. And when the dust finally began to settle, the deeper work surfaced—navigating the ache of loneliness while trusting that I had chosen this new life for a reason.

Looking back, I see that my white-knuckled grip on that first flight east was about more than a cat in a carrier. The worry that Kitty might disturb the passengers, my dread of making a scene—it was all part of something bigger that I managed to keep tucked away for years: my tendency to be a people-pleaser.

Let's get real. This was a huge move for a senior citizen—and it cracked me wide open. Suddenly, the urge to make everyone happy—to avoid disappointing anyone—went into overdrive. I saw how much of my energy I spent meeting others' expectations while quietly setting aside my own.

What followed was the slow, sometimes painful work of confronting those tendencies—and discovering how listening to my intuition could help me begin to let them go.

The ache of leaving California and the familiar rhythms I had built pressed heavily on me when I arrived in Washington, D.C. I bounced back and forth between excitement about this new adventure and grief over what I gave up.

THE WHISPERS BEGIN

Slowly, quietly, I began to recognize something more enduring—my soul-self. Wherever I lived, at every age, she walked beside me. My inner joy—my *joie de vivre*—never abandoned me. Even in the loneliest days, even in the upheaval of change, that spark was there, waiting for me to notice. Thank God she didn't give up on me, because I stumbled more than once along the way.

This move affected me in ways I'm only now beginning to discern. The loneliness and grief created a pause, a space where something new took root. In that silence, I heard the whispers within—gentle reminders that I didn't have to keep living for everyone else's expectations. *Have they been here all along, but I refused to listen?*

Those whispers guided me home to *myself.*

THE ALCHEMY OF AWARENESS

I used to think being kind meant saying yes to everyone. I bent to meet expectations, smoothed rough edges, and tried to keep the peace. It looked generous from the outside—but inside, it was exhausting.

Through my study of awareness, I saw this pattern for what it truly was. It wasn't harmless "niceness." It was a quiet betrayal of my own truth. And worse, it sometimes hurt the very people I loved most. Decisions made to avoid disappointing others often turned out to be wrong—for me and my family.

That realization landed hard. I can trace the pattern back decades, woven through nearly every season of my life. In fact, I can trace this pattern back to my ancestors, but that will be another book! *How much of myself have I given away by not listening within? How many times have I let fear of disapproval silence the whispers of my soul-self?*

And yet, awareness is alchemy. Now that I fully see the pattern, I can't unsee it. The pain of that truth became the spark of change. I experimented with a different approach: listening inward first, setting boundaries, letting my "yes" mean yes and my "no" mean no. Slowly, I discovered that honoring myself wasn't selfish at all—it was healing, for me and those I love.

Many of us are taught to override our quiet inner knowing—to prioritize logic, obligation, approval, or authority over our gut. No wonder intuition so often shows up in hindsight, whispering in your ear: *I tried to tell you.*

Through awareness practices, I cultivated a deeper connection with my intuition. I learned to stay present (still a challenge, but I'm working at it!). I practice listening to my body, emotions, and thoughts—and recognize the patterns they reveal.

As I stepped into a new community, I quickly discovered just how deeply those old patterns still had a grip on me.

REDISCOVERY AND BECOMING

When I moved across the country, I discovered a new church and joined a community, my heart open and with a deep longing. I met warm, kind-hearted people whom I continue to cherish. Yet somewhere in that process, something in me shifted.

I stopped listening to my intuition. Instead, I fell back into the familiar echo of old patterns: *Show up more. Give more. Say yes. Be what they need.* In my eagerness to belong—and, of course, to make friends—I lost touch with the still, small voice inside me, the one that always led me toward peace and truth.

No one asked me to burn out. No one expected me to give myself away. In fact, a few even noticed the warning signs and gently nudged me, but I brushed their kindness aside. And burnout came anyway—quietly, steadily—until I nearly unraveled.

That unraveling became my awakening. In the midst of exhaustion, my soul began to whisper: *Come back to me.* And for the first time in a long while, I listened.

I may return to church someday. But when I do, I will bring my whole self—not the one who performs or overextends, but the one who listens inward first, and trusts that voice to guide me forward.

Awareness opened my eyes; now life allows me to put it into practice. I don't have it all figured out yet—but I know this much: every time I choose to listen inward, I take one more step toward becoming the person I was always meant to be.

THE VOICE I'M LEARNING TO TRUST

I haven't walked away from faith—I've walked toward it in a deeper form. I've learned to trust my inner compass, my God-given intuition.

Dear Susan,

I see you. I know the ache and the questioning—the quiet guilt that whispers *you've stepped away from something sacred.* But here's what I want you to know:

You know you haven't walked away from God.
You've walked toward yourself.
Toward stillness.
Toward clarity.
Toward a form of faith that feels less like performance and more like peace.
You gave with your whole heart—so much that it began to fray.
You showed up for everyone, but forgot to show up for yourself.

Now you are stepping into something transformational.
Not an ending—but a beginning.
You are pausing. Listening.

And no matter what anyone thinks, this is not a falling away.
This is a return.
A return to the quiet, sacred place where God has always met you—in the sound of your own breath when the world is finally silent.

Yep, guilt will rise. That's okay.
But remember: guilt is not your soul speaking—it's old wiring.
Conviction leads to life. Guilt traps you in doubt.

You are not unfaithful.
You are faithful to the truth that something needed to change.
And in that change, something beautiful is being born.

Keep listening inward.
Your heart knows the way.
God is not disappointed in your becoming.
God is in your becoming.

I love you.

Listening inward didn't just bring clarity; it offered me medicine—life-giving practices that continue to restore joy and peace.

The Medicine

STRATEGIES FOR YOU, DEAR READER

Through awareness practices born from a genuine need to heal, I feel more authentic than ever before, and with that came an inner joy I haven't felt in years.

I see my soul-self perched high in the branches of an ancient Monterey pine, ponytails flying, fingers wrapped around a weathered rope, legs swinging me higher and higher toward the clouds. I hear her laughter on the wind, whispering with a smile: *Well, it took you long enough.*

Before I can hear the whispers of intuition, I must first quiet the noise around me—and within me. One of the simplest ways to begin, for me, is with the breath.

Our breath is always with us, steady and faithful, and it can become a doorway into calm awareness. I invite you to pause here and try one of these gentle practices.

First, set your intention. For example:

- *I open myself to quiet moments, trusting that stillness will reveal what I need to hear.*

- *I trust the whispers within me, even if they arrive softly or in ways I don't yet understand.*

- *I let go of expectations that do not belong to me, making room for my own deep knowing.*

Or choose words of your own. Let your intention be simple, kind, and true for you.

PRACTICE ONE: THE 4-4-4 BREATH

Imagine tracing the sides of a square with your breath:

- Inhale slowly through your nose for a count of four.

- Hold softly for a count of four.

- Exhale gently through your mouth for a count of four.

- Repeat for three to five rounds.

Notice how the rhythm steadies both body and mind.

PRACTICE TWO: HEART-CENTERED BREATHING

Place one hand lightly over your heart:

- Inhale through your nose for a count of five, imagining the breath flowing into your chest.

- Exhale gently for a count of five, releasing warmth and ease.

- With each exhale, silently add a word such as *peace, love,* and *ease.*

This practice calms the mind and opens the heart, creating space for intuition to arise.

When the body is calm and the heart open, you're better able to listen for the subtle voice within. From here, you can explore simple strategies for strengthening your connection to intuition:

1. **Create Quiet Spaces**
   Give yourself daily moments of stillness—such as morning silence, a mindful walk, or a pause before sleep.

- Reflective Prompt: *When and where in my day can I set aside a small space for silence?*

2. **Notice the Body's Signals**
   Intuition often speaks through sensations—manifesting as goosebumps, a racing heart, or a deep calm. Notice them without judgment.

- Reflective Prompt: *What physical sensations have I felt when I've known a strong "yes" or "no"?*

3. **Trust Small Whispers**
   Intuition isn't always dramatic. It may be a repeating thought, a persistent image, or a gentle nudge. Please keep track of them.

- Reflective Prompt: *What small, recurring thoughts or nudges have been appearing in my life lately?*

4. **Practice Gentle Discernment**
   Not every thought is intuitive. Ask: *Is this fear, desire, or deep knowing?* Over time, clarity grows.

- Reflective Prompt: *How can I tell the difference between anxious thoughts and deeper knowing?*

5. **Take One Brave Step**
    Acting on intuition may mean a single step—a phone call, a "no," or trying something new.

- Reflective Prompt: *What is one small, courageous action I feel drawn to take this week?*

6. **Reflect and Record**
    Keep an intuition journal. Record what you sense, how you respond, and what unfolds. Patterns will emerge.

- Reflective Prompt: *What do I notice when I look back at times I followed—or ignored—my intuition?*

CLOSING REFLECTION

We are all a work in progress. Transformation has come to me in my seventy-ninth year—right on time. I stand in the middle of it now. At times, it feels like walking through fog, with light shifting and reshaping the path ahead. I'm no longer where I was, and not yet where I'm going. But I'm awakening. And I'm excited to see where this leads.

I learned that my guilt was never about wrongdoing—it was about expectation. Not expectation from God, but from people. And that, I am gently letting go. As I release those weights, anxiety eases too.

What are you ready to release? What weight are you carrying that no longer serves you?

Listen to the whispers. They will always lead you home.

Susan L. Ernst recently relocated from California to Washington, D.C., to be closer to her family. After a distinguished 35+ year career as a commercial real estate appraiser, she has entered a new season of creativity and service. Today, Susan provides proofreading support for Brave Healer Productions and released her first solo book, *Called to Serve: Standing with Survivors and Protecting Children Still at Risk.* She is passionate about raising awareness and doing all she can in the fight against sex trafficking and child abuse.

A bestselling author, Susan was inspired to begin writing children's stories through her volunteer work in Cambodia at a rescue center for child survivors of sex trafficking. Her stories appear in all three volumes of *Brave Kids: Short Stories to Inspire Our Future World Changers* by lead author K.J. Kaschula. She also contributed to David McLeod's bestselling anthology, *Gifts of Wisdom: Practices for Healing and Empowerment,* with her chapter, *Throw Some Love at It!: Embracing Vulnerability on the Public Stage,* whiich reflects her heart for courage and connection.

Now exploring life on the East Coast, Susan finds joy in walking in nature, discovering new places, and spending time with her daughters, their partners, and her grandchildren.

CONNECT WITH SUSAN:

Website: https://www.susanernstauthor.com

Facebook: https://www.facebook.com/sernst992/

LinkedIn: https://www.linkedin.com/in/susan-ernst-57b87272/

Instagram: https://www.instagram.com/sernst992/

Chapter 6

Intuition Comes in All Shapes and Sizes
Access Yours to Get Heart-Centered Answers

MICHELE TATOS

My Story

"My wife sees dead people." The words slide effortlessly off my husband's tongue when asked what his wife (me) does for a living.

"I, um, teach guided meditation," tumbles awkwardly out of my mouth when I am asked what I do for a living.

What the hell?

Why is it that my husband has no problem telling his business buddies that I'm a practitioner of woo, but I keep my intuitive abilities as a closely guarded secret?

Even after all these years as an intuitive practitioner?

And by the way, my husband's answer is a terrible, yet funny and partially accurate, description of what I do.

Everyone is born with intuition, but intuition comes in all shapes and sizes. You, too, have your own story about how your wonderful gift of intuition has unfolded in your life. I hope hearing my story helps you remember and embrace your own.

MY SHAKY INTRODUCTION TO INTUITION

"Kat, wake up! Help me get this thing off my chest! Please! HELP!" I squeaked out because the terror reduced my voice to a low hiss.

"What are you talking about? I don't see anything," my sister sleepily replied.

"But he was here a second ago. He was sitting on my chest, and I couldn't move," I cried hysterically as my voice began returning to me.

"Go back to sleep. You were just having a bad dream," she responded.

At the age of five, my intuitive abilities were shut down before I even had a chance to begin processing them.

And the dismissals continued.

"Mom, Dad, wake up! Things are wandering around in my room! I can see them, and they're looking at me!" I screamed out as I finally mustered the courage to run into my parents' bedroom in the middle of the night.

"There's no one in your room, honey. You're just having a bad dream," my dad calmly responded.

"I was wide awake!" I yelled, unable to mask the fear and frustration in my tone.

"You can come sleep with us. We'll talk about it in the morning," my mom kindly said, trying to soothe my fear.

This happened early and often in my childhood, until I realized no one would believe me, and I decided to stop talking about it.

My parents and sister weren't mean or uncaring. They simply weren't seeing what I saw, so they assumed I was having nightmares or had an overactive imagination.

It was a logical assumption given how our society at large responds to anything that cannot be explicitly seen or measured.

PUTTING BLINDERS ON MY INTUITION

Bunny, you go here. Doggie, you go there. Timmy Turtle, you get to sleep on my chest.

I pretended none of it existed, tucking myself in each night with an army of stuffed animals surrounding me in my bed. I closed my eyes tight and told myself: *It's just your imagination!*

Eventually, I stopped seeing most of it. I say "most" as I couldn't get rid of the entity that used to sit on my chest. Well, at least not until I was in my thirties, and I began taking intuitive and energy management classes. With my teacher's help, I learned how to send him off. Oddly enough, during my recent trip to Ireland for this book, the entity and I reconnected and became friends! That wild story is a little later on in this chapter.

Seeing ghosts or having an entity sitting on your chest may seem like an extreme introduction to intuition, but I know this isn't an uncommon story. Several of my friends, as well as people I met along my spiritual path, have had similar experiences.

They were also similarly shut down by their families.

If I had someone in my life who explained what was happening to me and provided tools, my introduction to intuition and the spiritual realm could've played out very differently. Unfortunately, intuitive abilities weren't a topic openly discussed in the early seventies.

The basic definition of intuition is the ability to understand something immediately, without the need for conscious reasoning. However, that immediate understanding can take many different forms.

The ability to see or sense spirits is just one way of tapping into your intuition. When I put my blinders on to block out my nighttime visitors, I also took some of my basic intuition tools offline.

If I couldn't trust what I saw to be real, how could I trust my other intuitive senses?

Hence, for the next twenty-five years, I had limited access to my deep well of intuitive abilities.

TAKING MY BLINDERS OFF

"Your grounding is very shallow, as if you are hesitant to connect with Mother Earth, as if you don't know what your next steps will be," Glenda said.

"Your third chakra is beginning to come into alignment with your heart chakra. You're learning to own your personal power with grace and unconditional love. Learning how to be the benevolent queen, instead of the harsh and controlling shadow aspect of the archetypal queen," she continued.

And just like that, I was hooked.

Everything Glenda said in that one-hour consultation resonated deeply within me. It was exactly what I needed to hear.

"I want to learn to do what you do!" came flying out of my mouth.

Wait. What? Did I just say I wanted to learn to read chakras? I don't even know what chakras are.

My blinders loosened when I received that amazing gift of my first intuitive healing consultation for my thirtieth birthday. Glenda was a former co-worker who left to start a business as a teacher and healer. I was now one of her students.

I studied closely under Glenda for many years, learning to trust my intuition. I explored the beautiful intricacies of the energy body. I delved into the wild and wonderful mysteries of the spiritual realm and divine universe.

It was pretty bad-ass. Still is.

At some point, I decided I was ready, and I launched my business. Owning my intuitive abilities was way harder than I expected.

IMPOSTER SYNDROME REARS ITS UGLY HEAD

Ba-dum. Ba-dum. Ba-dum.

I'm pretty sure the stranger who is about to call me will be able to hear my loud, rapid heartbeat, even though she's several states away.

Should I tell her what I saw when I was previewing? Maybe not, because if it doesn't make sense to her, we will be starting on bad footing, and she'll think I'm a fraud.

Why did I agree to do this consultation? I'm so not ready yet.

My Weimaraner, Cigany, nudges me with his big ole head because he's picking up on my angst. Dogs are so intuitive.

The phone rings, and I hesitate for a heartbeat—a very loud heartbeat.

"Hi, so glad that we could make this happen," I say in that high-pitched voice that usually means the exact opposite of whatever I'm saying.

"I did a preview earlier today, which means I checked in with your guides and with my guides, to see if there was anything I should be aware of before your healing session. If it's okay with you, before we begin, I'm going to share what I saw."

Susan seemed a bit hesitant, "I've never done anything like this before, so I'm not sure how this works, but please share what you saw."

I'm all in at this point, so I might as well just go for it.

"I saw a girl, about twelve or thirteen years old, pointing to her long ponytail with a huge, proud grin on her face. She was adamant that I acknowledge her. Does that make any sense to you?"

I held my breath and got ready to crawl under a rock if she had no idea what I was talking about.

"Oh my god! My thirteen-year-old daughter just donated her hair to create wigs for cancer patients. They cut her ponytail off! She was so happy about it, and I was extremely proud of her."

And with that affirmation, my imposter syndrome paralysis melted away. I relaxed into my intuitive mojo and navigated a powerful healing with a woman living across the country from me—a woman I had neither met nor spoken to before that session.

How do you know that you aren't just making it up?

I can't tell you how many times I've been asked that.

It's the million-dollar question, isn't it?

I have yet to meet a single person who trusted their intuition from day one. I'm sure they're out there, but I haven't bumped into them yet. It usually takes practice, time, and relentless self-trust.

As I said before, we're all born with intuition. Yep, every single one of us. It's our internal survival guidance system, and our moral compass. It gently nudges us via whispers and gut feelings, encouraging us to become who we're meant to be. Transforming us, one intuitive hit at a time, into our higher selves.

I've spent over twenty-five years exploring my intuitive abilities, but I still have moments of "Am I making this up?"

WELCOME IN THE UNKNOWN

Why can't my body stop shaking and flailing? Someone's hands are on my heart, and two more hands are holding my feet and shaking them with a bit of force. What's going on?

"AAAAAAAHHHHH!" A primal scream rips out of my throat, but it really comes from the very seat of my soul.

The scream turns into a drawn-out howl, as part of me is still aware of the first-time breathwork participants in the room, and I don't want to terrify them.

Weird that I think a howl is less frightening than a scream.

My howls are being answered by the rest of my pack! That's awesome.

Okay. I'm okay.

My body shoots off one last explosive release, and then I lie there completely still.

Huh, that's strange. I usually can't stop moving during my shamanic breathwork.

I suddenly remembered hearing my spirit guides tell me to stop trying to control my journeys, which are individual spiritual experiences during shamanic breathwork.

Now that I'm no longer trying to control my journey, I'm simply sitting in the darkness, not moving a muscle.

WELCOME IN THE UNKNOWN! Repeats over and over.

Stop putting things in boxes of good or bad, angels or demons, light or dark. It's all the same.

Duality is just two sides of the same coin.

It's time to let go of fear and judgment, as they are keeping you from fully stepping into your intuitive powers.

It's time to accept that everything that happens is a way to change and evolve.

This is coming from a black angel, who I later discover is Morrigan, appearing as the crow goddess of death.

So much peace seeped into every cell in my body as these words were spoken.

Hi, remember me? says the entity who terrified me for more than half of my life.

He just popped up out of nowhere. Alrighty then.

Oh, I get it! You were helping me unlock my intuitive abilities. You wouldn't let me ignore them. Thank you! I really mean it.

I sat there in complete darkness, nothingness, and grace for the rest of the breathwork session.

This happened while I was in Ireland with many of the amazing authors in this book.

The shamanic breathwork mentioned above does not involve any hallucinogens, but it does put you in a very altered state.

I mentioned there were two people with their hands on me. I found out later that there was only one. I actually felt one of my guides' hands on my heart chakra. I usually only see and hear my guides, but this was the first time I truly felt them.

I'm still processing this experience, as it definitely felt like a leveling up of my intuitive abilities and my understanding of how the universe works. It also triggered my "Are you sure you aren't making it up?" reflex, but I squashed that old knee-jerk reaction pretty quickly. Yay me!

FULL CIRCLE

I started my journey fearful and mistrusting of my intuition, but I grew to embrace the magic of it all—entities, chakras, whispers from my higher self—all of it!

Now, when people ask me what I do, I will boldly answer, "I am an intuitive healer and consultant. I work with all aspects of the human energy body, including chakras, auras, spiritual guides, Akashic Records, contracts, cords, and past lives."

When people ask you about your intuitive abilities, do you want to confidently state, "I practice and use my intuitive abilities regularly, and they are improving my life"?

I hope the answer is yes; I created a fun and easy meditation to get you started.

The Medicine

Get ready to climb the staircase to the seat of your soul, and get the intuitive answer to every question you ever wished to ask your higher self.

Have a notepad and pen handy, and let's go!

- Make sure you are seated comfortably, with your feet lovingly connected to the ground—to Mother Earth.

- Close your eyes and take several slow and intentional breaths, in and out.

- Call back your attention from wherever it has wandered.

- Give yourself the gift of being here, in your body, ready to connect with your higher self.

- Take another beautiful, life-affirming breath, and imagine an iridescent bridge suddenly appears in front of you.

- Something about the colors and the vibration of the bridge is calling for you to walk over it.

- This magical bridge is taking you from your analyzer, your front office, where you make all your day-to-day decisions, into your own private, peaceful garden in the center of your head—your intuitive center, where you come to relax, feel safe, and rejuvenate. This is where your inner wisdom resides.

- Breathe in the calming scent.

- Notice how the temperature here is just right.

- Take a moment to look around and ensure your garden looks and feels exactly how you want it to.

- Maybe there are redwood trees and sparkling creeks.

- Maybe you are on a beach and you can smell the saltwater in the breeze.

- When it feels just right, take a look around and spot a stone path that lights up for you. It should be slightly off to the right, with colorful flowers growing on either side.

- Follow the path until you see a golden doorway. It's warm, bright, and welcoming.

- Reach out and grab the shining, smooth handle, and open the door.

- You should see, or sense, a spiral staircase that is lit up with a soft, inviting light.

- You begin easing down the staircase, one step at a time, holding on to the railing.

- When you reach the bottom, there's an open archway that appears to be gently pulsing.

- As you begin to walk through the archway, the pulsing becomes more intense. You feel it vibrating throughout your whole body.

- Straight ahead is a seat, with the softest-looking cushion, waiting for you to snuggle in.

- You effortlessly melt into the velvety loveliness.

- You feel nothing but unconditional love.

- You can hear the beating of your heart.

- You are the beating of your heart.

- You are sitting in your heart chakra.

- You are sitting in the seat of your soul.

- From this unbelievably peaceful place, you can ask any question.

- Immediately, you will be answered by your higher self.

- This is the answer that is best for your spiritual growth and development.

- This is your heart's desire.

- Go ahead, ask a question.

- Write the answer down quickly, before your analytical self starts to create roadblocks and alternate solutions that are safer, or what others would prefer you to do.

- Once you've written your answer down, settle back into your heart for another breath or two.

- Allow yourself to soak in how this feels.

- Notice how it feels different from sitting in your analyzer, making day-to-day decisions based on logic and social norms.

- Ask another question if you like.

- When you've had your fill of this loving goodness, this heart wisdom, slowly lift yourself out of the chair.

- Send a loving thanks to your higher self before walking back through the archway and toward the spiral staircase.

- Gently grasp the rail and begin your ascent back up the winding staircase.

- As you reach the top, follow the lighted stone path back to your personal garden.

- Take one last look around your garden before slowly walking across the iridescent bridge to land back in your body—back in your seat.

- Notice the sounds in the room.

- Begin wiggling your fingers and toes.

- When you're ready, stretch your hands up over your head, and open your eyes.

I hope you enjoyed this intimate connection with your intuition—with your heart's wisdom.

Remember, you can repeat this anytime you have an important decision to make, or any time you want to feel that deep connection to your higher self.

You can visit my website at https://beatreewithme.com and listen to the recording of this meditation in the Resources section.

I look forward to reading the story of your intuitive journey someday!

Michele Tatos is wildly passionate about the intricacies of the human energy body, a big believer in the magic of meditation, and knows working with your guides to heal absolutely rocks!

For over twenty-five years, Michele has provided energy-rebalancing consultations and guided meditations, giving people information and tools to make transformational decisions, change unhealthy patterns, and connect with their higher self and purpose.

Her sessions focus on improving the health of your grounding, shielding, chakras, and subtle bodies. She works closely with spirit guides to update soul contracts, cut cords, remove blockages, and heal present and past life trauma.

The first fifteen years of her adult life were spent serving in the mental health field in San Francisco, including a position as CEO of a mental health employment agency. She then embarked on another inspirational journey, working for a nonprofit that served individuals of all ages with developmental disabilities.

If she's not hanging with her family, playing some sport that has a ball in it, or reading a juicy sci-fi book, you can find Michele blissfully walking on a trail filled with trees, talking to her dog, her guides, or any other creature that crosses her path.

Her education includes an MBA, many psychology courses, even more alternative healing courses, and more than 25 years of energy and intuition training.

She has been published in four best-selling Amazon books.

CONNECT WITH MICHELE:

Website: https://www.beatreewithme.com/

Chapter 7

Walking With the Grim Reaper
Finding Balance Through Overwhelming Grief

SUSAN C. JENSEN, MA, SPIRITUAL DIRECTOR

"In the course of our relationship we . . .
make a new sanctuary within each of our stories—
a place where love survives unbearable loss."
~Carl Rogers

My Story

Her hands are like ice. I feverishly work to warm them between my hands in the hope of bringing vitality back to a listless body. As I observe her beautiful face marred by a breathing tube protruding from her mouth, I'm pulled into a deep black hole of grief and despair again, with no power to resist the descent.

I have a big lump in my throat as the doctor appears, "I'm not sure if you've been told, but your sister's tests reveal she's had a massive stroke and is brain-dead. There's no way she can come back from this."

Tears flood my eyes and rush down my cheeks—I can taste their bitter saltiness as the doctor continues, "Now you must decide on removing her breathing tube."

My nose is assaulted by the stench of medicine in this ER room; my ears by the buzzing and beeping of noisy hospital machines. My watery eyes can hardly focus on the papers I'm required to sign, and it's difficult for me to let go of my sister's hands. I feel another part of my heart being chiseled away, and I lament the fact that the Grim Reaper is present in my life once again.

I'm transported back to a time when the Grim Reaper took my first developing baby.

"Doctor, why am I spotting and bleeding when I'm pregnant?" I ask this with a tone of alarm.

The doctor replies, "This is not unusual and frequently happens to many women during pregnancy; your baby is just fine."

Once reassured, I asked him, "Can I still work while I'm spotting?" He responds, "Since your work as a keypunch operator is primarily sedentary, I see no reason why you shouldn't continue to work." I like my job because it's interesting, and my employer is North American Rockwell in Long Beach, California, which processes astronauts' data and information.

I am nearly four months pregnant, and I plan to work at least four more months. However, one night, while working a swing shift, I felt nauseous and clammy. I ran to the women's restroom and became alarmed when I saw clots of blood streaming down my legs. I grabbed paper towels to absorb the blood and walked awkwardly to my supervisor's office.

"Susan, what's wrong?" she asks with real concern in her voice while observing my situation.

"I need to use your phone to call my doctor," I reply.

With phone in hand, she asks, "What's the number?"

A sympathetic voice on the other end of the receiver says, "Mrs. Jensen, I will meet you at St. Mary's Hospital."

I punched out at work on the way to my car, shaking uncontrollably. I did my best to calm myself, but it wasn't easy. *If only we had two cars, my husband could pick me up here at work and drive me to the hospital!*

Feeling scared and alone with tears once again streaming down my cheeks, I somehow drive my car onto the busy Long Beach freeway. I don't get far before I hear police sirens and see flashing red lights in my car's rear-view mirror. I pull over to the right.

"Lady, do you know you're speeding? Going almost 100 miles per hour!"

"I know, officer," I shout with a panicky voice, "I'm on my way to the hospital to see my doctor because I'm hemorrhaging blood and about to lose my baby!"

He replies slowly and calmly, "Well, I want you to get there, but I want you to get there safely. So, I want you to follow me—can you do that for me, Ma'am?"

I shake my head yes, restart my car, and follow his flashing red light escort all the way to the hospital—while he *safely* drives almost 100 miles per hour himself!

I felt some relief as I entered St. Mary's Hospital and saw my husband's face. I rushed into his loving arms, saying, "Sweetheart, I can't believe this is happening, and on your birthday!"

He tenderly kissed me and whispered, "I know, I know."

My doctor scheduled the necessary hospital tests, which I immediately completed. I'm overcome with grief when these tests reveal there is no longer a heartbeat and that my developing baby is dead inside of me.

Distraught at this news, I scream at my doctor, "How can this be? My baby was okay a few days ago when I was in your office! You told me everything was okay. How is this happening?!"

My doctor explains matter-of-factly, "It's nature's way of getting rid of a bad piece of fruit, or in this case, a malformed baby." He continues, "You'll be able to try again, but right now your body will be poisoned if we do not do an immediate D&C."

Sobbing, I say, "No! I don't want you to take my baby. Maybe those tests are wrong!"

"I assure you they're not wrong," he patiently explains, "I've concurred with two other doctors, and we all agree your baby is no longer alive. There is no heartbeat, and since your own body has been unable to abort the fetus, sepsis will set in. For your own welfare, we need to perform an immediate D&C."

Losing my first baby unwillingly to the Grim Reaper was an extremely traumatic episode in my life, and it feels similar to my unwillingness to make it easier for the Grim Reaper to take my beloved sister, Virginia, by removing her breathing tube; however, soulfully, I do decide to remove her breathing tube because I know she's no longer truly alive. I succumb to the validity of all the hospital tests and agree with the consensus of the educated doctors.

As fate would have it, I'm assisted in this decision by Father Anthony, a Catholic priest and acting Chaplain of Queen of the Valley Hospital in Napa, California. While observing me praying at Virginia's ER bedside, trying to warm her hand, he approaches and says, "I am Father Anthony, would you like me to pray with you?"

"Thank you, Father," I reply, "and please will you pray for my sister, Virginia. I need to decide to remove her breathing tube, and part of me is resistant because I want her to recover and live."

"Yes, this is difficult," Father Anthony counsels, "but God will give you the strength to make the right decision for Virginia." He then asks, "Would you like Virginia to receive the Last Rites?"

I sit up straight at that question, "Oh, could you, Father?" I say with a glimmer of hope, "Virginia is a lapsed Catholic and angry at God for taking both her sons, but at least I will know I've done everything I could possibly do for her."

Tears stream down my face once more as her breathing tube is now removed. Virginia took a last breath the very next day, with me and another sister each holding her hands.

I'm filled with emotion and try to flee from the grief I feel over losing my dearest sister, Virginia. She's six years older and the sister who's been with me all my life. The sister who dealt with unimaginable grief over the Grim Reaper taking both of her sons, both of her husbands, as well as all of our grandparents, parents, numerous aunts and uncles, three nephews, and most of our eight siblings. Only three sisters are left, and I'm the oldest. I must now step into the shoes of the esteemed matriarch of our family.

"I don't like being the matriarch," my sister Virginia would say, "I don't care if I am the oldest, don't call me that!"

I, on the other hand, welcome the honor of that title. Both of my grandmothers were loving and wise matriarchs. One was of Irish-Scottish descent, and the other Spanish, French, and Mexican.

My Grandma Isabel scared me as a kid, asking, powerfully, with her hands on her hips, "Who do you think you are?" But now I've matured with age and become a grandmother myself to three precious granddaughters. I need to stand up and be who I am: a loving matriarch.

I recently returned from a trip to Ireland, and the last time I was there was with my sister, Virginia.

"Top of the mornin' to ye!" she said each day, trying to mimic an Irish accent.

"Likewise," I responded, "Top of the mornin' to you, too!"

I intuit Virginia's presence with me everywhere, especially as I travel through that lush green land filled with the stories of our ancestors. I hear her musical voice exclaiming, "Our Great-Great Grandmother was the Belle of Wexford!" to listeners in the Irish pub, where we sit, laugh, and sing, drinking wine. I even hugged an ancient tree for her and for my lovely granddaughters. But not just any trees, the hawthorn and magical trees in the fairy forest, where The White Lady resides, and fairies build whimsical forts using supernatural forces.

One of my granddaughters has a devotion to Ireland's patroness, St. Brigid. I'm pleasantly surprised to discover why. Symbolically, St. Brigid represents the young blossoms of spring, growth, eternal flame, holy wells, and new beginnings. That's where my twenty-two-year-old granddaughter finds herself in life right now: embarking on a new, exciting career of different possibilities.

Conversely, the matriarch, crone, hag, or grandmother represents the old woman of winter turbulence, endurance, wisdom, and endings. Both epitomize so much more in the world of alchemy—the innocence of youth forged by trial, misfortune, loss, and change, and the experience of old age forged by resilience, intuition, and transformation. Metaphorically, they aren't two opposites but one: a single entity recycling through herself, endlessly. Sometimes she appears as a Fairy Godmother or a witch. Sometimes she comes as the Grim Reaper—Death herself.

I have come to honor and respect the Grim Reaper's presence in my life, and with my grandmother's intuition, believe that we can look at Death like a crow—either as a thief or as a messenger. As a thief, Death comes and steals what is most valuable, so we're afraid. But seeing Death as a messenger holding the key, our beloved is waiting at the door to take us home. So, there is peace and tranquillity.

The Medicine

Some believe we rejoin God and our loved ones in Heaven, while others believe we recycle back to Earth in a different life form. My father would say, "After the Grim Reaper comes, I'll be pushing up daisies!"

Journal your answer to these questions:

What is your belief? Where do we go after our last breath?

There have been a multitude of books written on this subject. What books have you read? Plan to read at least one from the following:

- *On Death and Dying* by Elizabeth Kubler-Ross

- *Afterlife, the Other Side of Dying* by Morton T. Kelsey

- *Beyond Grief: Guide for Recovery from the Loss of a Loved One* by Carol Staudacher

- *A Grief Observed* by C.S. Lewis

- *While I Breathe, I Hope* by Dr. Richard R. Gaillardetz

Using my grandmother's intuition and training as a transpersonal psychotherapist and hypnotherapist, I offer the following guided meditation:

Find a safe place to relax where you won't be disturbed. Get comfortable, turn off your phone, and close window coverings. Place pets outside or in another room.

Focus on your breathing. Relax face and jaw. Relax temples, eyes, eyelids. Relax the back of the neck and shoulders. Relax your lower back. Relax arms and chest. Relax your stomach, legs, and toes.

Notice your breath. Are your breaths short and shallow? If so, take a deep breath and relax your breathing. Take a deep breath in and a deep breath out. Inhale in and inhale out.

Now, just relax your body even more, and experience each emotion as it surfaces and rises to the top. No need to resist.

Allow your body and mind to accept them as being a natural part of your process. Just let yourself flow with each and every emotion. See yourself with a heart full of compassion. Feel a greater kindness fill your heart, and let yourself feel more at peace, balanced, and more harmonious with life around you.

Let yourself release all of the anger and sadness you have been feeling. Let it go, just feel it pass, feel it flow through and pass out of you, no need to resist. As you let these emotions go, feel a new sense of peace emerge.

You know you are alright, you know you have the courage to move beyond your grief.

Now, just begin to imagine yourself beyond your sorrow. It's behind you now. You may see yourself with friends or family, or you may see yourself as stardust floating in the universe with your loved ones, or see yourself alone in your special place.

See yourself smiling, feeling at peace, feeling healthy and strong. Imagine yourself motivated, once again, with activities you enjoy. Your mind, body, and spirit heal each day. Each day, you grow stronger, healing, and recovering.

Feel yourself drift and float in a warm glow of healing energy. No need to resist, just drift and float. Now just enjoy your special place, take your time, and when you are ready, open your eyes, sense this room, feeling grateful, at peace, and happy to be alive.

ADDITIONAL GRANDMOTHER'S INTUITIVE MEDICINE:

- Take time to cry. This also applies to men—tough men can and do cry.

- Keep busy. Do purposeful work that occupies the mind and heart; volunteer.

- Join a grief group.

- Turn grief into creative energy. Join an art, dance, book club, or singing group.

- Record your thoughts in a journal. Writing can be very therapeutic.

- Take care of yourself. Eat well and exercise regularly.

- Spend time in nature, and if possible, do this as a daily practice.

- Find ways to be around animals. Play with a pet, or visit a petting zoo.

- Take advantage of the services offered by your religious community. Or, join a faith, meditation, or 12-step group in your area.

- Spend time with family, friends, or reach out to old and new friends.

- Get professional help if needed.

- Look at your face in the mirror each day and tell yourself, "I Love You!"

Even though I'm cognizant of walking with the Grim Reaper, I have learned not to fear death. There's no denying it hurts to lose those we love; however, a time of loss can be a time of learning unlike any other. It's important to remember living with loss is about beginnings as well as endings.

In my youthful, lead-colored years, I lived a trance-like existence in a world of dysfunction, fear, and denial. I am thankful for that existence because I know it was essential for the development of my authentic self.

As I mature into my golden Grandmother years, I am empowered by awareness and intuition, provided I stay resilient and awake to all the possibilities life has to offer. The great Carl Jung believed this cyclical search was the alchemist's goal of self-realization. Walking with the Grim Reaper and grieving is a matter of living, loving, and transforming.

Susan C. Jensen earned a Master of Arts from John F. Kennedy University in Transpersonal Psychotherapy, specializing in Somatic and Marriage and Family therapy; a Bachelor of Arts in Humanities from Dominican University; and an Associate of Arts in Addiction Studies from Diablo Valley College. She is a certified Hypnotherapist from Josie Hadley's Palo Alto School of Hypnotherapy; certified Alcohol and Drug Counselor from Diablo Valley College; certified Don Riso and Russ Hudson Enneagram Instructor; certified Jeremy Taylor Projective Dream Worker; certified Spiritual Director from La Casa De La Luz and Mercy Center; and a Commissioned Lay Minister for the Sacramento Diocese in California. While semi-retired, Susan is kept busy as a Spiritual Director, Lay Minister, Enneagram Instructor, and as a wife, mother, and grandmother—her most cherished job in life. Susan delights in the Arts, listening to music, and is a member of several choirs. Owning both a piano and a Celtic harp, she hopes one day to master them. Susan is a lifelong learner, enjoys reading, traveling, being in nature, and with pets. She has a very curious intellect and practices *Vipassana* (Insight) meditation and yoga at home and with friends at the senior center. Susan looks forward to daily walks by the Benicia waterfront. She is a long-time member of both the International Enneagram Association and Spiritual Directors International.

CONNECT WITH SUSAN:

Websites: https://www.internationalenneagram.org/

https://www.sdicompanions.org/

Email: thejonahconnection@gmail.com

Chapter 8

Coming of Age at Seventy
Step Over the Threshold of Fear to Soar

JENNIFER K. SPROUL, FOUNDER, GRACEING AGEFULLY™

*"Intuition comes disguised, sometimes as an answered prayer,
sometimes as a delightfully simple solution to a
seemingly complex problem."*
~Jennifer Sproul
(inspired by a writing prompt: "What is intuition?")

My Story

"Am I going to Ireland?"

The deadline loomed; I still wobbled.

It's the middle of one of the busiest seasons in real estate. Maybe I shouldn't. What will my clients think?

Ego, my protective (fearful) self, warned me I'd regret this decision.

"Are you going to be here for my follow-up medical tests?" Raymond implored me, aiming his puppy dog worried eyes directly at my heart.

My husband had undergone major surgery in April, and they would conduct follow-up scans six months later to make sure there was no spread of the cancer.

"The tests are in October. I'll be back on September 25th, in plenty of time for your tests," I assured him.

The money was a worry earlier, but as the deadline approached, unexpected windfalls landed in our accounts.

It was still a lot of money (especially for a solo traveler).

What makes you think you deserve a trip to Europe by yourself? I kept asking myself. We hadn't taken a *real* vacation together in five years.

That last thought stood in the doorway to my commitment, like a giant bouncer, hands on his hips, blocking the doorway. His head tilted down, his eyes glared at me with disgust as if to say, "Selfish woman, how *dare* you?"

Behind him, though, I saw something. It wasn't clear, but in the fog on the other side of the bouncer was a woman's finger beckoning and a tiny voice whispering:

The bouncer's an illusion. You can push him out of the way like a feather. You won't regret it.

I felt a knowing wink.

I pushed the bouncer aside with ease, just like she said. I jumped through the doorway, the point of no return.

Once in, like everything else in my life, I knew I'd make it work. I've mostly had that "what's-the-worst-that-can-happen" mindset followed by the "you can always get out of it; it's only money, you're not going to die" attitude.

This is the story of my journey to Ireland to write a chapter in a collaborative book titled *The Alchemy of Intuition*.

Eleven authors, led by a psychotherapist/shamanic priestess, over the course of ten days, were introduced to the four stages of alchemy based on Jungian psychology:

DEATH, PURIFICATION, RISE OF CONSCIOUSNESS, and INTEGRATION/TRANSFORMATION.

This is the story that unfolded for me and continues to unfold:

DEATH
LETTING GO OF WHAT NO LONGER SERVES

In the first half of my life, I never wanted to make trouble. I kept my voice down. I flew under the radar. If ego spoke, I listened and obeyed. I was a good girl.

At sixty, I had what I now recognize as an intuitive hit that changed the course of my life.

I could live to one hundred and twenty. I'm only halfway. I have as many years ahead as I've already lived. It's like a do-over. I have time to get it "right" the second time around.

I was reborn.

My generation, the Baby Boomers, is the first, I believe, that can live, on average, one hundred years or more.

Fast forward ten years. I'm seventy. I liken this to a "new adolescence."

My TRUE self was born and is now coming of age. This is my second half. My higher self, a.k.a. intuition, is calling. When intuition calls, ego tries to protect me.

I'm learning to set aside my ego, with gratitude for trying to protect me, and follow my intuition.

DEATH OF THE MASKS

The masks we wear are part of a kind of hologram (a three-dimensional image we project). Our hologram is what we want the external world to see. It's the image we think the external world expects of us and accepts.

Our hologram masks our truth, even from ourselves.

Some of my masks include makeup, manicures, pedicures, designer clothing, cars, jewelry, and accessories. We also have behavior masks, which I won't go into here.

Suffice it to say, as we get older, the masking can become more aggressive, even harmful (think plastic surgery/invasive procedures).

Our hologram is what we think the external world wants us to be. It's also what we hope the world will see. Sadly, it keeps us from seeing what's inside.

I practiced unmasking for months. I was just getting comfortable not wearing makeup or having my nails and toes manicured, as I had for my entire adult life.

Before going, I decided I'd show up unmasked to meet my fellow authors. I threw my makeup bag in like a life jacket, in case of an emergency. In the end, I never touched it.

This group would meet me without my masks.

Each day, I faced my unmasked image in the mirror. I had to push aside my screaming ego and walk into the world unmasked. Each day, it got easier. Each day, I came closer to accepting my reflection in the mirror.

THE WORK OF LETTING GO
SLEEPLESS IN DUBLIN DAY 1

Was that a knock?

Sue's voice, a hushed whisper, "Jen, you're late!" Her voice sounded protective, disappointed, and ashamed (for me) all at once.

Dripping from the shower I just took, wrapped in a towel, I slid the door open a crack.

"I thought it started at 5:30!"

"No, 4:50 and everyone is there except you!"

Sue had a look that said, "We are in big trouble, and it's just the first night."

I shooed her off and thanked her as if to say, "I'll take the walk of shame alone."

Frantic, I plugged my hair dryer into the converter. At least I'd dry my hair before descending to the dark courtroom where I would be judged for not paying attention (troublemaker). I imagined the spotlight would shine on me as I entered the dark, quiet room of *attentive* authors. It would light me up like a Christmas tree as I shrank into my small self, hoping not to be noticed.

SNAP! No whoosh from the dryer; all power to the outlets *off!*

Alrighty then, this is a test of the emergency unmasking system.

I threw on my clothes and took the elevator to the main level.

Where's the room?

I'm getting a little more panicked. The concierge points me to a conference room.

The room is dark and very quiet. I push gently on the door, hoping not to call any more attention to myself. There's an empty chair next to the woman with the purple streaks in her pretty gray hair.

"Sorry, sorry," I whisper. *Not sorry,* I think. *I'm already apologizing, ugh.*

Purple streaks, a.k.a. Ruthie, reaches out and takes my hand; she gives me a knowing "twink" (my new word for a twinkle and a wink which only a fairy can do!).

Looking me in the eye, she says, "You look like a **wild** woman." She bestows it as a kind of honor. I immediately know I'm accepted. I know I belong here.

That act of courage—leaving behind my masks and apologies and being accepted by the group—gave me the strength to push ego aside and let my true self show up.

Soon after arriving at our next destination, Deerstone Eco Resort, we were led through guided shamanic breathwork. I was told that the circular breathing technique has an effect similar to ayahuasca, without the ingestion of drugs. Once it started, the room shook with crying, howling like wolves, and writhing on the floor. Afterward, we processed what came up.

I still vividly remember being three years old and being left with trusted family friends—strangers to me—while the rest of my family went on vacation.

During the breathwork, the pain of that experience came alive as if I were there again. The breathing method reopened the wound. It brought me right back to convulsive sobbing. I could barely breathe, and tears flowed endlessly. For my processing, the guide asked me to select two participants to represent my parents, who are now deceased.

This is the account of that experience:

Why did you leave me with those strangers?

I'm crying, the plea erupting from my heart. Wracked with sobs and tears, I gasp for breath. I still feel, deep in my core, the unquenchable sobs of three-year-old me.

Sixty-seven years later, I cry to two near strangers acting as proxies for my dead parents while others watch.

My mother's proxy looks like my real mother. My father's proxy—a woman—looks clumsy and uncomfortable with my emotional outburst (pretty accurate, I'd say).

My mother's proxy looks genuinely ashamed, anguished. I can feel she's not acting.

"If I had any idea how much it hurt you, I never would have left you," she weeps.

I see she's suffering. The act that inflicted this pain on me is irreversible. I see she feels powerless in the face of this truth.

I can finally forgive her.

A deep sigh escapes from my chest.

A crack opened in the locked container that held my heart for sixty-seven years. I have worked with energy healers to release this before. I feel something different this time.

This time it is complete.

Scar tissue formed around my heart when my family left me with friends while they took a vacation. A three-year-old only knows her mother is not there to comfort her in the dark.

Fear of abandonment became my lifelong subconscious protector.

If I don't let them in, they can't hurt me.

I have lived proudly most of my adult life, independent and self-sufficient.

Until now, I thought independence was a superpower.

I learned it was my Achilles' heel.

I am opening my heart at last.

I am clearing the blocks.

I am ready for purification.

PURIFICATION: CLEARING, CLEANSING, AND DETOXING THE DISINTEGRATING BATHING SUIT

THE RIVER BOYNE/HOT BOX EXPERIENCE

The thought of putting on a bathing suit (body shame) on an already too-cold-for-swimwear day, *and* sliding into a cold, muddy river? *I don't think so!*

"Nope, not doing it!" I said before even getting to the scene.

Laura threw me a bone, "You can wear pants over your bathing suit and just pull up the bottom and go in up to your ankles."

Then, I'm supposed to go into a super-hot sauna, a.k.a., the HOT BOX (don't even start).

"No way, not interested. I will go there, but I'm not doing it!"

Sue chimes in, "Me either! Ugh! I don't want to!"

Next thing, she's already changed into her suit in the community locker room.

I glare at her, my eyes burning a hole in her stupid suit.

"Traitor," I mumble to myself as I pull the curtain around me to change into mine.

My bathing suit was fine when I packed it. Today, as I stuffed it reluctantly into my backpack, I noticed a small tear in the fabric on the back, as if to say, "Don't bother trying to cover up or hold in your naked body."

As I pulled it on, the small tear parted like the Red Sea all the way down to my butt. I pulled my pants on. The straps kept the front up, but it billowed like a sail.

I had to laugh. I went out and into the hottest sauna for about a minute.

I emerged and stepped into the River Boyne to my shins.

I laughed at myself.

My bathing suit did the work of taking off another mask for me. As if in a ceremony, I peeled off what remained of my bathing suit, balled it up, and threw it in the trash.

Cleared, cleansed, and released.

A channel to source energy was open; I was ready for the "rise of consciousness."

RISE OF CONSCIOUSNESS
GUIDES, ANGELS, AND SOURCE, OH MY!

"Can you tell me what my spirit animal is?" I asked Michele, a medium who "sees dead people" and a lot of other things. She was divinely placed in my space during this trip.

Several of us landed randomly together in the cabins and lodges. We felt it was divinely ordained, given our propensity to be loud, laughing at inappropriate times, and enjoying a bit of Irish whiskey.

Michele talked about her spirit animals as if they were visible to all of us. She sees them.

"Not like I see you, it's different, but it is visual," she explains.

She agreed to perform what I call her "soul x-ray" on me.

I was thrilled.

"Come up now to my room." We had about thirty minutes before dinner.

Michele already introduced us to the friendly ghosts that inhabited Rockfield House.

"Don't worry, they're just curious. You can ask them to stay away, and they will."

"We don't have a lot of time, so I'm just going to tell you what I see that's right in front of me," she began.

"Okay, I'm ready!" I was really excited. I don't have that kind of visual sense, so to have someone who could tell me what they see in my soul? I was in!

"State your name three times." That gives her permission to look.

Her hands wave around the whole time. She stared at me intently.

What's she seeing? Do I want to know? Maybe it's dark.

I keep experiencing that stepping into fear and doubt transports me to another level.

In the next few minutes, I learn I have guides she can see, a wolf and an angel.

I was a witch in another lifetime, and my astral body was stuck in the area of my heart chakra. I had a very vivid dream about this over a year ago.

I learn I need to summon my guides and ask for help. They are always there, but I must ask for their help.

That night, I slid into my bed and visualized my guides. I asked them to protect me and keep the supposedly friendly ghosts away. I feared falling asleep. I feared I'd stop breathing. I've stopped breathing in my sleep before, due to sleep apnea. I wake up gasping sometimes.

I see and feel myself as a newborn in the arms of an angel. I feel safe and warm. I breathe easily.

This night, I knew my guides wouldn't let any of those things happen.

I slept so deeply, without interruption, until my alarm went off. At home, I never need an alarm.

I've suffered from insomnia for thirty years. I don't remember the last time I slept as deeply as I did that night.

CLOSING THOUGHTS

Over the course of ten days, living with and baring my soul to strangers—now friends—opened a previously blocked channel to higher consciousness.

The channel from the Earth to my crown chakra and beyond is wide open.

The energy flows through my open heart.

The work brought the flow, peace, and calm I sought.

Thirty years of sleeplessness are behind me.

Now, on the nights I wake at three a.m., I know it's a higher consciousness calling, and I listen.

At seventy, I'm coming of age.

The second half of my life is guided by Source (intuition).

I am an explorer.

Five hundred years ago, explorers set out to prove the world wasn't flat because they *knew* (intuition).

I am exploring INNER SPACE, the new infinite frontier!

The Medicine

I use *intuition* and *Source* interchangeably.

Source energy is always present. Like a fish in water, you don't recognize it; you swim in it.

When a baby is born, they're driven by source energy, pure **love.** Look at a newborn, what do you feel? **Love.**

Babies *learn* to fear. They *learn* to control. They *learn* to protect themselves from danger.

You are the product of that learning. Inside you is a newborn hidden from the world by ego and masks.

Source, guides, angels, and higher self are always available. You need to ask them for help.

You can explore inner space—the field of infinite possibilities—by accessing intuition starting now.

ACCESSING INTUITION

1. THE PRACTICE

   Thirty minutes of SILENCE without distractions, every morning.

   The best time to access Source is when you first wake up. You're most receptive in the state between sleep and full wakefulness.

2. CLEAR THE CLUTTER

   As you practice 30 minutes of undistracted silence *every* day, you notice thoughts.

   It's natural to attach and follow them down the path of fear, worry, pain, etc. Catch yourself; practice letting go of the thought.
   Let go of judgment. Thank yourself for noticing and continue.

   Visualization: Imagine your thoughts are in a river. You're standing on the bank, watching them flow by. They come into view and flow by, out of view. Let them go down the river until they disappear.

   Initially, the clutter of thoughts can be overwhelming.

   After 30 minutes of silence, they'll come rushing in.

   When they do, go to Step 3.

3. WRITE

   Write the thoughts down. Don't worry about making sense. Try to capture as many words and phrases as possible, not all complete thoughts.

   This is journaling. Specifically, this is what Julia Cameron calls "morning pages" in her book, *The Artist's Way.*

   This is a powerful tool to unblock creativity.

   This is a powerful tool to unblock source energy.

   If you don't want to write, speak into a recorder—just get it out.

Promise: There will be a time you no longer need Step 3 for clutter clearing.

4. LISTEN

Listen and stay present.

You are now vibrating at a frequency that will access higher consciousness (intuition).

For more inspiration and thoughts on thriving in the second half of life, and to receive my monthly blog, subscribe to: https://graceingagefully.com.

Jennifer K. Sproul is the founder of Graceing Agefully™, a platform dedicated to changing the culture of aging. At sixty, Jennifer had an intuitive hit that she could live to one hundred and twenty years. If so, she realized she was only halfway. She began to share her experiences of changing her mindset about getting old. From running her first full marathon at age fifty-eight to beginning a writing journey and becoming a published author at sixty-six, she continually challenges the idea that we decline as we age.

The Alchemy of Intuition is the fourth collaborative book to which she has contributed a chapter. Each chapter tells a never-before-told story of transformation in her life.

Jennifer is an explorer of all things that enable her to understand more about how her mind works. She studies human design, astrology, yoga, hypnotherapy, enneagram, IFS (Internal Family Systems), meditation, and now Jungian psychology for clues to expansion in the second half of life.

Her program "Living a Well-Integrated Life" has become the foundational practice for her expansion.

Jennifer is a Realtor® in the Washington, D.C. metropolitan area. She lives in Gaithersburg, Maryland, with her husband, Raymond, and two cats, Sam and Jack.

Jennifer is envisioning her first solo book, and she's on the threshold of creating an older female Superhero. Stay tuned.

CONNECT WITH JENNIFER:

Facebook: https://www.facebook.com/jennifer.sproul.58

Email: jennifer@graceingagefully.com

Chapter 9

Hopeful Leaps of Faith
Transform Intrusive Thoughts to a Safe Place in Two Steps

MARTA KOWALSKA

My Story

POLAND, 1994

"It's all your fault!" My father roared, his voice echoing off the walls.

He swayed; a half-empty bottle of cheap liquor gripped in his hand. His knuckles were bone white. His face was a mask of purple and red. A glob of spittle flew from his lips.

I squeezed my body flat against the cool, humming steel of the refrigerator. A shudder ran from the crown of my head to my heels. My breath hitched. My hands were fisted at my sides, nails digging into my palms—a silent, useless protest.

Not a single word escaped my throat.

He slammed the bottle onto the chipped counter.

"Food!" The demand was a guttural bark.

My mother moved with the unsettling quiet of a ghost, her back perfectly straight, eyes fixed on the task. A plate materialized in front of him, the steam from the meal mingling with the heavy, sour stench that coated the air.

The room reeked of stale alcohol, a smell that had long ago become the permanent, suffocating wallpaper of our home. He didn't use a fork; he shoveled a mound of food into his mouth, then immediately tilted his head back, taking a long, defiant gulp from his bottle.

My thirteen-year-old legs were a sudden, desperate blur. I didn't stop to think or look back. The hallway was a tunnel, and the door to my room was the only light at the end.

I burst inside and slammed it shut. The latch was a pathetic barrier. I sank onto the floor, pressing my ear against the wood, listening to the muffled, terrifying sounds of the life my mother still catered to.

USA, 2024

"It's your fault!" My husband bellowed, the spittle from his mouth spraying across the table.

He punctuated each word with a violent shake of his hand. His eyes, normally a gentle blue, were now cold and wide open. He kicked a trash bin; beer cans rattled inside.

I felt a chill crawl up my spine, even as the heat bled through the open window behind him. The memory of old dread mixed with new fear. I closed my eyes and a single, silent tear slid down my cheek. I waited for the next one to fall.

He was on his feet now, stumbling. He didn't raise his hand, but I watched my own reflection in the table's polished surface, my eyes wide with a terror that looked back at me.

The glass of water beside me trembled, not from my hand, but from the force of his fury. I didn't wait for the volume to spike again. My gaze locked onto the bedroom door—my only exit.

Without a word, I backed away slowly, my hands held low and ready, my focus entirely on the space between us. The moment I reached the doorway, I pivoted and fled inside, pulling the door shut with a sharp snick of the latch.

From the other side, a chair scraped violently across the floor, a frustrated screech of metal on tile. The heavy, defeated sigh that followed confirmed his rage hadn't moved. I stayed pressed against the cool wood, my body shaking as the silence resumed.

A few minutes later, the townhouse's front door slammed shut with a finality that rattled the windows. A long, shuddering sigh of relief escaped my lungs.

The house is quiet. I'm safe.

For now.

The damp, crumpled paper in my hand felt suddenly inadequate. I tossed the used Kleenex onto the growing, snowy mound on the coffee table. *Forty-three years.* I leaned my forehead against the cool glass of the window, the faint chill a strange comfort against the heat of my skin.

My birthday.

Instead of a cake with candles, a guttural sob shook my chest, tasting bitter and old.

What the fuck did I do wrong?

The question wasn't a whisper; it was a shriek trapped behind my teeth.

How did I end up in the same situation again?

A thousand miles separated me from the childhood home and the cheap liquor that stained the air, yet the hollow, sinking dread in my stomach was an identical weight to the one I carried at thirteen. The space around me was different—cleaner, quieter—but the fear was a familiar ghost, whispering the same story.

I turned back to the stack of manila folders on the counter—documents packed, birth certificate, bank statements, and a thick file labeled "Legal."

My eyes drifted to the clock: *Twenty minutes until the call with the divorce lawyer.*

There was nowhere to go.

My gaze fell upon a postcard tacked to the corkboard—a sun-drenched photograph of a cliffside in San Diego, California. I remembered the effortless blue of the Pacific, the way the setting sun turned the sand to liquid gold, and how, for just a few hours, the knot in my chest entirely disappeared.

A sudden, sharp clarity settled over me, cutting through the panic. I would go there. San Diego was five hundred miles away, an entirely new world where I knew no one.

Five hundred miles. My chin lifted a fraction. That distance, I decided, would be enough. It had to be enough to breathe, enough to feel safe.

IRELAND, 2025

A sharp click, then darkness. The sudden silence in the hotel room was deafening, broken only by the frantic beat of my own heart.

Fuck, it's my fault the power just went out!

My hand still hovered over the kettle switch, a phantom heat rising from the now-silent appliance.

I shouldn't turn the kettle on, what the fuck was I thinking?! I should've known better!

A flush crept up my neck, hot and mortifying.

The old mansion creaked around us, each groan of timber amplifying my guilt. Our "luxury" Irish getaway—a grand, albeit aging, estate—now felt like a giant, echoing tomb. We were on the third floor, and the abrupt plunge into blackness suggested the problem wasn't localized to just my room.

The whole damn floor, I just knew it.

I opened my door and gazed into the dark hallway. A soft chuckle broke through the oppressive quiet.

"It's *not* your fault!" Jennifer's voice, light and melodic, cut through my spiraling thoughts.

Even in the gloom, I felt the warmth of her gaze. When my eyes finally adjusted, her smile was a beacon, a gentle curve that banished the shadows. Her radiant blue eyes, even in the dimness, sparkled with a joy and mischief that seemed entirely out of place, yet utterly characteristic of her. The tension in my shoulders eased.

* * *

The air in the hotel's dining room was thick with the scent of melted wax and sugar. Eleven voices, slightly off-key but full of heart, swelled around me:

"Happy birthday to you. . .happy birthday, dear Marta. . ."

I leaned in, my cheeks hurting from the wide, genuine smile I couldn't contain, and blew out the flames on the cake. The small explosion of smoke and cheers signaled the close of the song.

I opened my eyes to the faces surrounding me—a newly found sisterhood, my rookery, forged in the shared laughter and quiet understanding of this Irish retreat. This was my forty-fourth birthday, and I never felt so rich.

The laughter died down, giving way to a comfortable silence. Tomorrow, the bubble would burst. We'd pack our bags and drive to Dublin airport, scattering back to our respective corners of the world. Mine was waiting for me: San Diego, my sunny, warm paradise.

I swirled the last sip of tea in my mug. The warmth spread through my hands, but a deeper, settling warmth spread through my soul. The phantom grip of the past, the anchor I dragged for decades, felt suddenly loose.

I thought of my father. I didn't want to see his face ever again—that much was a settled, cold certainty. But the hot, consuming weight of anger I carried for him? I decided to just set it down.

It wasn't serving me; it was just a chain. I did the same for my ex-husband, letting the last of the resentment drift away like the smoke from the candles. The chain went slack. The anchor was lifted.

A quiet certainty bloomed in my chest, a truth I finally owned.

It's not my fault.
It's not your fault.

The twin affirmations felt less like words and more like the sound of a door clicking shut on an empty, dark room.

I am light.

I am free.

I'm going home.

The Medicine

The decision was made. The path was clear. I was leaving my soon-to-be ex-husband. And yet, the doubts kept coming, a relentless tide of anxiety that threatened to pull me under.

How do I get out of a hole?

The words of my Buddhist teachers echoed in my mind: *First, you must stop digging.*

But how? I made the choice, I was following through, I was moving out. Still, my mind, a frantic miner, kept at it.

Then, a flicker of an idea. Instead of trying to halt the thought, I could change its direction. Thoughts have energy, and like energy, they can't be stopped. But I could transform them. I began to build my safe place.

My new ideal living room has huge windows that let in sunshine, a stark contrast to the darkness I lived in. The walls are a calming, serene blue. In the corner sits the most comfortable chair imaginable, a soft haven for reading and journaling.

It was a detail-by-detail construction, a meticulous act of creation. And it worked. When my mind started to stray towards the fear or grief, I pulled it back, focusing on the texture of a throw pillow or the precise shade of paint.

The more I built, the easier it became to return.

This was a practice—a daily, often hourly—act of redirecting my focus. Like building a muscle, it requires repetition. I learned that the key was to focus on the same positive vision, building on it again and again.

Switching from decorating my ideal home to crocheting led to confusion. The goal was to build a single, solid safe place, a place I could always return to, a sanctuary that was mine and mine alone—a place no one could reach.

THE 2-STEP FORMULA FOR FREEDOM

This simple framework, I realized, was a universal tool. It could work for any type of intrusive thought, for any fucking thing that held me captive. The key was consistently building a detailed, compelling safe space. The formula was straightforward:

1. **Catch it:** Identify the intrusive thought.

2. **Redirect it:** Immediately shift focus to the safe place.

To make it work, you need a powerful "safe place." What do you love to do? What brings you joy? What are you passionate about? Use that to build a retreat so vivid and compelling that your mind can't resist the redirection.

A GENTLE PATH

Patience and kindness became my new tools. I caught myself in a spiral of intrusive thoughts, and instead of getting frustrated, I simply acknowledged the lapse.

It's okay to fail, as long as I get back up. There is enough negativity in the world without adding more from within. I began to reward myself for catching these thoughts and deliberately steering them back to my ideal home.

With practice, the redirection became faster and less of a struggle. The intrusive thought was like a stray dog, and my safe place was the leash, gently pulling it back.

FORGIVENESS

The ultimate purpose of this practice wasn't just to manage thoughts, but to let go of the unhealthy attachments for good. For me, that meant forgiveness. Forgiving myself for being in that situation and forgiving others for their part in it.

Forgiveness, like peeling an onion, has many layers. Each act of transforming a negative thought into my safe place was a layer being peeled away. It lightened the baggage, making room for a deeper, more profound sense of freedom.

Are you ready to build your safe place? Take five minutes right now to choose core elements that resonate with you. What are the feelings, colors, scents, and sounds that belong in your safe place? The power lies in repetition. Start building that muscle now.

Marta Kowalska's passion is guiding others toward a higher quality of life—a mission forged by a unique blend of scientific discipline and profound inner work. Born and raised in Poland, Marta holds a master's and engineering degrees in Computer Science.

For a decade, she immersed herself in Diamond Way Buddhism, completing the demanding Ngöndro foundation practices. These meditation techniques became the core tools that allowed her to access her intuition and cultivate the invaluable ability to find beauty and clarity even in life's darkest moments.

Professionally, Marta has spent the last decade as an engineer in the medical device field. In this role, she contributes to patient well-being, helping those with chronic pain achieve relief as quickly as possible and sustain that state for as long as possible. Her work is a real-world application of her commitment to easing suffering.

Now based in the San Diego Metro Area, California, Marta enjoys grounding her days with sunset walks on the beach. She integrates her technical background, spiritual insights, and life experience to help people navigate their own internal challenges.

CONNECT WITH MARTA:

Email: Hopeful.Leaps.Of.Faith@gmail.com

Chapter 10

Opening to Intuition
Using Love and Trust to Unlock Inner Wisdom
RACHEL KAUFMAN, MPH, ACC

"It's all in you."
~ A wise groundhog

My Story

I held tightly to the amethyst pendulum with my left hand, suspending it over the open palm of my right hand. The pendulum remained still.

"Think of a question and try to receive a yes or no response from your pendulum." I looked around the large, thickly carpeted basement at the other women who had joined me for the sixth sensory playgroup meet-up, and most people gathered were succeeding. The pendulum, which humans have used for thousands of years, is a powerful intuitive tool for receiving messages from the Divine through your subconscious.

Why can't I do this? What is stopping me?!

I regularly attended this intuitive playgroup with a few friends to strengthen my intuition, and things usually flowed for me, but today I was frustrated.

Maybe the pendulum is not for me. I was about to give up trying when the woman leading the group came over to check on me. "How's it going with your pendulum, Rachel?" I think she saw the disappointment on my face.

"Not well. My pendulum isn't moving." I felt stuck, but I didn't know why. What she told me next was something I'll never forget and was perhaps a pivotal moment in my intuitive awakening.

LOVE

"Think of someone you love, take some deep breaths, and see if that helps move the pendulum." At the time, my husband and I were dating seriously, so his face popped into my head. He looked at me lovingly, and I felt warmth spread into my heart.

My pendulum is moving! I breathed a sigh of relief.

For the rest of that afternoon, I practiced using this new (for me) tool to tap into my subconscious and see what answers came up.

So why didn't it swing for me initially? My energy flow was blocked for some reason. Stress, negative emotions, thoughts, traumas, and other negative experiences can lower our vibration. Being sick and eating unhealthy foods can also block our energy flow, as they are low-vibration.

Being stuck feels constrictive. Have you ever felt a lump in your throat? Maybe you felt a tightness or loss of steady breath when you didn't say something you wanted to?

In spiritual terms, that lump is an energetic blockage. It means that your chi, or life force, isn't flowing through the area where you feel the constriction in your body.

On the other hand, being in the *flow* feels great. You're floating, time doesn't matter, and you feel free. Your body and mind are boundless. You're vibing at a high level. Who doesn't want to feel that?

What can you do to find more flow and positive energy?

One way is to use positive emotions to move your energy toward a higher vibration. After all, emotions are energy in motion. Letting feelings like love and gratitude surge through your body can help flush out and release low vibrational energy that has built up. A physical hug feels good because it stimulates the release of the love hormone oxytocin. Similarly, love and gratitude can lower stress hormones, ease anxiety and depression, and strengthen our overall immune system. I know when I'm vibing high, I feel more curious, generous, grounded, and gentle with myself and others.

TRUST

My pendulum experience was over 18 years ago, when I began to work to strengthen my intuition. It was love that helped me get *unstuck,* and because it worked, my *trust* in myself and my abilities increased.

We've all heard the saying "trust your gut." This really means *trusting your intuition,* or sixth sense. This trust builds up over time, and each experience is like a stepping stone, carrying you to higher elevations. The more I trusted in mine, the stronger it grew, and continues to grow.

Each time you really listen, sense, and feel your way rather than just use your brain, you build up *trust* in your intuition. This strengthens your ability to use it to make choices more aligned with your core values and your soul's unique journey.

Many students have asked me, "How do I know when a thought or message is coming from fear or intuition?" I enjoy answering this as the answer is simple yet powerful.

Fear is an emotion that often arrives in a swirl of chaos and negativity, and it often feels heavy in our bodies because it's a low vibration.

When you have a fearful, negative thought (*My son is late arriving home. Maybe he's injured?!),* you might feel your heartbeat speed up, skip a beat, or feel a knot of dread in your stomach. This is fear—worrying without any evidence.

Intuition, on the other hand, arrives gently, often as a quiet whisper in your mind—a certain knowing that the thought is true. You may feel grounded and calm when the thought arrives.

My phone rang. *I know it's my friend Amy calling.* I knew without looking at the caller ID. I picked up the phone, and it was her. My intuition is already connected to her without my conscious mind knowing.

How do we decipher the difference between fear and intuition?

My advice is to check in with *how* your body feels at that moment. "Am I feeling calm and relaxed, or scared and agitated?" In the case of worrying about my son, it was total fear. He arrived home safely soon after.

We often ignore what our senses tell us because we're scared, skeptical, or a mix of both. Sometimes it's hard to trust something we can't see, yet we somehow trust that Wi-fi, electricity, and other technologies are real, because we see results. Our TV turns on, and our friends call us on our mobile from across the world. The energetic world is the same, but we often want results to trust it's real.

Do you have an example of when you received information that you trusted but could not see?

Here is one of mine. Another day at the sixth sensory playgroup, when I still doubted my intuition, we did an exercise that helped me believe in it. About 20 of us were divided into pairs, and the person leading the exercise instructed us to "Look at your partner for a minute to get a sense of them and then imagine them in a landscape."

I stared at the older Latina woman sitting on the carpeted floor across from me, whom I had just met.

I hope this works; it seems a bit silly.

"Times up!" I shared with her what I saw in my mind's eye, hoping it wasn't too far off. I described it to her.

"I saw a rural area, and a gravel road lined by trees with beautiful fall leaves, leading to a stone gate further up the road. I felt a sense of calmness and peace in the scene."

She looked back at me with wide eyes as I asked, "Does that mean anything to you?" expecting it to be a bit off.

Her feedback, once again, reminded me to trust what I receive.

She replied, surprised, "I am about to retire and that is the place I'm retiring to!"

I felt shocked and exhilarated at the same time.

This stuff actually works!

I felt something shift within me—perhaps an increase in my confidence.

I can do this! I was accurate with this lady!

I began to trust the process a bit more and became more excited about continuing to receive the signs the Universe was sending me. It was up to me to listen or ignore; I decided to listen.

UNLOCKING INNER WISDOM

It's all in you. Years ago, during my senior year of college, I was guided through meditation by a friend while dealing with heartbreak. We had escaped to my family's mountain house so we could relax and snowboard, and so I could heal emotionally. We arrived at the start of a significant snowstorm; the fresh powder was perfect for snowboarding, but not for driving. We stayed in the mountains for several more days than planned, which turned out for the best.

One night while we relaxed in the hot tub, feeling the soothing contrast of hot water on our skin, and breathing in the cold, snowy, pine-scented air, he asked, "Can I guide you on a meditation?"

Why not? It can't hurt, and we have nothing else to do!

I closed my eyes, and his gentle voice began guiding me. "I'd like you to picture a tree, then imagine moving down its roots, where you will meet a spirit animal who will bring you a message."

Sure, let's see what happens. I was doubtful I'd receive anything.

As we meditated, I visualized a beautiful, large tree. I slowly began to follow its ancient roots deep into the Earth. As I traveled down, he instructed, "Now stop and meet your spirit animal." Suddenly, I saw a groundhog! The groundhog came closer and calmly said to me, "It's all in you." Short, to the point, and profound.

It's all in me. I repeated slowly to myself, soaking in the message.

"Now come back up to the surface through the roots of the tree."

As we sat together in the hot tub in the stillness of the night, I felt a peace I hadn't felt in a long time. The groundhog's message resonated because I connected with my *higher self.* This true self exists at a higher level than the soul and doesn't get bogged down in negative human emotions such as grief, anger, and jealousy. At the higher self-level, there is only *love.*

The saying goes, "We are energetic beings having a physical journey." The groundhog reminded me of what I now live by—we already hold all the answers, we need to listen for them. As a healer and life coach, I'm here to remind you: *It's all in you, too.*

So how can you listen better?

Shamanic practices and some cool researchers around the world have proven that reconnecting with nature, the self, and the spiritual world is crucial for good health and well-being. Meditation, energy-healing sessions, being in nature, or thinking of someone you love are a few ways to ground, find stillness, reconnect with Source, and *listen.*

Throughout the years, I've received images, words, feelings, smells, and messages from ancestors and spirit guides that deeply resonated (with me and clients). The key is not to doubt these sensory inputs, but to welcome them, or at least be curious about what their meaning is to you.

Recently, I worked with a client who was stuck deciding whether she should share some information she learned with a neighbor. While she lay on the massage table, relaxing and enjoying the Reiki energy, I received a series of images.

First, I saw a rose in my mind's eye. *I wonder what this means to her.* As I continued the healing session, I clearly saw the Great Wall of China.

Now I was intrigued! *This is going to be interesting to share with her. I have no idea what these two images have to do with each other.*

"Oh wow, that decision I was talking about earlier is with a neighbor named Rose who is Chinese!" she said with amused shock. "I guess this is the confirmation I was looking for! I'll talk with her soon." She left feeling at peace with this new decision that she had worried about for days.

It is normal for doubts to spring up. *What if I let love and trust flow through me, but I still don't feel it or know what to do?*

Don't worry, that's perfectly fine. The miracle of intuition is that it's often the little things that matter. Paying attention to that little voice saying, *"Slow down,"* in your head while you're driving on the highway, or choosing to make tea because your body craves it but your brain wants coffee, is often just as important as paying attention when making big life decisions.

I am still amazed at how it all works, even now!

Accessing inner wisdom is possible, but we often block it by letting the background noise, negative thoughts, and other stressors take the driver's seat. The good news is that with practice and awareness, we can find a clear road ahead. Now it's your time to take a test drive and see how inviting love and trust can increase access to your higher self.

The Medicine

USING A PENDULUM TO SEEK ANSWERS

You can use a pendulum to tap into the answers your body and soul already know, but your brain hasn't figured out yet. It can help balance the energy flow between your mind, body, and spirit. If you're a healer, it's a useful tool to assess your clients' energy flow as well. Whatever your intention for using it, it's one of several holistic tools and techniques you can use to support your intuitive journey and make embodied decisions.

Before we start, here's a list of what you'll need:

- A pendulum: Find yours online or in-person at a metaphysical store that sells crystals.

- Selenite stone: Place the pendulum on top of a piece of selenite to cleanse and recharge the crystal pendulum, especially after purchasing it. Cleanse 12-24 hours (not required but recommended).

- A quiet space to focus and find stillness, and 15-20 minutes of time.

- Let go of expectations: This is just for fun—don't get too stressed out if it doesn't work right away or if it's not for you!

STEP 1: FIND STILLNESS AND ACCESS LOVE.

- A great way to access your intuition is to find your center, or inner calm. Find a quiet space in your house—maybe somewhere you usually meditate, or at least somewhere you won't be disturbed by family, pets, or technology.

- Feel free to do a short meditation, although it's not required.

- Find a comfortable sitting position, legs uncrossed and feet on the floor.

- Begin to breathe in through your nose slowly, and out through your mouth, even more slowly. The slower the better, as it calms your nervous system.

- Repeat until you feel calmer and more grounded.

- If you wish, think of someone you love and who loves you, and feel them in your heart. You may see their name or face, or both. Trust your intuition and use the first person who pops in. If you prefer to picture a beloved pet or a landscape that brings you peace, use that instead.

STEP 2: CALIBRATE YOUR PENDULUM.

Now that you're more relaxed, let's calibrate your pendulum and sync it to your body and energy field. A good way to find your *yes* is to think of something that's true for you; to find your *no,* think about something false. For example, I would say, "My name is Rachel" to find my *yes.* I discovered that my *'yes' means the pendulum swings in a clockwise circle.* Alternatively, to find my *no,* I would say the wrong name, such as, "My name is Sam." My pendulum usually swings back and forth for a *no.* As everyone's energy works differently and can change day to day, I recommend recalibrating your pendulum every time you use it.

Try this method now and see how it goes!

Now that you know which way your pendulum moves for your *yes* and *no,* proceed to the next step.

STEP 3: ASK IT A QUESTION.

- Most pendulums have a small metal or crystal ball attached to the top of their cord. Hold the ball gently but firmly with your fingers in a pinched shape with whichever hand you prefer.

- Hold it steady and without moving over the palm of your other hand, keeping your mind clear and calm.

- Think of a question. I recommend starting with a simple one, such as, *Do I want tea or coffee right now?*

- Test each answer separately.

    o   For example, start with, *I want tea.* Take your time and see if you get a *yes* or a *no.* It usually takes at least ten seconds for the mind to sync with the body, so be patient. Once you have movement, let the pendulum swing over your open palm for at least 20 seconds.

    o   Now test the other possible answer. Make sure the pendulum is not moving above your palm before you say to yourself, *I want coffee,* and see what happens.

o   Sometimes a *yes* swing can turn into a *no,* or vice versa; or a *yes* or *no* swing becomes stronger or weaker, depending on what your system is telling you. It's all good, let your body speak its truth.

o   Sometimes the pendulum will swing the same for both answers. In this case, test them again separately. If it's the same answer again, then you may want (or not want) both equally. In that case, your brain may need to be the tie breaker!

The pendulum is one of many tools we can use to help us perceive *beyond* our five senses and find the answers we seek. The truth is, however, we don't need tools to access our intuition, as *it's all in us.* Every minute of the day, our bodies and energy fields are sensing and perceiving subtle shifts in vibrations and energy from the earth and people around us, whether we notice or not. The more we allow positive emotions such as love and gratitude to flow through us, the easier it will be to access and trust our inner wisdom, which makes all the difference.

Rachel Kaufman, MPH, ACC, is a professional life coach, Usui Reiki Master, reflexologist, Insight Acupressure practitioner, teacher, and author. Rachel received the Rite of the Womb Munay-Ki initiation and is a Womb Keeper, and has also studied the use of essential oils, crystals, and shamanic techniques, all of which she incorporates into healing sessions when needed. She has supported hundreds of clients over the past 20-plus years to find more resilience, calmness, and balance in their daily lives.

Rachel earned an MPH in International Public Health and worked in that field for many years, but she was born to be a transformational healer and coach, so she founded Integrated Healing Vibes, LLC, to fulfill her dream of working full-time as a healer, life coach, and teacher/mentor. Her unique blend of skills and experience allows her to access many tools to customize each session to what her client needs most. Rachel's overall goal for her offerings, which include individual coaching and healing sessions, classes, and healing retreats, is to provide guidance, support, and tools to help her clients and students find more alignment with their core values and true selves. She also encourages them to trust in themselves, their intuition, and the signs from the universe.

Rachel is a featured author in the anthology *Her Badass Story 2*. Her chapter is titled "A Birth Story: From Darkness to Light, Fear to Joy, and Everything in Between." Rachel is honored to offer her embodied intuitive wisdom to readers through her stories and medicine. When she is not working, she's playing or resting. Dancing, traveling, reading, breathing in mountain air, practicing Qigong and Yoga, and receiving hugs from her family and the family dog fulfill her.

CONNECT WITH RACHEL:

Website: https://www.integratedhealingvibes.com

Facebook: https://www.facebook.com/rachel.kaufmanparra

Instagram: https://www.instagram.com/integrated_healing_vibes

LinkedIn: https://linkedin.com/in/rachel-kaufman-coaching-healing

Chapter 11

The Secret Portal
What No One Tells You About Sex

JAYME LYNN, CREATIVE WELLNESS FACILITATOR

My Story

No one tells you that the same energy that breaks your heart can also bring you home to your body.

I want to leave.

But we are celebrating my birthday. I can't.

So, I sit at a table in my own home, surrounded by people who are closest to me, and I feel like I may as well be from another planet. We're all gathered to celebrate my birthday, but all I want is to be swallowed up by the weight of my blankets and lost in my bed, void of all life.

An ocean wave gathers momentum below the surface, threatening to crash ashore. Waves of tension whirl up my limbs to form white knuckles atop clenched fists. I shift uncomfortably in my seat.

Every emotion is merging. A warning. *Why am I still sitting here?*

Breathe.

Inhale. Exhale.

It will be over soon.

It's as if I am an immovable island—surrounded by life blooming, yet my bones feel hollow. There is a current raging inside me from waves of loss. Grief is swallowing me whole, one breath at a time.

Is this just how life is going to be now?

The conversation bounced back and forth like a ping pong ball across the table. Words poured out between spread lips, but no sound reached my fair-skinned ears. The room grew bigger with each shortened breath and shrank.

I hate this.

One by one, the table cleared. Lights out. Door locked.

My shoulders shake with each shallow breath, a pressure valve releasing with the flick of the deadbolt.

I'm alone. Finally.

The tightness travels upward—belly to ribs to chest—tightening its grip. Unmovable. All that's left is to surrender to the tide.

B r e a t h e.

I was utterly frozen on my kitchen floor.

Eyes unmoving—even to blink.

Time ceased.

Something familiar stirred within me—a quiet force, an echo of myself—urging me to stand. I felt my body move towards the bed over the hundred-year-old wood floor, and my mind struggled to catch up. Everyone was gone, but I sensed that I was not alone.

The blankets hissed as I slid my bare and weary body between them.

How easily I could now give myself over to the endless ocean of sadness.

Breathe—a voice—mine, yet not mine.

The same soft voice guided my hands to caress and hold myself as a lover would. Inch by inch, the tension from the imaginary ropes holding my arms and legs, suffocating my chest, started to loosen.

Each breath, breaking free from fear's grip.

Each breath, a coastal breeze kisses land.

It is safe to let more in. My hands move slowly and deliberately to where feeling takes hold, tracing the edges of sensation.

It feels uncertain—almost unsafe—to let pleasure in. Part of me would rather stay in the numbness, where nothing moves or asks too much.

But the familiar voice rose again somewhere inside, soft and sure: *Trust.*

I drink in another breath. My shoulders sink deeper into the pillow.

E x h a l e.

Each pass is a rising of sensation and emotion—a dance of energy twirling and dipping. The tightness returns and leaves just as quickly. Tears pool in my gut, threatening a tsunami. Anxiety crawls up my legs. Pleasure weaves in and around and through it all.

How can this be?

Surrender, the familiar voice whispers. *It doesn't need to make sense.*

Rising and falling, ebbing and flowing—sensation and emotion merge.

Time ceases. The bedroom is gone, and I'm in a void space where all creation is made, encompassed by darkness, soothing and familiar.

The release comes, and with it, salt water of my own making.

In an instant, I'm back in my body—my face soaked, eyes aching from the tears cascading down my cheeks. The threatening tsunami in my gut released.

Naked and alone, yet held in loving arms. The same soft voice returns—steady, certain.

I've got you.

Lightning strikes of sensation meld into a warm liquid invisible to my eyes, coating every crevice of my limp body.

A familiar curve finds the corners of my mouth.

Am I smiling?

Without warning, laughter erupts—a geyser of release—intimate and odd.

The hissing blankets wrap around my exhausted body—sweet and tender as a kiss. And once more, I hear that warm, familiar voice: *You can hold more than you know. Trust in your body's wisdom to show you the way.*

No one tells you that the same energy that breaks your heart can also bring you home to your body.

On my birthday, I experienced a merging of heavy emotions with those of creation and joy—what some might call sexual energy. I believe this merging is what enables transformation. I went from feeling completely numb—my body unable to access the sadness for fear of what it might bring—to swimming in pleasure, where the sorrow and joy began to merge through the movement of sexual energy.

I practice welcoming every feeling, big or small, and honor them as the messengers they are. I now know how to work with them intentionally. Doing so creates safety in my body while gently unlearning shame around what I "should" feel.

When I speak about sexual energy, I'm not referring only to sex itself. Sexual energy—what many traditions call *Eros*—is the pulse of creation that lives inside every being—the same current that stirs desire, animates creativity, and fuels new life. The raw life force moves through our bodies, inviting us to feel, express, and connect. Allowing this energy to move freely nourishes every part of us—heart, mind, and body. Sometimes it appears as sensual pleasure, but just as often, the quiet spark inspires art, sparks ideas, or helps us rise from grief. It's the energy of aliveness—the body's saying, "I am still here."

Learning to meet this energy with awareness transforms it from something private or taboo into a sacred force of renewal. It teaches us that pleasure and pain, creation and loss, aren't opposites but partners in the dance of life. Sexual energy, at its essence, is the rhythm of becoming—the power that creates, destroys, and recreates us, again and again.

Curious about how I ended up in a pool of grief on my kitchen floor? A couple of years ago, the women in my life fell away like petals in slow motion. My last living grandmother, then two beloved aunts—all gone within thirteen months. It was a year of grief, and, when I finally let it touch me, a year of grace. The grief has been like a wave crashing onto the shore and receding out to sea, even now.

When my grandmother died, and then my aunts soon after, I oscillated between closing down and feeling the most alive. I didn't know how I "should" feel. I felt everything—the ache, the love, the strange flicker of aliveness that pulsed beneath the sorrow. At first, this collision of opposites confused me—how my heart could break and bloom together.

I remember sitting in my car one afternoon, completely undone, realizing that my inner child was falling apart. Imagine a six-year-old girl trying to make sense of it all. Her whole world—the people she trusted always to be there—was disappearing. In that moment, I held her in my mind's eye, her hand in mine, and together we began to walk the path of grief at our own pace.

Life has a way of moving too quickly, rushing past the moments that breathe animation into our story. I feel it, too, when I'm swimming in a sea of sexual energy—the surge of a new creative idea that silences everything else on my to-do list. In the midst of love-making, time disappears; there's only one moment, stretching into forever.

And then there is loss, where I remember: *I am still alive.* When I remember just how precious every moment is, the quiet question that follows is: *Will I say yes to being alive? Will I live my most whole truth without shame of what it looks like to others?*

Loss, like love, is a portal deeper into life.

Grief often masquerades as sadness, then anger, then sadness again throughout my days. Sometimes it paralyzes me for days, leaving me unable to think clearly or function in my world. Pleasure, I've learned, is one of the most powerful ways to move it. Loss has taught me how to honor my process and its ever-shifting flow.

When I reached my own edge of sorrow, I sensed the hum of life still brewing beneath it. At that moment, I had a choice: *Swim back out to sea or explore the pulse of life crackling below the crust.*

For a long time, I thought grief took me away from living before returning me to who I was before. But grief doesn't return us to anything; it reshapes us. It shows us how much more space the heart can hold when we stop resisting what it feels.

Over time, I learned to meet grief not as an enemy to survive, but as a teacher—one that invited me deeper into the body, breath, and movement. The same energy that once felt unbearable became the current that carried me.

Sexual energy reshapes us, too. It burns away pretense, softens the edges, and shows what it means to feel fully alive inside our skin. Where grief cracks the heart open, sexual energy floods it with light. Both are portals—one through pain, one through pleasure—leading to the same place: presence.

It's no secret that pleasure often comes wrapped in a cocoon of shame—especially for those of us raised to believe sex or sexual energy is sinful. Honestly, some of me still wrestles with the shame instilled so young. I see how this shame has spread and tells me how I should feel or express myself.

What I know to be true now is this: sexual energy is my birthright. It is life. To be human is to be in pleasure, to create art with words, paint, and photographs; laughter and connection; and a life I can look back on, at my final threshold, and say, "Yes. I'm proud of the life I created—one centered in pleasure, truth, and the courage to enter the dark places I once feared."

Grief, who once felt like an imposter sent to ruin everything, is now the friend who reminds us how to live—with more aliveness, truth, and more me.

Both grief and pleasure work in tandem—expanding and contracting, breathing in and out, mirroring the natural rhythm of the universe. Through them, I still grow my capacity to hold it all: the softening of sadness, the fire of anger, the opening into joy. With time, I now see these heavier emotions not as enemies but as guides. Sadness holds me when I need to rest; anger points the way to what I value.

In the end, grief and pleasure teach me the same lesson: Wholeness lives where we dare to feel.

This is where medicine lives: in allowing the body to become the altar where life and loss meet, in recognizing that our sexual energy, our creative life force, isn't something separate from our grief—it's what helps it move, metabolize, and transform. They are in a divine partnership in service to wholeness.

This practice is for you if you are in a season of grief, heartbreak, or transition. It's not about fixing or escaping. It's an invitation to listen—to let the body show you what it already knows. I invite you to be courageous and allow your body's ancient wisdom to guide you.

The body remembers what the mind forgets.

I used to think healing was about letting go, but now I know it's about compassionately welcoming every experience, thought, feeling, and emotion. In the wholeness of my fully being alive, I am always healed, whole, and never broken.

Energy doesn't disappear; it transforms. What once felt like heartbreak became alchemy—a portal through which grief, love, and pleasure all found their place.

What follows is the practice that has evolved from my experiences with life's challenging seasons—*The Secret Portal.*

The Medicine

THE SECRET PORTAL PRACTICE

If you prefer to be guided by an audio version of this practice, visit

www.curiousjaymelynn.squarespace.com and look under "Resources" for **The Secret Portal** audio link. You'll also find a **felt-sense vocabulary list** to help you describe sensations in the body. If you'd like to be guided by music, a Spotify playlist companion for this practice is also available.

1. Find a private place where you won't be disturbed—maybe your car, bedroom, bathroom, or even somewhere in nature.

2. Get comfortable and begin by noticing your natural breath without judgment.

3. When you're ready, gradually lengthen your inhale and exhale, allowing your exhale to become slightly longer than your inhale.

4. Ask yourself: *What emotion wants to be felt right now?*
   Be patient if there isn't an instant answer, or if there are many.

5. Notice where that emotion lives in your body.
   Begin to describe how it feels (you can use the felt-sense vocabulary list if needed). If accessible, notice how it looks in your mind's eye.

6. If other emotions arise in connection, allow them to.
   Give your body space to feel and express what's coming up fully—this might look like tears, laughter, sound, or movement. Take as much time as you need here and trust your unique process.

7. When you're ready, invite in pleasure and/or joy.

   Option One: Begin moving your body intuitively, without thought—let it dance you.

   Option Two: Engage in self-pleasure in whatever feels nourishing and supportive.

8. Continue breathing through the emotions. Notice the oscillation between the alive emotions and sensations in your body. Trust your body to guide you for as long as it needs to.

9. When you're ready, gently return to stillness and rest.
Optional: Journal your experience or share it with a trusted friend or family member.

Return to this practice whenever you navigate big emotions or wish to transmute memories stored in the body.

When I think back to seasons of grief, I don't remember the pain as much as the space that opened inside me. The voice was right—I could hold more than I ever knew.

Jayme Lynn is a creative wellness facilitator, writer, and designer devoted to helping others discover the truth of who they are through the body, beauty, and presence.

Blending her background in interior design, photography, and creative direction, she approaches life as a living ritual. Each space, image, and word becomes an invitation to remember that beauty is not a luxury—it's a reflection of our aliveness. Her work bridges the seen and unseen, the tangible and the felt, guiding others to inhabit their truth with courage, sensuality, and grace.

As a certified sex, love, and relationship coach and a student of Tantric philosophy and practice, Jayme weaves the wisdom of Eros—the life force that animates all creation—into her work. She invites people to explore how this creative, sexual energy can become a source of healing, inspiration, and deep connection.

Through her offerings, she invites people to explore the places where art meets embodiment: grief softens into tenderness, desire awakens creativity, and authenticity feels safe enough to be seen. Her approach is intuitive and body-centered, blending movement, breath, ritual, and creative expression to help others feel safe in their truth.

At the heart of her work is the belief that truth is beautiful, and that it is possible—and deeply healing—to live from that truth. She holds space for those ready to honor their emotions as sacred messengers and to meet themselves not through fixing or striving, but through deep listening and gentle embodiment.

When she's not guiding others, you can find her writing near a window, tending to her home as a temple, or lost behind the lens, capturing the light that lives in ordinary moments.

CONNECT WITH JAYME:

Website: http://www.curiousjaymelynn.squarespace.com

Social Media: @Curious_Jayme

Podcast: Learned From Love

Email: CuriousJaymeLynn@gmail.com

Chapter 12

You Are the Pathfinder
Recovering Your Joy and Moving Forward

DUSTIN GRAHAM

My Story

"Hey man, you got a lighter I can borrow?" The young man asked as he approached. I pumped gas at a Shell station somewhere in the Navajo Nation in northern Arizona one stormy evening. I was at the part of the lighter cycle every smoker has when they're just lousy with lighters, so I gave him one and said, "Here ya go, brother, you keep this—it's my gift to you."

"You have a cool truck," he said—magic words to me, an instant friend.

"Thanks!" I said, and he asked if I was traveling north. Intuition kicked in—absolutely, *I have to give this brother a ride.*

"I am. Would you like a ride?"

He did. That decision dramatically changed the trajectory of my life.

Days earlier, I was camping in the largest contiguous Ponderosa pine forest in the world. A cool afternoon, with a light breeze rustling through the trees and the sunlight dancing in the droplets hanging on the pine needles from a morning shower. I was just about a year on the other side of the biggest transition I'd ever gone through in life up to that point, completely dismantling it all and leaving everything I knew behind to strike out as a nomad in an effort to feed my soul. The path before me held infinite potential, brimming with excitement. This particular afternoon held an incredibly disruptive life quake.

My phone chirped—the message that was waiting for me collapsed my reality in an instant, a devastating injury to a lifelong wound I still carried. "D, we have to take a separation."

The person I anchored myself to through that previous enormous transition had cast me out of their life with almost no explanation. It was as though the entire world went still—no birds, no breeze, no breath. The beautiful picture I held in my head and in my heart of what my future looked like turned to ash and slipped through my fingers. The path I walked crumbled beneath my feet and washed away. Despite the state I found myself in, I saw the divinity in what took place. I saw exactly how this served my highest good, but that didn't mean I had to like it.

Being a truck-based wilderness nomad at the time, working a remote job from the most beautiful natural splendors the American West had to offer, I packed up camp at the end of the week and hit the road for Colorado. While I was well aware that what I was actually doing was fleeing the loss—running from the feelings—I was also diving headlong into adventure. Adventure was always where my purest joy resided—the kind of joy that was mine, the kind of joy that required nothing of anyone else—so I set out to immerse myself in it.

As I passed through the Navajo Nation in northern Arizona and stopped for fuel, I picked up a hitchhiker. It was at that moment I stepped onto the path of my soul mission. This young man was headed to Idaho. We spent three wonderful days together on the road, beginning with seeing an owl as we drove deep into the reservation to his mother's home for him to gather some last-minute things for his journey. The owl was an omen we both saw very differently—for me, it was light and hope; for him, it was darkness and despair. Our individual perceptions of this seemed to hold true for both of us.

That first night, as we parted ways in Blanding, Utah, he asked me where I was going the next day.

"I plan to sleep tomorrow in Grand Junction, Colorado."

"My sister lives near Grand Junction and might give me a ride the rest of the way to Idaho. Can I come with you?"

Excited at the idea of spending more road time with his company, I said, "You sure can, *but* I'm doing a big off-road adventure tomorrow, and I don't know how long it will take or what it will entail. You in for that?"

He thought it sounded fun and was in.

Jerrold ended up being my copilot for the first bucket-list item I ever accomplished. We drove the Top of the World Trail in Moab, Utah—a harrowing adventure for my mildly modified truck. It was technical and brutal, and it took us most of the day. My truck was my home at the time, and doing this trail carried immense risk. This trail was so far beyond anything I had driven before; if Jerrold had not been with me, I would've quit by the second major obstacle.

I spent seven hours white-knuckling with my nervous system drenched in adrenaline. By the time we got to the top, I was wrung out. The whole point of this adventure was to take the iconic picture of my truck perched on what is essentially a stone diving board sticking out of the top of a 2,500-foot cliff, as so many others have done. Mission accomplished.

As I backed my truck off this very steep ledge, loaded down with enough gear to live year-round full-time, I tested my brakes, and the combination of gravity, cargo, and a strong reverse gear left me unable to bring the truck to a complete stop. While I wasn't careening and could stop once the terrain leveled out, this sent me into a quiet panic. Suddenly, every obstacle I climbed up with tires squealing and frame dragging flashed through my mind—*I have to go back down all that, and gravity might not be my friend after all.*

Jerrold and I previously planned to have a ceremony at the top—a blending of his Indigenous spirituality with whatever you'd call my spirituality. I forgot about this plan. I parked in a flat spot at the top, near the trees and far from the edge of this mountain peak we were on, to let my nerves settle while we prepared lunch. As he and I were deeply in tune with each other at that point, Jerrold picked up on my vibe.

"Dude, you okay?"

"Yes," I said.

He paused for a beat and raised an eyebrow. "Are you sure?" he asked.

I replied, "Well, I mean, no, I'm not—but I will be."

He then reminded me about the ceremony and suggested we hold off on lunch until after, and I wholeheartedly agreed. It was blisteringly hot and arid, the breeze drying our sweat as fast as we produced it. Together we smudged, blessed each other, the land, and the people close to us, and then we separated to each finish in our own personal way.

Never being one to actually pray, I prayed that day. "Let Jerrold, me, and my truck get off that mountain safe, sound, and unscathed."

Not five minutes after jumping back in the air-conditioned truck to eat lunch, another truck came up the trail—the first one we had seen—a prayer answered in real time. Relief flooded me—"Hello, new friends!" I relaxed in an instant. Having another experienced driver in their own rig to drive down with as a team was the best thing I could've hoped for.

This trek was symbolic in many ways—overcoming obstacles, adapting to challenges, and fostering a sacred brotherhood.

Jerrold and I parted ways in Grand Junction, Colorado. It was a heartfelt goodbye, a deep hug, a few tears, and beautiful words. There aren't many things that highlight the depth and quality of a connection quite like a farewell.

Next, in the Arapaho National Forest in the high Rockies, at a spot I discovered years back and always wanted to camp in, I arrived at this majestic place, 10,400 feet in elevation. I was greeted with hummingbirds, rainbows, and wildflowers. The air, while crisp and thin, was thick with the smell of pine, rain, earth, and wildflowers. Warm sun competed with the cold breeze on my skin—I found paradise in the clouds. Still, the loss in my heart tugged at me.

I realized then that I shed all of my practices. I built the foundation of my spiritual path around the light of the person who discarded me. With that foundation gone, I had to rebuild it for myself and of myself, around my own light. In retrospect, that's how I should've created it in the first place—but this is how we learn.

From Colorado, I continued bombing around the western half of the continent, fleeing what I couldn't yet bring myself to face—the work of transmuting this loss and stepping into the growth that would follow. Utah, Idaho, Montana, Wyoming, Washington—endless road, both paved and unpaved, stretched before me in whatever direction I chose to go, welcoming me, beckoning me. I met amazing people, I had magical experiences, but still, the loss was there—ever-present in the background, fading but steadfast.

Originally, I planned to head into Canada, but the logistics were daunting and stressful. In Montana, I realized: *If I'm supposed to go to Canada,* it would be easier. Immediately followed by: *I have to go to Rainier*—another place I always wanted to go. That decision to shift my trajectory was a tipping point I felt in my internal world, but didn't understand yet.

Following my internal joy compass, I found myself camped on the side of Mount Rainier three weeks later. There's a pattern I've noticed in my travels—when I'm in places of internal transition, I usually discover near my campsites a memorial built to someone who passed on, deep in the wilderness, in the middle of nowhere. It's a sign that I've left an old version of myself behind—this spot was no different.

I stumbled across fresh bear scat about thirty yards from where I set up camp, which resulted in more chores than usual before bed each night. About midweek, another flash of intuition came—*Dustin, you have observed yourself in this loss long enough; you're on the edge of being stuck in it; you have all the tools in the world to transmute this tragedy into magic*—pick *a thing and do it.*

So I lit a candle in my tent, gazed into it for a moment, listening to the orchestra of wildlife in the stillness of the evening, feeling the moist cool air on my skin and the warmth of the candle on my face. I then entered a brief meditation followed by short breathwork. Before, I was worried that my connection to Spirit would be gone, but it had merely atrophied, as anything does when left unused. Afterwards, I felt amazing—I felt alive in a way that I didn't know I had lost.

Later—"Yikes, I almost forgot to do my bear chores for the evening!" I left the tent. It was full nighttime in the Pacific Northwest during the season when the sky is eternally overcast. Jumping down the ladder from my rooftop tent, I felt something was different. I looked up and saw not only that the sky was clear, but that the aurora was out. I nearly fell to my knees, staggered by its beauty. This was my second bucket-list item checked off—this time entirely unintentional—a pat on the back from reality itself as a reward for stepping back onto my path of growth and healing.

From that moment on, everything was an upward swing—a beautiful symphony of orchestrated synchronicity. I picked my way back south, ultimately aiming for Sedona again. I missed it and was ready to shift the balance in my life toward more solitude and adventure, with a stronger community and home base.

I followed the same internal joy compass—*I have to go to Mount Shasta now.* Never questioning where I was being guided, I hit the road again, and there on Shasta, somehow, I had a hit of higher knowledge of exactly where my next place would be. Within two days of that intuitive spark, I received a message from someone offering me a beautiful place to call home in Sedona—exactly the place I saw in my vision and in precisely the manner I expected to receive it. Naturally, the timing of my move-in would be perfect, as all such synchronicity tends to be. I set an intention: *This time around, I'm going to immerse myself in the community of Sedona—become part of it.*

Over the next few weeks, I adventured the rest of my way to Southern California to visit a friend in Camarillo. On the way there, while struggling to find a spot to camp for the weekend near Sequoia National Park so I could check off the last item on my bucket list, a friend I had made seven months earlier in Arizona messaged me: "Hey dude, we got some land in California. If you're ever passing through, stop by!"

I was entirely unsurprised to find out that not only was it on my route to Sequoia National Forest, but it was within an hour's drive of it. Thus, my original bucket list was complete in the span of about ten weeks.

Exceptionally road-worn at this point, I booked a hotel room in the valley for a week to nurture and recharge. Throughout that week, I watched out my window as an actual circus was constructed in the lot adjacent to the hotel, and that Friday, I went and had so much fun. Much of it was in Spanish and geared almost entirely toward selling trinkets to small children, but instead of dampening my joy, it elevated it.

Choice after choice, place after place, magic and synchronicity compounded. I was on a ride that I never wanted to end, and so far, it hasn't.

Eventually returning to Sedona, I joined a men's full moon hike up one of the major energy vortexes of this incredible place. This hike was the original excuse for my return to Sedona. It was wonderful—I connected with these men in a way similar to Jerrold, and it opened something in me. These new brothers told me about something called the Red Rock Brotherhood. Through it, I discovered a weekly men's group that gathered every Friday.

After signing up for the weekly men's group, the founder of the nonprofit overseeing the group asked, "We don't have a facilitator for the group anymore. Would you be interested?"

How about that, I AM interested! Who even am I anymore? And so began the path I'm currently on.

It took my group a while to gain traction. For about two months, I went on hikes by myself because no one showed up. Of course, that's fine—I go hiking by myself all the time and thoroughly enjoy it. I wasn't disappointed by the lack of turnout. I suspect that's because I didn't have much ego invested in this endeavor. However, in the springtime, men showed up.

I now also participate in and occasionally lead a virtual men's group with brothers across the country and beyond. As a result, men have reached out to me to request regularly scheduled support calls, which I've agreed to. In that, I discovered a passion—supporting men struggling on the path and helping them return to joy. I found myself in a sea of sacred brotherhood. It's something I struggle to describe, but it's incredibly fulfilling—perhaps more fulfilling than anything else I've ever done. I treasure these connections we forged.

Following my joy compass led me into so much magic, with new, amazing, unexpected things coming to me from every direction. I still feel that words are inadequate to express how profound all of this has been for me, but through this pursuit of joy, I found my mission, tribe, and passion. I'm awash in a sea of gratitude and love every day. You can be too—for you are The Pathfinder.

The Medicine

The path lies in the journey of answering one question: "What brings you joy that requires nothing of anyone else?"

Answering this question takes radical self-honesty. Where is your joy? Not what gives you relief. Not escape. Not numbing. Joy.

Joy that requires nothing of anyone—not their permission, presence, or blessing.

Your body will help you find the answers. If you feel excitement when you think about doing something, that's probably joy. If you feel relief, it's escape or numbing. If you feel fear, look underneath it—often there's excitement hiding there, waiting to be reclaimed.

It's not the easiest question to answer, but it might be one of the most important. Because once you know the things that bring you joy independent of anyone else, you begin to remember who you were before the world told you who to be.

So here's the practice:

- Pause. Get quiet for two minutes—no phone, no music, no distractions.

- Ask yourself out loud: "What would bring me joy in this moment that requires nothing of anyone else?"

- Listen to your body's first response. Don't think. Feel.

- Write down three things that arise—they can be as small as sunlight on your skin or a song that moves through you.

- Do one of them today. Even for sixty seconds.

That's it. That's the path. Every time you return to that question and act on it, you take one more step back home to yourself. The journey of finding that answer is filled with magic at every turn.

So—what's your joy?

Dustin Graham is a men's coach, group facilitator, and founder of Pathfinder Support for Men, a practice dedicated to helping men see clearly and move forward with purpose. Through his work, Dustin creates spaces of honesty, reflection, and grounded growth—guiding men toward mental clarity, emotional awareness, physical grounding, and spiritual alignment.

A Reflector in Human Design, Dustin's strength lies in his ability to mirror truth back to others. His coaching style is rooted in deep listening, presence, and the belief that clarity emerges when we slow down enough to truly see ourselves.

After life-altering experiences that stripped away everything familiar, Dustin rebuilt from the inside out. Living nomadically across the American West, he learned the language of solitude, resilience, and trust in his own intuition. That journey became the foundation for Pathfinder Support for Men and his commitment to guiding others through their own initiations of change.

Now based in Sedona, Arizona, Dustin leads The Sedona Men's Group and continues to explore the intersections of intuition, healing, and purpose. His writing and coaching invite men to walk the path of authentic self-discovery—one rooted not in fixing what's broken, but in remembering what's always been whole.

CONNECT WITH DUSTIN:

Facebook: https://www.Facebook.com/PathfinderSupportForMen

Email: DLux.Outdoors@gmail.com

Instagram: https://www.instagram@DLux.Outdoors

YouTube: https://YouTube.com/@D-LuxOutdoors

Chapter 13

A Desire for Alchemy
Ignite and Embody Your Most Authentic Self

MORGAN COSTLEY, MSOM, LAC, LMT

Once I finally sat down to write this chapter, there was so much more to write and so much less to forgive.

I sat. I let it breathe in me—this moment, the past moments—all of it was necessary to be here right now on this beautiful day. Let's play.

My Story

The assembly was gathered. The buzz and hustle of the elementary school crowd was unsettled. I looked out at a sea of tiny heads giggling and humming, all sitting cross-legged in the auditorium. Principal Mathers was giving a speech on school education in a brown bear costume. I looked down at my legs sitting cross-legged in my red and green polka-dot tights. The bottoms of my feet were stained with dust. I pinched myself. I could not feel my legs. They were like glass. My 7-year-old brain tried to reason with myself.

I was going to be in the way once everyone got up. I was always in the way.

She concluded her speech and invited everyone to return to class. I used all my tiny strength to push myself up with the weight of my arms. My legs sank like quicksand into the linoleum floor. I toppled directly on top of Jeremy Meyers, next to me. I was horrified. My face went hot. I heard giggles. I fumbled, apologized, shifted back down to the ground, and waited. People tripped over me. I waited until everyone was out of the assembly before rolling over like a dead fish. I began to hit my legs with my fists with all my force.

I was going to be late.

It was a good 10 minutes before I felt the familiar sharp knives, then pins and needles. I gritted my teeth and kept going.

Why was I the only one this happened to?

I felt different. I always felt different.

I was a quiet little girl with a lot of inner gumption and minimal outer expression. I tiptoed around people, struggling to feel at home in my own body. I had something called a Tethered Spinal Cord. It bound me up, tugging at me from the inside, tightening my core from my head to my lower back, often leaving my legs numb. Inhabiting a body far too small for the whole of me diminished my presence in the world.

It felt like a relentless tug-of-war inside my body, my head, and my lower half pulled apart as if neither was allowed to truly belong to the other. I lacked the legs to stand on to create, or the head to articulate in the world.

As I grew up, I experienced growth spurts, I became increasingly less present in my body, and over time, other forces took over—Lyme, parasites, viral load, bacteria, and other people's pain. My blood-brain barrier and the dura around my head were fragile and permeable, so everything coming at me was heightened—weather, allergens, and mold. The constriction in my spinal cord dissolved my boundaries, and this reflected spiritually and energetically. My body mirrored my spirit, extremely permeable, absorbing, and feeling everything. I held space for everything but myself. I was tethered to cycles of pain.

I became very frail in my early thirties. My health declined rapidly, my vitality dimming a little more each day. Over several years, night sweats ravaged my sleep. Weight slipped away. I felt myself dissolving from my own life. Little did I know that my body's unraveling also served as a sacred invitation, a catalyst for a profound spiritual awakening.

I began to explore different spiritual practices and circles, seeking to understand, to heal, and to reclaim a sense of wholeness. It was exhilarating to explore the unseen realms and develop new abilities, yet the deeper I went, the further I drifted from my own body and healing. Eventually, I felt as though I'd become a single grain of sand – light, scattered, and barely anchored to the earth. Existing in the world grew harder with each passing day.

In searching for a way back into my body, I began to study everything that lived between the visible and the invisible – the matter and mystery of what makes and unmakes us. I became fluent in the language of illness and energy, tracing patterns from the micro to macro level. I studied mold, Lyme, bacteria, parasites, and the medicines that help reclaim the body from them. I learned the soul's anatomy, Chinese medicine, ancestral and herbal traditions, and the resonant power of sound. I built strong relationships with guides, practiced as a medium and healer, and held sacred space for others. My intuition sharpened, and I became the space where others came to find wholeness, even as I drifted from my own. As I guided others through their healing with care and devotion, I struggled to offer myself the same grace. I found myself asking why healing could touch others so deeply while eluding me. My patients grew stronger while I quietly faded, still searching for the piece of healing I could not yet embody.

I was sitting on the porch, watching rain trace the outline of the mountains. My body ached, but something inside me whispered, *This is the beginning.*

Embodiment was my greatest challenge—and ultimately my greatest passion. I realized the work I had done for years needed to come home to my cells. I had to alchemize my soul with my body. The spiritual work I had done for years had to take root, weaving through every fiber of my being. Fully integrated, I had to choose life.

The official diagnosis of a tethered spinal cord did not come until my thirties. I happened upon a practitioner who understood what I could barely articulate—who'd become an expert in this syndrome that was taking so much from me. From our first session, my body felt profoundly witnessed – so much so that I went home and wept for hours. I'd never felt so seen, and in that seeing, a part of me that had been lost quietly began to return. When she placed her hand over my spine, warmth spread upward. I wanted to pull away and hide, but tears spilled instead. "You actually see me," I whispered, and for the first time, I believed it.

With each session, she gently began to unwind my tethering. The release was never permanent, but it lasted a little longer each time. My body began to fill out and hum with new life. I felt lighter, yet somehow fuller – more me. I believe all the work I did healing parts of my soul prepared me for this, allowing me to receive embodiment as something sacred. It was beyond enlivening. The density of pain began to lift, and over time, I learned how to release it myself.

Through this process, I finally understood why it had once been so easy to check out of life. Returning to my body was not merely healing – it was reclamation. The duality was rich. My body had become a mirror for the tension between the soul and the body.

What if the soul and the body could lighten the burden of living through cohesion?

What if the soul and the body could dance?

That longing to merge the soul and body became the turning point. It was then that I began to understand what true alchemy meant—not as an idea, but as a living practice.

ARE YOU DANCING? ARE YOU SINGING?

These were the first questions asked by the ancient Earth-based medicines. Before anything else, they wanted to know whether life itself was moving through my form. I began learning what it meant to alchemize my soul-body with my living body by inviting movement, voice, and expression back into the places where silence and stillness had taken hold.

These questions became more than metaphors—they became daily invitations. I realized that healing wasn't something to think about; it was something to move, breathe, and create with. From there, my healing journey became a practice. It wasn't enough to understand alchemy—I had to live it in my body.

DUALITY

To find true wholeness, we must allow our external and internal selves to coexist, to find new ground in a more authentic way of living. No part of you is wrong. Healing asks us to integrate and assimilate these hidden parts rather than deny them—especially the ones we avoid or judge as unworthy. It is the merging of opposites—soul and body, light and density—that marks the beginning of true alchemy. Where these two meet, something new is born. This is where energy transforms, flushing the system with vitality and softening what has long felt rigid or painful. Through witnessing rather than resisting, we return to resonance, to presence, to self.

AMPLIFY LIFE, NOT THE PATHOLOGY

In my practice, I began to amplify life rather than pathology. My gaze shifted. It moved beyond symptoms, pain, and stories, and towards the true and eternal essence within a person. I began to see my patients not as fractured beings, but as whole souls temporarily entangled in life's shadows. When I looked deeper, I could see a person's original makeup— the brilliance of who they truly were—the radiance and fullness of their soul, and the self that had never been harmed. And as I witnessed their wholeness, they began to remember it too.

The healing deepened—not because I absorbed their pain, but because I learned to witness without sacrificing myself. I didn't have to run their pain through my body to help them heal. I could remain in my wholeness and simply see them, and that seeing became medicine. I gifted them with the sacred process of self-witnessing—a remembering of the truth that had always been theirs. The alchemy began here for them: their current version met their most eternal, centered self—the one who is always whole, healed, and free. And through that transformational witnessing, I began to witness myself, too.

The Medicine

Find a space that feels safe and sacred. Clear it, cleanse it, and allow it to hold the container of your practice.

WITNESS THE SOUL

First, remember that your eternal soul—the part closest to Source—is always whole and always free. It is the pure essence of you. It is a place within you that has never been broken and never forgotten. It is always loving.

We begin by sensing where the sovereignty of our existence lives; where the core frequency of who we are originates, our first unfolding from Source. This is where the possibility for alchemy and transformation resides.

Let go of any worries or judgements about how it shows up for you.

Shift your gaze to be *the witness* of self. Let it reveal itself to you. What does it feel like? Taste like? Sound like? Connect to your senses and let it be exactly what it shows up as today.

Notice the parts of you that show up to resist or tell a different story.

Let them also give you information.

And remember, this is a practice.
It unfolds over time.
There is no rush or perfect picture.

THE ALIVE—BODY

Next, we're connecting to the *alive* body. This is the physical body that is earthly; that walks, breathes, and feels through the world. For some, connecting to the body can be uncomfortable or unfamiliar. Be gentle with yourself here. Let what arises be enough for that moment. There is no need to push; only to notice.

What does your *alive* body feel like?
What is your body trying to tell you?
Is it sharing information, a story, or a memory?

What does your body want?

ALCHEMIZE

Now, invite the part of you that is calling the loudest. A story or experience—the one that does not want you to fully arrive, that inhibits you from the whole experience of being here.

Ask it what it needs.

Then, gently remind this part that your soul is here too.

Let your eternal self witness it – not to fix it and not to silence it, but simply to see it.

What does your soul's presence want to let it know? Write it out or draw it out. Let it be expressed in words – stream of consciousness or through an art form.

Let yourself be surprised by what comes through.

THE DANCE—BRING IT BACK TO THE BODY

As emotions surface, remember: movement transforms stagnation. Let your body tell its side of the story.

Be as gentle with your body as it asks you to be.

Listen closely.

If all it wants in this moment is breath, let breath be enough.

If your body wants to dance, find a space where it can move freely and give it room to dance.

MUSIC IS KEY

Let rhythm be your medicine; let it lead the way.
Drumming can also help awaken what is held.

Feel the emotion as you dance with it. Notice your sacred—dancing alongside you, holding space for what rises.

What does this part want you to hear?
Let your body move to the truth of the emotion that appears.
Where it lives in the body, breathe into it.
Let any sounds come through, a sigh, a shake, a roar, a cry.
Let movement loosen what has been held within.
Stomp. Pound the ground beneath you.

Connect with the part that hurts—let it move you.
Connect with your soul, let it help you.

Take a moment in between.
Drink water.
Assimilate what has shifted.

Alchemy lives in the cycle—between movement and expression, between body and soul.

Writing and creating are part of the expression. Dancing and singing alchemize what you are ready to witness and shift, changing your physical cells with its expression.

SINGING AND TONING

Make tones and sounds. You don't have to be in a perfect tone. It isn't about sounding any one way. To ease into it, you can gently hum. A gentle breath, shaped into an ahh or an ohm tone, can help connect the heart and the root. Let whatever wants to come out, come out.

It can be large or small, raw or tender. This practice isn't about performance. It's about listening to your body and allowing sound to rise from feeling.

Notice what tone the hurt part wants to express. Does it want to moan, groan, or roar? Maybe it wants to scream and yell. Let the sound move through you. Let it reclaim the spaces that once held silence or pain.

If a song drifts into your awareness, follow it—let it guide you.

Turn it on, and sing along.

Each sound, each tone may call for something different depending on the part of you that is being met. Listen closely with your body and what it longs to express.

Connect with your eternal Self and let it witness you in this process. Does it want to make a sound, a tone, a vibration? Let it. This is not about sounding perfect. It is about allowing what is real to move through you.

After releasing through sound and movement, come back to stillness. Integration is where the medicine takes root.

AFTER THE PRACTICE—SIMPLE MEDICINES TO HELP YOU ASSIMILATE

Micro shifts are enough. You may return to the same place a few times.

Alchemize only what you are ready to shift.

Try to love yourself through every stage. It is not about a result or a perfect outcome.

Remember, there is always full permission to make a mess if that is what wants to come out.

SUPPORTING THE BODY'S RELEASE

Every ceremony needs its integration. The following simple medicines help you root the transformation into daily life.

When the expression feels complete, let your cells know:

This is the new me.

Drink water with a pinch of sea salt. Chew on a lemon wedge or add it to your water.

Allow yourself to cleanse and replenish what has moved.

- *Lymph Tone II* by Energetix—this helps to unwind and heal ancestral line patterns in the lymph.

- Cordyceps—To support vitality and remind you of your power.

- Dandelion tea—to nourish the kidneys as they filter emotional and energetic release.

To ground the change into your root and heart chakras, your foundation:

- Beet juice or beet powder in water

- A heart-opening tea. I personally prefer Czystek tea, which helps the heart open to what is new and welcome it

Essence Alchemy has a trauma kit (the Mt. Shasta Kit) that can help with the assimilation of trauma and old patterns.

Honor the guidance of your body and your trusted practitioners as you choose what remedies are right to incorporate for you.

MAKE SURE YOU HAVE A SUPPORT SYSTEM

You do not have to do this alone. Some journeys are meant to be witnessed in a space held with care by a trusted practitioner. Some life experiences can feel too overwhelming to meet alone.

You may begin the process with a practitioner or therapist who can support you.

Keep support close by.
You never have to begin with the hardest thing.
Start small. Trust your pacing.
Begin where there is room to breathe.

I celebrate you.

Morgan Costley is a Chinese medicine practitioner based in Portland, Oregon. She has multidimensional healing practices that merge herbal medicine, homeopathy, NAET, and frequency medicine with Earth-based practices. She works to get to the root of physical and emotional ailments and bring back a sense of wholeness.

CONNECT WITH MORGAN:

For a more in-depth continuation of the medicine, with artistic writing and a creative process to alchemize the soul and an 'alive body,' I invite you to continue to the PDF on my website.

Website: https://www.wildriverhealingarts.com

Facebook: Wild River Healing Arts-Morgan Costley

Dance/Movement Playlists on Spotify: Morgan Costley

Chapter 14

There's a Prophecy for You—This is How to Meet It
Recognizing the Glimpse of Your Soul's Calling

CAROLINE ARCO, A GUIDE FOR MODERN LIGHTWORKERS

My Story

If you could go back, would you erase your awareness of the spiritual world?

Would you return to the safety of not knowing, to a life unshaken by mystery?

Before you glimpsed the unseen, before you felt that unmistakable shift that changes everything—the one that rearranges your senses, questions your sanity, and pulls you into a path you can never un-walk?

Sometimes I wonder: *Would I trade the weight of awakening for the comfort of not?*

I know I didn't choose to believe in the spiritual world.

But as you'll read in this chapter, belief had nothing to do with it. Magic found me early—sudden, undeniable, and far too grand to dismiss. It cracked my world open, and there was no turning away from what I saw.

Still, I sometimes catch myself wondering what it would be like to live as most people do—the ones whose lives seem so normal.

No endless sense of mystery pressing against the edges of reality. . .

No awareness of energy moving through every moment. . .

No communion with unseen realms and beings—that strange, shimmering world that is as intoxicating as it is disorienting.

How peaceful it must be to just be *normal,* to pour cereal each morning, complain about work, gossip about the neighbor, and fall asleep unburdened by the knowledge that everything—*everything*—is so alive.

My mother was one of those people, beautifully grounded in the ordinary.

She worked as a university professor, a position she held with deep pride. For a woman in rural Brazil in the late eighties, that was no small feat.

Her life was everything it was meant to be: stable, respectable, predictable. Except for one thing—me.

Her only child, gifted in many things, but not in the one she prized most: traditional education.

I resisted school with every cell in my body. The idea of being told what to do and then having my worth graded by how well I conformed made my whole body rebel.

When I was fifteen, we were asked to fill out a form at school, declaring what we wanted to study in college. I remember staring at that blank page, twirling a strand of hair around my finger, chewing gum that had long lost its flavor as if waiting for someone to give me an answer.

I thought, and thought, and thought.

And I wrote. . .

. . . nothing.

My teacher must have noticed—and, in her own way, appreciated both my struggle and my honesty. After class, she called me aside and offered something that would quietly alter the course of my life.

"We fund a small school in the slums," she told me. "They need a theater teacher. I'll warn you—it won't be easy. Those kids have lived things you can't imagine. Don't wear anything fancy. Just go as yourself. If you can stay the course, I think you'll be brilliant."

So I found myself, two weeks later, wearing an orange pair of All Stars that had been sitting in my closet since eighth grade, standing in the middle of a rickety wooden room, waiting to meet the kids I'd spend the next year with.

The air smelled of dust and chalk. The wooden walls were chipped and uneven, their paint long surrendered to time. Everything about that room felt far from the world I knew—yet I could sense I was exactly where I needed to be.

As the children began to arrive, I felt an instinctive pull to step back. Their energy was dense, defiant, and achingly real. I knew I wasn't meant to command the space, but to witness it.

These children were not like me. They knew hurt. Their eyes carried stories far too heavy for their years. Stories of hunger, of violence, of a life that had demanded resilience long before joy. They weren't free; they were surviving.

And the mark they carried changed me instantly. It made me more present, more real—like I had finally found something that mattered. Something that deserved to be seen.

In that moment, I understood privilege for the first time.

I felt the wall between us—made of nothing but luck and circumstance. A wall that shouldn't be there. That was stealing lives that still had so much to live.

And I felt angry. The rage of injustice roared through me like thunder waiting to break. I didn't know what I could do, but I knew I had to do something. I was going to do something.

The first few weeks were hard. Building trust when trust itself had always been dangerous was no small task. But little by little, that wooden room began to turn into a portal of change.

We started working on a story, and every kid was eager to take the lead. We wrote it together, and the children chose the theme: **Planet Earth as a mother, asking her children for help.**

During rehearsals, ideas ran wild.

"I'll be a tree," one shouted. "I'll grow so tall I'll touch the sun and stop global warming!"

"I'll be a river," another said. "I'll flow so fast I'll bring life to every dry land!"

In that wooden room, everything felt possible. The walls that once held their pain now echoed with laughter, ideas, and imagination.

And over that year, from chaos and cardboard, a play was born.

On opening night, every seat in the theater was filled. Families in pressed shirts and polished shoes sat beside mothers in worn sandals and work uniforms. The air felt different—this wasn't a night for us. It was a night for them. For the children to finally be seen.

From backstage, I watched them step into the spotlight. I'd heard their lines a hundred times, but that night, it sounded new. Their bodies glowed with pride.

After each act, they'd rush toward me, beaming:

"Did you see that?" they shouted. "I was so good at it!"

Watching them, I knew it. Those weren't the same kids I first met in that wooden room. That night, they were no longer their stories, trauma, or pain. They were—finally, and maybe for the first time—free.

And I found the answer I was meant to write on that empty form all along.

This. This is what I want to do for a living.

I want to help people experience moments of change—moments that set them free.

And that's how, at the ripe old age of sixteen, certain I had life all figured out, I made a plan: move to the big city, become an actress and a teacher, and help people feel the power of transformation through art.

My parents didn't believe me at first. They thought it was "just a phase." But when I graduated high school and started planning my move to São Paulo, reality came crashing down.

"You're not going," they said. "This plan is madness. We're cutting all funds until you figure out what to do with your life. Go to your room and don't come out until you have an answer."

So I did.

I spent a week locked inside that pink room, surrounded by things that no longer felt like mine, meeting grief face to face, whispering questions to a presence that never seemed to answer.

Please. . .show me what to do.

If I'm wrong, take the desire away. If I'm right, give me a sign.

I didn't know what hopelessness felt like until then. It came suddenly. One moment, I had a plan—a pull—something that finally felt worthy of pursuit. And the next, nothing.

That was my first experience of the dark void. That place of no answers. The one that exists to open our world to the possibility of *more*, but first, inevitably brings us into the reality of *less*.

My dark void, at eighteen, was vast.

I couldn't eat. So I fasted, drank water, and wondered if there would ever be a life worth going back out to.

On the seventh night, a storm brewed outside my bedroom window. I watched as the grey clouds advanced like an army—powerful and unrelenting, announcing their arrival, ready for battle. The wind grew fierce, making the branches of the tree knock against the glass in a steady rhythm that called me closer.

I was being summoned by that storm, her anger thrumming through me as my own. She arrived like a wise sister—fierce and tender all at once—reaching through the wind to remind me: *don't you dare give up on what you came here for.*

I opened the window and let the wind tangle my hair. The thunder and my breath became one relentless voice. I wasn't alone anymore. There was power here, and it wasn't just my own.

As the rain struck my face with its sharp drops, I let out a scream.

Show me the way, it said.

That night, I fell asleep in peace - for the first time.

* * *

The next morning, I woke to the sound of a ringing bell.

I jumped out of bed, still floating between worlds. The number on the screen began with "11."

That was the area code for São Paulo—the place I longed to be more than anywhere.

Who could it possibly be?

Why are they calling me now?

I picked up the phone, still returning to my body.

"Hello, Caroline?" I heard a male voice on the other end. "It's me, Raony. I don't know why, but my dad asked me to call you. Are you okay? Do you need anything?"

I was stunned. Raony was the only person I knew who lived in São Paulo. We met briefly a year before and hadn't spoken since. And he was calling me. Now?

I told him what I was going through.

I really need to go. I know I need to be there, but I don't have money or a place to stay.

"If you can make your way here, you can stay at my place," he said. "My mum will take care of you like family. I promise."

That was the thread of hope I needed.

Still in my pajamas, I called my best friend and my old nanny. I explained everything—how badly I needed to leave. They both agreed: I should go. I packed my bag in disbelief.

This is so fast. So scary. Is this how God is speaking to me?

I left home that afternoon and headed to the bus stop. Arriving there, I found my best friend waiting. She gave me some cash—enough for a bus ticket and a meal when I arrived—along with a letter.

In it, she wrote:

"I know how hard this has been for you. And I just want to say: I believe it. I don't even know what—but I believe it. I know you'll do well because your heart is in the right place. And when you feel like you can't do it on your own, take this piece of my heart with you. You are never alone."

I made the eighteen-hour bus journey through heavy tears. I couldn't understand the strength that carried me. I had no idea what was to come—but I knew: *This is my path.*

When I arrived in São Paulo the next morning, I made my way to Raony's home. His mother welcomed me with a set table of fresh milk and bread. She was a gentle woman who asked me questions but never pushed for answers. I was quiet most of the time, carrying the shame of being there under such circumstances.

I entered the room she prepared for me—a big space with a soft bed and a palpable sense of care. And I felt, for the first time since I left, that maybe I'd be okay.

The very next day, I got a job at an events agency. São Paulo was kind to me those first weeks. Opportunities came easily, money flowed, and I never went without.

But inside me, the ache grew stronger. I left my hometown and everything I knew behind. I was estranged from my parents, who, though they lacked the skills to handle it, I knew loved me deeply.

One evening, I sat in that bedroom, feeling the weight of it all. Tears flowed endlessly—of overwhelm, confusion, and more than anything, love.

Then the door opened, and Raony's parents walked in. His father, an older man with a quiet, mysterious presence, looked at me. It was the first time I saw him since arriving.

"Sit down," he said. "I need to tell you something."

"When my son first met you, my soul recognized yours. We were partners in a past life, and share a strong soul connection. I knew you needed my help, and that's why I asked him to call you."

His words pierced through me with an energy that words cannot describe—it was the first time I felt it. The force of the Divine entered, shaking reality as I knew it, and leaving me with that ruthless sense of the Holy mystery that is impossible to ignore.

I looked into his eyes, and I *saw* it. This was the man I used to have visions about. The scene was always the same: coming out of a caravan in the dark, starless sky, sitting across a fire, sharing a tea; a recurring dream I've had for as long as I can remember.

I couldn't question him. There was no room to. This was magic making its presence known. This was the sacred current. It waited for the moment I had no choice but to see it.

That day, he gave me a prophecy:

"You are to become a healer. You are here to help people remember the Divine. On this journey, you will discover many gifts that won't make sense to most, but you must use them. There are beings from other planets coming, and they will help you find your way. When they come, you just have to answer."

I'm writing this story eighteen years after that day.

For the past eight years, I've served people full-time as a healer and mentor, helping them find their purpose and open their lives to magic. What I do today is exactly what that man told me all those years ago.

I'm still following the pull of inspiration I first felt while watching those children on that stage:

I help people experience moments of change—the kind you never return from.

My work is my greatest honor. And it's more than that.

It's the answer to a calling—a living prophecy accepted by my soul long before I ever knew what a soul truly was.

I hope this story anchors the truth that you are meant to believe in magic—to feel the force of the Divine running through you, and as you.

Even when the path feels hard, confusing, like an endless void of questions without answers:

The Divine is working perfectly through you.

Keep listening.

There's a prophecy for you.

Answer it.

The Medicine

There is a prophecy for you, and it has always been waiting to be answered.

This prophecy lives in the space between words—in the quiet knowing you've carried since childhood, in the invisible presence that grounds in the moments when it matters most.

Your intuition is the bridge to these seeds of knowing. Contrary to popular belief, intuition isn't abstract or mystical—it's *precise, reliable,* and *measurable.*

It's a tool of guidance, and some would say, the very **operating system humans were designed to live by** to thrive, evolve, and participate intelligently in creation. When you choose to live by intuition, you answer not only the prayer of your soul but the collective call of humanity's evolution.

As we enter this medicine space, I invite you to activate both your **logical mind** and your **imagination.**

Imagination is the home of intuition. A real sixth sense, a channel that translates the language of your soul into the physical world. When you pair imagination with a strong, love-based intention, it becomes the most direct way to receive guidance from your deeper self.

PART ONE—THE JOURNEY WITHIN

Begin by visiting the link below and experiencing the **"Journey to Your Sacred Inner Garden"** meditation.

https://www.arcoteachings.com/ascension-series

This garden is a threshold—the meeting point between your conscious mind and the realm where your soul lives.

When you enter that space, bring with you this question:

"What is the truth I am here to uncover?"

Hold it gently, with curiosity. Trust what you receive, even if it feels abstract—the soul often speaks in metaphors.

When you return, take a few moments to journal your experience.

PART TWO—THE INTEGRATION

To anchor what you received, enter a soft, receptive state once more. Slow your breath, feel your body, and journal through these prompts:

- What are the truths I've always known, even when I couldn't explain them?

- What gifts have always come naturally to me?

- Which qualities or ways of being do I love most about myself?

- What impact do I have on others—how does my energy move people, change the atmosphere, or make them feel, often in ways I don't even notice?

- If I could create one change in the world, what would it be—and why does that matter to me?

Your prophecy is not a single answer; it's a thread woven through many expressions of your life.

Return to your imagination often. Let it become a daily practice—a familiar landscape where you meet yourself with presence. And most importantly, when you receive guidance there, **answer it.** Take action, however small. Embodiment is how prophecy becomes reality.

It has been an honor to share this space with you!

Thank you for still believing and acting from magic.

Because this (humans who are willing to be living prophecies) is the exact medicine the world is praying for.

With love,

Caroline Arco

Caroline Arco is a spiritual mentor, writer, and thought leader pioneering a new era of frequency-first living and light leadership. As the founder of ARCO, a global mentorship company serving over 4,000 clients worldwide, her work bridges mysticism and embodiment—helping spiritual seekers move beyond awakening into true spiritual stewardship rooted in sovereignty, integrity, and power.

For more than a decade, Caroline has guided individuals and communities through teachings on manifestation, emotional alchemy, energetic mastery, and soul leadership. Known for bringing depth and clarity to the spiritual field, she reframes lightwork as both a path of service and a blueprint for collective transformation.

She is a Certified Reiki Master Teacher, an ICF-accredited Life Coach, a Past Lives Healer, and a Breathwork Facilitator. Her work weaves the ancient with the modern, honoring intuition as humanity's original intelligence and embodiment as the key to sustainable change.

Through her programs, events, and her Substack series *Beyond the Rainbow Bridge,* Caroline explores spiritual leadership, grief as initiation, and the evolution of consciousness. Her message is clear: lightwork is not an escape from the world—it's how we rebuild it.

She lives on a tropical island in southern Brazil with her Dutch husband and their dogs, leading a life that mirrors her teachings—**Heaven on Earth is each person's right, and we are the ones to reclaim it.**

CONNECT WITH CAROLINE ARCO:

Website: https://www.arcoteachings.com/

Facebook: https://www.facebook.com/caroline.arco

Instagram: https://www.instagram.com/arcoteachings/

Free Ascension Series: https://www.arcoteachings.com/ascension-series

Chapter 15

I Want My Life Back!
Beyond Chronic Illness with Biomagnetism Energy Healing

BETH WILSON, CBT, LMP

My Story

"I need your help," The woman cried without introduction.

A lovely woman with dark circles beneath tear-filled indigo eyes waited for me to open the door.

Her voice trembled. Her eyes pleaded. I'd seen that look of anguish many times during my twelve years as a Biomagnetism practitioner.

"I want my life back!" Kamia's tone was insistent. She hoped for a miracle, counting on me to heal the dreaded sickness that plagued her. The weight of her desperation hung in the air.

"I'm Kamia. I need your help. Please."

"Of course," I responded, noting the five enormous binders in her arms. She strained under their weight.

"I've heard so many good things about you and Biomagnetism. I'm at my wits' end. I've got three children to raise. I'm of little help to my husband." She paused. "I hope you can help me get better."

She noticed my raised eyebrows as I stared at the load in her arms.

"These are filled with all my medical records and lab reports. No one can help. No one knows what to do."

Kamia was desperate to jump off the medical merry-go-round. She needed relief.

Now.

"I've been to more doctors than I can count over the past decade. I've spent tens of thousands of dollars with limited results. Beth, please tell me you can help."

With a warm smile, I ushered her into my office. We had work to do. "I believe I can."

A glimmer of hope lit her haggard face.

Like so many others who came to me with Lyme disease and other chronic illnesses, she was searching for answers. Deliverance from her daily suffering couldn't come soon enough.

Though a bit intimidated by the complexity and intricacies of her version of Lyme disease, I felt confident I could assist her. I just wasn't exactly sure how.

"Have a seat, Kamia, and we'll take a few minutes to assess your situation."

"Thank you, Beth. Where do I begin?" Kamia's voice cracked as she struggled not to cry.

"Tell me about your history as well as current symptoms," I responded, pen in hand.

"All of them?"

I felt her becoming overwhelmed as she sifted through the extensive list of complaints, straining to retrieve them from her unreliable brain.

"I have chronic fatigue, most days I'm bedridden, frequent infections, restless sleep, mast cell activation. . ." She paused for a moment, attempting to remember. "Memory problems, Lyme disease and co-infections, including brain fog, joint pain, mood swings, and muscle weakness, to name a few."

"The usual suspects," I responded. "Let's get you on the table so I can see what your body wants to address first. The body is extremely intelligent. Its wisdom will guide me."

I sensed that an extensive review of all her maladies wouldn't take us where we needed to go. Her body had the answers, not an overtaxed mind swimming with a plethora of diagnostic labels.

Once prone, I placed a pair of specialized booties on her feet for kinesthetic muscle testing.

"I'll be putting my hands on your ankles so I can communicate more deeply with your body. Is that alright with you?"

"Yes. Yes!"

I laid my hands on her sock-covered ankles, took a deep breath, and listened—not with my ears but with my intuition. Immediately, I made contact. The communications began to flow effortlessly. Transmissions came into me like fish being gently poured from a water bucket into a meandering stream.

I witnessed pictures of her life: a mother's death at a young age, living in Northern Africa, and the cultural confusion she experienced in such a distant land.

I felt her exhaustion and the internal agitation from the strain of holding on minute by minute. Having had Lyme for over ten years myself, I understood her struggle intimately. The perplexing battle that raged within—a battle others could rarely comprehend.

It was a lonely and terrifying illness that, if not arrested or at least significantly ameliorated, could reduce one's life to pure survival.

I scanned her head, neck, upper body, diaphragm, pelvis, backside, legs, and feet. Each area of her anatomy provided me with ample information about her condition. I'd need to form a comprehensive picture of the issues plaguing her.

Borrelia, yes; Babesia, yes; West Nile, yes; Ehrlichia, yes; Bartonella, yes; Tick Fever, yes; Epstein-Barr, yes; Tularemia, yes; parasites, yes; mold, lots of mold exposure.

The poor woman was overrun with pathogens. No wonder she floundered. Her immune system was doing its best, but it was overburdened. Though tempted to clear as much as I could during the initial session to bring her immediate relief, I knew better. Kamia was fragile and, as a result, needed gentle, personalized, focused care.

From my mind, I telepathically spoke to her body, mind, and spirit employing a wellness system known as "Bioenergetics."

There was no resistance. Kamia's entire being made it abundantly clear that she wanted to get well. She wanted to heal. Her body understood what I asked, and it quickly moved into alignment, waiting for the magnets to be strategically placed.

"Show me," I asked silently. "Show me."

Within seconds, I saw a picture in my mind's eye. Only one pair of magnets would be needed for her first session. Black on the right kidney and red on the left kidney. Negative on the right, positive on the left. I rocked her feet up and down, using kinesiology once again to confirm the information I received.

Yep, one pair is all she requires.

The interaction of the magnetic polarities would stimulate the hydrogen molecules within her cells, bringing her pH into balance; thus, the environment would become inhospitable to a number of pathogens that were creating distortions within her.

The art and science of the Biomagnetism system is simple yet profound. When integrated with my intuitive talents, a powerful environment for healing was created in service of my clients. I never tired of it.

Each individual brought in a unique array of symptoms, maladies, and conditions. When their bodies willingly cooperated with me, I easily determined how best to use the magnets on their behalf. Kamia was willing. Her body spoke effortlessly, pouring forth copious amounts of wisdom to guide me.

"Only one pair?" she asked suspiciously.

"Yes, that's all you need for today," I told her, sliding the magnets into place beneath her. "We don't want to overdo. Step by step, Kamia. Trust me."

Her eyes softened, knowing I supported her wellness journey.

"I'm going to leave you on the table to rest for about thirty minutes and let the magnets do their magic, okay? I'll put on some music if you like. Please, just relax, Kamia. This is your time for quiet and rejuvenation."

"Okay." Her taut body slowly released its fear and stress.

As I began to exit the treatment room, Kamia spoke of her past. Without any prompting, she told me, "My mother died when I was only nine years old." Tears slid down her face. "My brother and I had to go live with my father in Tanzania. We eventually moved to Egypt. Both places, though beautiful and full of family and friends, were difficult for me. I didn't know the language. The culture was so different, foreign. It was a hard time for me."

Her words verified the images I saw running through my mind when I tuned into her body with my intuitive abilities. Just speaking the words in a safe place lessened the impact of the trauma she carried within her.

Thirty-five minutes passed. I quietly returned to the treatment room. Kamia was right where I left her and, even from a distance, I sensed a more vital energy emanating from her.

"How are you feeling?" I whispered.

"I feel good, relaxed," she responded, the jagged edge in her voice now gone.

"Take your time getting up. If you need any assistance, please let me know. You might feel a bit light-headed or slightly off balance since it's your first session," I gently warned.

As Kamia sat up and wriggled off the massage table, I saw that the color had returned to her skin, her eyes were brighter, and no longer drooping. As is common with Biomagnetism, her face, once tilted downward from the heaviness of the illness, now turned upward.

"Beth, I feel as if a weight has been lifted off my shoulders," she told me with a radiant smile, "I'm back online. For the first time in ten years, I'm back online!"

Before I could respond, she hugged me, tears of happiness and relief streaming down her face.

That night she slept soundly. Within a month, after three sessions, she functioned normally throughout an entire day, participating in a variety of activities with her children.

"I even cleaned out a closet for three hours, just because I had the energy, just because I felt like it," she laughed heartily in the telling and re-telling of it.

"My husband doesn't have to drive me everywhere. I can go for walks with my family. You've given me my life back!"

Those were the same words I shouted over fifteen years ago when Biomagnetism returned me to health. It altered the abysmal trajectory I was on due to Lyme's Disease and Complex Chronic Illness. The change was so dramatic that I decided to train for 4 years to become a Biomagnetism and Lyme Magnetic Protocol practitioner.

Employing this modality enabled me to strengthen and expand my medical intuitive gifts—gifts I was born with that I regularly apply to humans and animals alike in my practice. The work is incredibly rewarding.

While not everyone experiences a miracle, the impact is significant nevertheless. For those who are willing and open, healing is available. It's a beautiful process whereby the learning never ends. I'm honored to walk the wellness path with those who come to me.

Together, we transform their inner light, even if it's been dimmed by illness, so they can shine more brightly once again.

The Medicine

When we become hollow bones, there is no limit to what the Higher Powers can do in and through us in spiritual things.
~Chief Frank Fools Crow, Oglala Sioux

Intuition is often referred to as "the still, small voice inside," but it can also be substantial *cosmic downloads* that move into your consciousness like lightning bolts or fluid streams of salient information. While there are similar traits in the way intuition appears in people's lives throughout history, everyone's relationship with intuition is unique and personal, despite the mystical commonalities.

Becoming a *hollow bone* is a tall order, often requiring rigorous daily practice. Yet, one need not be a seasoned medicine man or woman to develop a strong relationship with intuition. Because it resides both within and around you, it's available 24/7.

The key is learning to listen—sometimes in quiet spaces, other times in the midst of chaos—so you can distinguish the voice of intuition from all the other noise: compulsive self-talk, worries, and mental chatter.

Right now, take a moment to listen to the thoughts running through your mind as you read these words. Are you analyzing ideas? Allowing distractions? Thinking of chores left undone? Maybe all of the above?

Instead of attempting to banish these voices, acquaint yourself with the quality of each one. Treat every voice as an individual with its own tone, cadence, and vernacular.

Then, as though clearing brush in a jungle, see if you can mentally separate those communications vying for your attention. Create enough space for a more elemental voice to emerge. *Intuition is the voice of knowing,* whether it comes in words, sensations, vivid images, meaningful spiritual guidance, or in a form distinct to you. Discover it.

Can you grow quiet enough to hear it? Do you hear it now? If so, what is its quality and tenor? Does it have a personality? Does it feel both part of you and separate from you, emanating from within or beyond your body and mind?

If you have difficulty locating it, ask it to speak to you. The voice of intuition carries a distinct resonance—a spiritual frequency—whether its personality is sassy or serious. Seek it out. Ask it to find you. Invite conversation with the language of Spirit, the language of consciousness.

You may receive an immediate response, or simply a feeling that your answer is on its way. Keep listening, not just with your ears, but with your entire being.

Some tools or practices to assist in contacting intuition: tarot, meditation, nature, healing others, or communing with animals. Trust that you can expand your intuition for knowledge, information, guidance, and answers.

A SIMPLE PRACTICE

1. **Find a quiet place to lie down.** Allow your body to relax and release the stress of the day.

2. **Listen to the messages of the mind.**

3. **Invite and activate your intuition:**
   "I ask for a connection to divine knowing. Speak to me. I'm listening."

4. **Identify the various voices in your mind.** Notice each one's resonance and personality. Then request that all chatter leave, except for the intuitive voice—its images, sensations, and knowing presence.

5. **Ask for its messages.** Write them down and promise Spirit you will keep the channel open. Be willing to receive. Willingness is the threshold to communication. Let the Universe know you are ready to be in conversation.

6. **Check for clarity.** When you're comfortable with regular communication, you can verify responses using muscle testing, a pendulum, or other means of divining energy.

7. **Try the Sway Technique:**

   • Stand with your hands at your sides.

   • Say, "I'm James Dean." Since you are not, your body should sway backward for *no*.

   • Then say your real name, and your body should sway forward for *yes*. If it sways backward, you may be a contrarian. In other words, a forward motion, for you, indicates a *no*. Test it out. Trust your responses.

   • Finally, ask: "Is this information correct? Is it in my highest good?" Do you sway forward or backward? Honor your answer.

This process helps to strengthen and deepen your connection and communication with intuitive transmissions.

Listen, and be heard. The Universe is waiting for you. Trust it will respond.

Beth Wilson is an intuitive guide, energy healer, best-selling author, and Biomagnetism practitioner. Her work is spirit-driven and deeply personal, offering support, guidance, and healing for those navigating transformational shifts, emotional blocks, or a desire to align more fully with soul expression.

She began her career in the U.S. Congress, eventually moving into publishing.

Her first book, *Meditations for New Mothers,* was a runaway international best-seller. Beth published four additional parenting books to great success. During media tours—radio, television, and speaking engagements—she enjoyed connecting with others and giving voice to the anxieties, joys, and challenges of parenthood.

Determined to present cutting-edge ideas to a broad audience, she launched *Quantum Leaps.* The podcast went to #1 in six weeks. Beth then hosted a Bay Area television show, *In the Sisterhood,* offering a new voice for women. She also appeared as a regular guest on ABC's *View from the Bay,* writing segments to provide guidance and advice based on her books.

Next, Beth wrote and produced a wryly absurd comedy news show for women, *The Feminine Front.* Her media talents caught the attention of Hollywood. She was offered a national TV show highlighting her humor alongside her intuitive talents and mediumship abilities. Diagnosed with Lyme, she was forced to turn it down.

Biomagnetism returned her to health. Beth trained extensively with Dr. Goiz to become a skilled Biomagnetism practitioner. Currently, she has a thriving international practice that incorporates a variety of energy medicine systems alongside her intuitive talents.

Her latest book, *Escaping Crazytown: A Spiritual Adventure of Courage, Comedy and Cosmic Love,* chronicles her colorful life growing up with a famous narcissistic mother while revealing the extent of Beth's incredible intuitive gifts and her relationship with Spirit. The book will be released in February 2026.

CONNECT WITH BETH:

Websites: https://bethwilsonlifecoach.com/

https://biomagnetismhealingarts.com/

Chapter 16

Someone Hold Me, Please
The Gift of a Sacred Despacho

NATALIE V. PETERSEN

My Story

"Is that why you turned your back on your mother and your family here?"

The words leapt off the screen and seared my heart, just as they were intended. Random but with such purpose, left by the asker in the middle of the night, the way it was staged indicated they were not looking for an answer more than to wound me. The comment on my publicly posted video percolated while I slept and now oozed its condemnation down through the pixels, puddling at the edge of my monitor.

You don't know me. You don't have a clue. . .oh shit.

My mind began to shake inside my skull, my stomach lurched, and the adrenaline that accompanies the anxiety with which I've lived for most of my adult life climbed from the bottom of my feet up through every last inch of my body. On the heels of this surge came the grief I held, bottled for so many, many years. It was a grief of a kind that swallows humans whole, and it wracked my spirit and body for many weeks.

Oh, Mom. Mom, please. Hold me, Mom. I feel so alone.

I dropped out of the chair in one motion, the wheels beneath it sending it smashing into the wall behind me. My body folded in on itself, and my hands caught my fall. The cluttered floor of my home office felt safer than sitting exposed in the window where someone might catch sight of me losing my grip, losing my edge—finally, losing my mind.

* * *

In the long, painful days following my father's death, I didn't dare take my eyes off my mother. When she moved, I moved with her, not physically, but my eyes kept track of her every step. I feared my father's abrupt end to his life would trigger her to make a similar decision about living. She had, on several occasions before, tried unsuccessfully to un-alive herself, after all. I wasn't going to lose both my parents to suicide.

The dynamics of my young family were volatile and completely rearranged as addiction and untreated mental illness took their toll. In shoring up against the confusion, I made a reputation for being the strong one, the matter-of-fact, always-have-a-plan one, the one who plotted next steps, directed traffic, and controlled the volume, the glare, the pressure, the heat, and the air. I had hands on dials, feet on pedals, and my own care came far beyond last.

"I have my own back, thanks," I'd tell you. No one would take me out. I was determined in all cases to be the last one standing, she who had made it, no matter the damage to her soul.

On one of those early evenings of bewilderment that comes in the wake of such tragedy, my mom finally lay down on her bed to rest, to stare, to try and create a space where she could get away from the reality of her beloved's death.

I entered the bedroom softly, trying not to disturb what peace she may have found, with a blanket in my hands. We visited a clinic earlier in the day to retrieve a prescription for her anxiety. I counted the pills left in the container sitting beside a burning cigarette in the handmade ashtray on the bedside table.

My mom's face was swollen and so very sad, and her blonde hair feathered out over my dad's pillow. Her body twitched in physical and emotional exhaustion. Her eyes were closed, but I saw she was awake, deep in grief.

"Why?" The word left her barely parted lips.

I went around to what had been her side of their small bed in the little bedroom my parents shared. As I crawled in behind her, I lay my own body gently against hers, my front to her back, wrapping one arm around her waist and crossing one leg gently over hers. Burying my face in her neck, I breathed in my mother's turmoil, and we exhaled together in one long, labored groan.

"I've got you, Mom. Breathe."

"Why. . ." She whispered to me, to him, to no one.

I encouraged her to get away from my dad. In the months leading up to his suicide, I begged my mom to separate from him, to put distance between them and their drinking and the chaos that became their relationship. There were indications of more than verbal and mental abuse, and the house reeked of volatility and dysfunction. Now here I was wrapped around the pieces that were left, broken open, splayed out in total disarray.

How will I hold this one together? I hadn't a clue.

I went to move, thinking she had finally dozed off, and her hand grabbed for mine. She was confused about who I was for a few moments. Looking over her shoulder through bloodshot, weary eyes, she realized it was me, not him.

We wouldn't come back from this—not fully. Part of her love left with him that Valentine's Day. Some things break and never go back together the same way. I wanted to be the balm. The healer. The one who made sense of senseless things. But I was still young myself, a young woman trying to mother her own mother while holding the shards of a family that never had enough glue.

* * *

Picking up the phone, tapping out the text, character by character, took on weight with each passing second, but I knew I needed help. I needed to be held. For the first time in my life that I can remember, I just wanted to be held.

I had been spiraling for days, and nothing I did eased the anxiety and dread that sat on my chest like a massive pallet of cement blocks. Breathing was a chore, my diaphragm tired and sore from constant tension. My hands shook, and as I hit Send, I shuddered in one soaking wet exhale.

"Are you around this morning?" I asked my older female friend, Nancy, praying she'd answer quickly, lest I lose my momentum and the space in between my question and her reply become too great a chasm to cross.

"Yes, Sherry is here with me. You're welcome to come by." Her words were soft and welcoming, assuring me it was safe to go, to find solace and safety in the arms of mothers. Not my mother, she'd been gone for over a year now, but mothers of my time, women who knew me for me now, not for some sad or angry accusation slung at me from across miles of misinformation and the missing truth of my story.

Climbing into the car, the sunbaked insides enveloped me like a too-heavy blanket. My body trembled in relief, and my nervous system roiled in anticipation. I carefully and purposely drove myself away from the house into the arms of the woman I knew my body and spirit needed. My mother passed, and with my wound wide open, I sought the medicine of my ancestors.

* * *

The door opened, and the two women came forward.

One took my feet and hands, rubbing warmth into my skin, helping me stay in my body when all I wanted was to flee. The other wrapped herself around me from behind, chest to my back, breath syncing with mine, and hummed low into the space between our ribs.

Voo.
Shhhh.
Let it go, baby.

They whispered prayers, sang lullabies older than any language I speak. Their voices vibrated through my bones.

Earth my body
Water my blood
Air my breath and
Fire my spirit

"Take the energies that are not wanted here and go," they intoned. "Leave this one to flow. She is loved. She is safe."

Time stood still. And I slept. Not deeply. Not long. But enough to reset the system and to breathe like it mattered again.

As I dozed, a sound bath emerged from below, tuning forks, bells, wave runners, and a drum. The sound of a gentle man's dozing off joined mine just long enough to let me know he loved me, too.

Later, when I could stand, I wrapped myself in a blanket and joined them, tired, weak, and dazed.

How precious the gift of this unconditional love. How simple and pure it is to give to someone in need. They exchanged glances and knowing nods.

"This is why we are here. You were right to come. You don't have to leave. You always have a home."

"We see you. We honor you. We are you."

"Have you eaten? Have you bathed? Meditated?" Their attentiveness was soft and patient.

"Yes, yes, yes, I believe so," I answered. "What else is there to do to make the ground feel firm instead of sliding out from beneath me?"

"We will build a sacred Despacho."

A handmade blanket of beautiful colors was laid on the floor. They brought a basket of materials from inside and outside and explained the sacred ritual.

"When we build and release a Despacho, we are saying: I see what was carried. I release what does not belong to me. I thank those who walked before me. I honor their love, their mistakes, their humanity. And I choose to live free."

On my knees on the floor in gratitude and wonder, I joined the beautiful older women in creating the offering that would help relieve my soul.

"Who do I pray to?" I asked.

"To the ones who are listening," they answered. "To the ones who hear." We took three deep breaths together, exhaling all negative energy from my inner space. Atop a dollar bill, more was placed.

Bay leaves to each side represented the divine masculine and divine feminine in balance, in divine balance within each of us. Around the outside, a cotton edge protected the offering from outside influence. Fresh lavender and sage lay in a beautiful circle. Sunflower seeds, rice, pumpkin seeds, corn flour, and more. Cranberries and sugar and flowers, too, as gifts and tributes.

Beautifully laid, easily made. Rose, precious rose, to represent my heart. In the middle, a clay face of a female guardian from long ago, hand-shaped from the Earth. Florida water cleansed my face and cleared my mind.

When we were done, we folded the Despacho, end over end, side over side, careful to contain the gifts. The air was quiet, and our breathing was calm. We tied the bundle gently, then wrapped it again in the beautiful, handmade cloth. Sherry reached across the now-empty space between us and placed it in my hands.

"Take this bundle, this offering, this package of your worries and fears wrapped in gifts for the ancestors and burn it. Let the flames take the gifts inside up into the heavens. Let the ancestors and guides carry and ease your load, for you are never alone.

"Listen to the wisdom of your foremothers: we never truly leave the womb. Rather, the womb is a shared space where we come home to be safe, where the Divine Mother wraps her loving arms around you, looks into your face, and proclaims: You are a miracle, sweet child of mine. From me you were born, to me you'll return.

"Nothing can take your peace, nothing can erase your sweet spirit. Lift your face into the sun and know. You are loved. You are held."

The next morning, I journeyed to the top of a nearby mountain with the bundle. I gathered grass and small sticks to create a fire. Carefully and purposefully, I laid the offering in the middle. As the smoke wafted up and the flames took hold, the wind picked up, and a small, unfamiliar bird landed nearby to watch. The sky above was crystal clear, and the sun drenched my back as I watched and listened to the sacred Despacho open up, crackling and expanding in the heat. I watched as the edges of the sweet offering of flowers, grains, sweets, paper, and clay turned black and then white ash. I waited until the last of the offering was gone, and I took a deep, cleansing breath.

"So it is, and so it shall be."

I did not walk down the mountain the same woman who climbed it. Something in me was witnessed, carried, returned, now with my foremothers at my back.

I didn't go searching for a Despacho. I searched for something else entirely—my intuition, maybe. My voice. My own mother's reassuring spirit. I couldn't name it exactly, but my body begged for release, for reconnection, for a ritual that might open something ancient in me. And as I've learned to trust—when the call is real, the answer appears.

I was invited to a sacred space held by women who knew deeply: healing doesn't have to come through words, logic, or linear plans. Sometimes it comes by laying down grief in a bundle of sweetness and setting it on fire.

That's what this story is. That's what this chapter is. A remembering. A teaching. A guide back to the knowing that never left you.

The Medicine

The word *despacho* means "dispatch" or "offering" in Spanish, but its origin is much older. The Despacho ceremony comes from the Andean spiritual traditions of Peru, especially the Q'ero people, descendants of the Inka. These ceremonies are often led by Paqos—Andean mystics who work with the spirit of the land (Pachamama), the Apus (mountain spirits), and the ancestors.

In its original form, a Despacho is a sacred mandala of gratitude and reciprocity, made with natural elements and prayers, offered to the Earth, ancestors, or unseen guides. It's not a "spell" or a "manifestation tool." It's a prayer, a conversation, a release. It's a humble way to say:

"I see you. I thank you. I am ready to carry this no more."

This is a spiritual practice that welcomes anyone with intention and respect. I am a student, a listener, and a sharer of what I received with permission and reverence. What I offer below is an adapted ritual for personal or communal use, rooted in the energy of gratitude, release, and intention. I share it not as a replacement, but as a doorway.

As you consider building your own sacred Despacho, I invite you to ask:

- Who might you release?

- What pain or pattern are you willing to surrender?

- What sweetness do you want to offer in gratitude?

Gather what you need, preferably biodegradable, as we want it all to return to our Mother Earth. Here are suggestions:

- A sheet of paper or natural cloth as your base; the Q'eros use coca leaves on a hand-woven piece of cloth, which is part of the shaman's "mesa" or healing bundle

- A dollar bill (or symbolic currency) as a base layer of value

- Bay leaves (masculine and feminine balance)

- Lavender, sage (cleansing, calm, clarity)

- Grains, sunflower and pumpkin seeds, rice, cornmeal (fertility, nourishment)

- Cranberries, raisins, sugar (sweetness and joy)

- Fresh or dried flowers (love and beauty)

- A rose or rose petal (symbol of your heart)

- A clay figure, stone, or symbolic token (representation of you or a protector)

- Florida water or sacred cleansing spray

Once you have gathered your materials, find a quiet place to sit undisturbed. The shamans call in the directions of the Four Winds. You can use prayer to open the space, or if you prefer, you can create the sacred container in whatever way feels natural for you.

Light candles. Burn sage or incense. Ring chimes. Chant. Sing. Hum. Call in whatever invisible support you wish. Perhaps that is God, Goddess, Jesus, Buddha, spirit guides, angels, animal totems. Mother Earth does not discriminate when she is being blessed.

While building your Despacho, take your time. Lay out your cloth or paper on a clean surface. Place the currency at the center. On top, begin layering items in a circular or intuitive pattern. There is no wrong way. Let spirit speak through your hands, and let your heart guide you.

As you place each item, name a feeling, a memory, a worry, or a gift. Breathe into each with your intentions.

- "I lay down fear."

- "I offer gratitude for my mother."

- "I surrender my need to control what is not mine."

In the center, place your clay figure or symbolic item. Mist or anoint yourself and the offering with Florida water or breath.

Listen. Receive any messages you're meant to receive. Be open to the mystery. If you have any requests you'd like to make of Pachamama or the Apus, this is an appropriate time. Just remember that the Despacho is not about getting what you want; rather, it's a ceremony of giving and gratitude.

Fold your Despacho like a sacred letter—corner to corner, edge to edge. Wrap it in your cloth and tie with a string or yarn. Hold it close to your heart and say:

"May this offering rise. May my prayers be heard. May I be lightened."

When it is time, release your Despacho carefully and with respect for the ritual. Choose a method that speaks to you. Burn it in a fire-safe container. Or bury it in the earth. Even offer it to a body of flowing water.

In whatever way you choose, let it go with gratitude.

Afterward, find some quiet time to journal. What might be possible now that this weight is gone?

And again, listen. The ancestors speak in dreams and symbols. You may feel their whisper in the wind, in birdsong, in your own breath.

You don't have to carry it all. You never did.

You are seen. You are free. You are held.

Natalie V. Petersen, or Natalie P. to friends, is a communications strategist, bestselling author, speaker, podcast host, and spiritual misfit and mentor with a rebellious heart and a reverent soul. She's the creator of *Healing-Curious Humans,* a growing movement that explores the wide-open landscape of personal transformation, non-religious spiritual practices, and radical self-reclamation.

With a background spanning media, marketing, storytelling, and mental health advocacy, Natalie helps people name their truth, own their voice, and live lives that actually fit. She doesn't teach from a pedestal—she walks beside you as an accomplice.

Natalie believes that healing doesn't happen in a vacuum and that wholeness is a community project. Her own story is a fierce and tender reckoning with generational conditioning, religious programming, mental health cycles, and what it means to live fully awake in a world that prefers you asleep.

Through *Healing-Curious Humans,* her signature mentorship offerings, and her unfiltered podcast *Think Out Loud with Me,* Natalie creates brave, irreverent, loving spaces for people to get curious, get honest, and get free. Whether she's guiding you through the Wheel of Wellbeing, handing you a microphone, or helping you rewrite your origin story, her work is rooted in one thing: we are not broken—we are becoming.

She lives in Loveland, Colorado, where she's raising kids, goofing off with her sweetheart, building weird sacred shit, and calling in a new kind of leadership: human-first, Spirit-led, and wildly alive.

CONNECT WITH NATALIE:

Website: https://www.1qr.com/nataliep

Chapter 17

Portals of Flesh and Fire
Conversations Between the Seen and Sensed

TERI FREESMEYER, METAPHYSICAL LMT, RMT, INTUITIVE HEALER

My Story

The restaurant hums with low conversations as Suzy and I catch up on life events, the clinking of chopsticks against porcelain chimes in the background. The faint hiss of the wok and the swinging doors of the kitchen hustle fade in and out. The sun blasts its rays through the windows on its westward journey.

My eyes begin to sting—sharp, intrusive, like a rush of fiery wind laced with smoke. The heat creeps up my neck and floods my face. My ears throb, my cheeks flame. I try to stay focused on Suzy's tales of—grandkids say the darnedest things—but her words dissolve into a heated distraction of body static.

I blink a few times, trying to stir up some soothing tears, "Suz. . .are your eyes stinging? Mine are burning like crazy. Is there something in the air?" She pauses her anecdotes quizzically. She shakes her head, "I don't notice anything. Are you okay?"

"Are they burning something in the kitchen, maybe? I don't know, it seems chemical-like, more so than charred egg rolls?" My voice cracks halfway between confusion and panic.

Suzy's eyes widen as she startles, "Oh my god—your face is so red, like beet red! Are you having a hot flash?"

"Maybe," I murmur, pressing my hand to my cheek, sweat beads on my brow. It was a feasible explanation. I was in the ripe age of possibility. "Feels like I'm on fire."

THE SENSATION PEAKS

An eruption of heat and pressure, my face is flush—and then it slowly ebbs. I have a quick reprieve, then another surge moves through. Different from the first slow evolution up the neck and face. This one was like a sudden searing whole-hand smack on a sunburned face, with a lingering slap of heat. I keep touching my temple, my brow, my ear—searching for the irritant on my tender skin.

I wave to the server to have my glass refilled. I dunk a napkin into the cool water to wipe my face and neck. Still concerned, Suzy inquires if the bizarre hot flash has passed. "Let's try to finish dinner before I spontaneously combust," I exclaim. After dinner and a movie, we bid our goodbyes as I drop Suzy off at her place. I wait in my car until she's safely inside.

The full moon and the haze of streetlights illuminate the night. Out of the corner of my eye, shadows flit past the rear bumper. I pause, giving them time to clear the drive and move on down the sidewalk. What's taking them so long? "Geez, come on," I huff with annoyance.

REAL OR REALM

"What are they doing back there?" I whisper to no one. My breathy exhale fogs the glass. Then a realization—there are no people. In the physical realm, anyway. My whole body tingles. Something or someone is trying to get my attention.

As if summoned by cinematic magic, an owl sweeps down the middle of the streetlight-lit avenue. Its wingspan slices through the night air. The owl is at eye level to my car door window. "Whoa, what is going on?" My heart sputters.

I'm stopped at the longest traffic light downtown—one that holds you hostage long enough to poke my impatience. I turn my phone back on. A message blinks from my friend Cheryl in Arizona. Her voice is urgent, layered with frenzied worry. "Someone's been hurt. Call me when you can."

The light turns green.

I head to my apartment complex. The night feels thick with omens. As I coast toward my parking space, over the apex of my building, an owl dives over the rooftop and straight through the center of my parking spot. I can sense the whoosh as the shadow passes right over my sunroof—two owls in one night. "Alright, universe. You have my attention." I was certain my Hogwarts invitation would be on the stoop.

I returned Cheryl's call. Her words tumbled out in a cry. "It's my sister-in-law, Kimberly, in Michigan—flash fire. Burn wounds—her face, her eyes, her ears. We don't know how bad it is."

As she speaks, the echoes of earlier replay—stinging eyes, flaming cheeks, and tender skin.

Cheryl's breath catches. "Tell me if this is too much to ask. Can you check in on her, please? My brother and their girls are beside themselves. I don't know what to do to help them. I instantly thought of you. I asked my brother for permission to see if you get anything."

"Her face is bad. They don't know if she has any damage to her airways or lungs." Cheryl is frantic, her voice cracking in heartache for her family, all of them wrapped in uncertainty.

"Oh, honey. I'm so sorry. Of course, I will check in with my guides and let you know what I get."

I listen, holding space for my dear friend as she relays the phone messages between her brother, Ben, her nieces, and me. "They have Kimberly in the burn unit and sedated to assess her wounds. On top of the flashback from the bonfire, she stuck her head in the pool to make sure the fire was out."

Hmmm, perhaps the second round of sensation?

"Call or text if you get anything. I don't care what time it is. I love you. Thank you. Gotta go; my niece is calling." Cheryl ends the call.

BEYOND THE VEILS AND ZIP CODES

The air in my bedroom thickens. I smell chemicals—sharp and acrid, like lighter fluid. I taste metal, then salt. My inner vision flickers with color—blue flames then white light.

I reach out with prayerful intent, requesting my higher self and guides obtain Kimberly's higher self's permission to observe and clarify whether there is anything I can share. The ear feels strange, melted into the temple— panic, confusion, floating, ahh.

I called Cheryl and walked her through my strange events here in Illinois: sensations at the restaurant, images of people milling behind my car, and the two owls. "I'm still feeling the ear," I mutter. "It has the majority of my attention. I feel like the eye area has some blistering, but I feel like it will be okay."

I hear the clacking of the keyboard. Cheryl tells me she's documenting the details for her brother. She has it on a spreadsheet with the timelines. Her brother is skeptical of the entire field of holistic and energetic medicine. He trusts Cheryl and is open to her suggestions.

Cheryl was always trying to get me to document my intuitive experiences. It happened too often for me to consider, but she would frequently do so when we daydreamed and brainstormed writing *You Can't Make This Up* books.

"Do you think she is going to make it through this? My brother said she hasn't responded. Tell her we love her, if it's her time, I understand, but we want her back," Cheryl pleads.

I blurt before I can stop myself, "Carolina, maybe? Older, slight accent or unique speech, protective. Grandmother, perhaps? She is with her from the spirit realm, comforting her while she is out of her body. Feels like a grandmother."

"Let me text, Ben, sounds right."

Cheryl gasps. "Yes! Grandmother Caroline. I don't remember where she was from, but yes, a distinct dialect. They were close when Kimmy was young."

"I'm asking her to help her get back in her body if it's not her time to go," I reply.

A surge of energy shoots through my backside, prickling sharply. "Ouch!" I shriek loudly from the sting. "Did she just get a shot of something in the butt?"

Cheryl types madly and confirms. "They just gave her an injection. My brother just said, "How the hell did you know that?"

I breathe, grounding myself. "Alright, sweetheart," I whisper to Kimberly, in spirit, "You're not alone. The doctors are helping. You're safe. If it's not your time to go, come back into your body. Your grandmother's right there with you, but you need to get into your body. It might feel uncomfortable at first, but there are a lot of people there who love you and are there to help you."

I feel her confusion and uncertainty, then a sense of her returning to her body.

Cheryl—the tech-savvy mystic—documents the entire exchange: times, messages, physical sensations. Every eerie synchronicity was cross-checked on her time-space continuum spreadsheet of the unseen. Her brother, still skeptical, conceded to faith through the cracks of disbelief. Kimberly survived her injuries. The ear required several skin grafts due to the severity of the injury. Her eyes healed with only a few slight scars at the temple.

I, too, am forever changed. A new level of empathic understanding has taken shape.

THE DANCE OF THE SOUL

It hasn't always been easy to trust my intuition, particularly through the wisdom of my body. Navigating the years of an extremely sensitive nervous system and suppression of intuitive impressions created some trauma and hyper-vigilance. My soul, however, knew the way. You may have heard the theory that you teach what you need to learn.

I had a perfect platform as a massage therapist, spa director, and educator. My desire to learn, my creative mind, and my love of teaching have served me well as a stage for alchemy. I was intuitively led on a journey that awakened my intuition and a yearning to understand it better.

I received messages, images, and sensory input as I worked with my clients and their bodies. Guides, angels, and messengers often appeared even before the client arrived for their session. I resisted sharing these impressions until I could no longer hold back the nudge. It was as if someone was pushing it up out of my throat. Just say it.

I drew in a particular niche for autoimmune, chronic pain challenges, and inner child healing. My mom had been diagnosed with an autoimmune disease. As her primary caregiver, I sought ways to support her where allopathic medicine left off and fell short. This evolved into sensing the body metaphysically, listening to the body's symbolic language, and detecting subconscious and unconscious clues to work through stored energy and trauma, to free up life force.

I joke, I should put on my business card, "I help people laugh, cry, and poop because we need to let crap go." Clients were left wide-eyed and perplexed yet grateful, saying this was unlike any massage or spa treatment they'd ever had. They may or may not return, but they did refer their people.

The spa staff would bring their clients to me. "Can you do that stuff you know on my client? I told them they needed to have one of your healing sessions."

As my extrasensory gifts grew, I vowed to live my life consciously guided by my intuition. I have followed the inner spark and intuitive signs along the way. I've had to learn to discern when resistance arises, what kind of resistance. The kind that makes you dig in your heels or want to hide.

Or the kind that lights a fire in the heart or under your ass because you know it's the next right leap.

In 2007, after a twenty-year career in the spa industry, I quit my job. I moved to Arizona, where I met my soul sister, Cheryl. I planned to take a year-long sabbatical to study metaphysics and energy medicine. It turned into a three-year, intuitively led masterclass in life: learning, traveling, speaking, and teaching. I continued developing my private practice, classes, and retreats while deepening my understanding of metaphysical language.

I continued to be led across the country and work remotely around the world—fascinating magic unfolding for this small-town girl. I would meet someone at one event or session who would lead me to the next. More than once, the bigger work was not the events I thought I was called there for. Eventually, I was guided back to Illinois by a message clearly carved in concrete. I will save a few of those stories for the next book.

It's been a journey to feel comfortable in this vehicle of the flesh. It doesn't always look or feel the way I'd like, or the way I was taught it should be. I spent my early years feeling all the feels, so I disconnected from my body, thinking it was safer than feeling. It took deep inner work to find the way back to my heart, and I could easily default here and still not be embodied. This is an ongoing practice.

I stay curious and I trust what I get. I understand how I am the tool. I appreciate my body as a profoundly masterful, intuitive guide. My intuition and perceptive sensitivity are my medicine. My apothecary of the physical and subtle realms.

I listen and collaborate with my higher self, my spiritual team, and my client's higher self. I follow the source and go from there. I use my metaphysical gifts along with holistic arts to customize each session, class, or retreat. I am grateful to my soul for continuing to guide me to the people, places, and pieces to support sharing my life's work.

The Medicine

THE ART OF RECEIVING AND TRANSFORMING ENERGY
TOOLS TO EMBODY YOUR INTUITIVE SUPERPOWERS

Find your own way with it. Make adaptations as you are guided. Return to the first two often.

1. TRUST: Trust what you get—my number one rule is to always keep a flexible mind. Trust what you get, even if you don't have the context. Stay curious.

2. NEUTRALITY: We apply meaning based on our life experiences, beliefs, opinions, biases, and symbolic references. Everything is neutral until we assign a meaning. Stay curious, allow your symbolic references to evolve. Continue to do your inner work on your beliefs, biases, and other mental constructs.

3. CONNECT TO YOUR ZENITH: Connect with your grounding techniques, your higher self and guides, your center, zero-point, or true north. Whatever that is for you today. Keep exploring and connecting with the felt sense. Stay present to what's working and what needs to be adapted.

   Practice: Imagine unplugging your energetic power strip from the mass consciousness and plugging into your own higher self. Let your body feel your vertical axis anchoring you to the Earth's core. Pull your energy in from the external, the horizontal field, and align it with your life force center. I call this my zenith. Explore the way it works best for you.

4. BUOYANT QUESTIONS: Know your inner yes, no, and maybe as a base reference. Be curious when you may need a clarifying question. This is where buoyant questions can help. Interview your sensations or nudges with open-ended questions.

   Practice: Here are a few examples I find potent.

   "What kind of no?"

This could be: No way. No, not the proper framework. No, not right now. No or know? No, not for you to know or understand at this point. No, not relevant or going to happen. Or other.

"Where is this sensation coming from? Is it inside or outside?"

This has been a powerful game-changer for my physically empathic senses. It helps me navigate varying levels of intuition depending on what I am referencing.

For instance, "Where is this pain coming from? How much of this pain is inside of me or outside of me?"

"What part of this feeling, emotion, or sensation is mine to process?"

Pause and breathe. Allow for what is not yours to shift. Just because we can pick up on something doesn't mean it's ours to process, share, or navigate. Reminder to check your boundaries. This has definitely been a learning curve on what is mine to speak into.

"What is the most important thing for me to know or share today?"

Always a good place to start your day, session, project, or writing.

If a question stops you, rephrase or ask a buoyant question.

5. Embody the Heart: "Follow your heart. Drop into your heart. Come from the heart." However, as this became easier, I noticed I could remain disconnected from the rest of my body. When I can ground my heart energy throughout my body, I'm more fully connected to my inner knowing and have full access to my body's intuitive wisdom.

   Practice: Bring one hand to your heart and the other to your navel. Relax here, breathe, and invite the heart energy to expand into the belly or solar plexus area until you sense a shift. This may be a yawn, a warming, tingling, shiver, relaxation, or some other way you notice.

   Next, one hand on your heart and the other on your throat center. Relax here, breathe, pause for the shift.

Repeat with one hand on the heart and the other below the navel.

Continue moving along the body to the brow, the root at the base of the spine, or the top of the legs with intention, the crown of the head, and the bottom of the feet so that you can feel on solid ground.

Explore the ways this may work best for you. Pause at the joints or focus awareness on the back of your body. Start at the crown, working downward, or at the feet, working upward.

Contact me to attend a free workshop or to schedule a private session at Terifreesmeyer@gmail.com

***Watch for my upcoming Brave Healer Transformation School course:

Mastering the Art of the Subtle Senses

https://bravehealertransformationschool.com/

Teri Freesmeyer, LMT, RMT, RYT-200, HypnoCoach®

Metaphysical Educator * Author * Artist * Speaker

Teri Freesmeyer is an intuitive healer offering transformational bodywork and coaching, drawing on a variety of metaphysical gifts, skills, and holistic healing arts. With over three decades of experience, Teri masterfully blends her massage and bodywork skills, metaphysics, somatic intelligence, and spiritual alchemy. Her integrative approach draws from energy psychology, trauma-healing resources, soul coaching, yoga, hypnosis, sound healing, and more—sacredly woven with compassion, creativity, and curiosity.

Teri skillfully leads her sessions and programs with her vibrant palette, serving as an Intentional Creativity® Teacher, a Transformation Game® Facilitator, an Avana Method® Medical Intuitive, and a Shamanic Breathwork® Facilitator. She merges intuitive guidance, embodiment modalities, and a playful yet directed multidimensional approach to personal evolution.

As a channel and coach, Teri brings subtle energies into form by guiding and supporting you in freeing life force energy, whether for healing, self-discovery, or authentic expression. She is the founder of The Art of Receiving and Transforming Energy Academy (aka The ART Academy), a community cultivated and devoted to awakening intuition, exploring energy medicine, and developing our innate metaphysical language. Through her classes, retreats, and private sessions, she invites individuals to reconnect with their divine essence and the living artistry of the soul through creative expression.

Teri's work spans generations—from trauma recovery to ancestral lineage, elder care to inner child work—sacredly held in her joyous presence, dancing between the esoteric and the direct interaction of daily life. Teri embodies the essence of the healing arts. Her offer is a customizable platform of possibilities. Whether reading the chakras or your toes, guiding your transformation map or the discovery of your subtle senses, dare to discover what you might unveil.

CONNECT WITH TERI:

Website: https://www.terifreesmeyer.com/

Email: terifreesmeyer@gmail.com

•

Chapter 18

Heartbreak as Initiation
The Sound of Becoming

VANESSA PACHECO, SOUND HEALER

My Story

The excitement I felt when I got off work early that day was something I could hardly contain.

I can't wait to surprise him!

I remember driving home, the windows down, music blasting, the world around me glowing with golden light. Life felt blissful, simple, full, and alive. The sunlight poured through the windshield like liquid honey, my hair whipping in the wind as I sang along to the radio. Somewhere beneath that joy, though, was a flicker I couldn't name. It was the kind of whisper your intuition gives when it senses a storm before the clouds appear.

When I parked and walked through the door, something shifted. My intuition slapped me across the face; the air felt different, heavy, off.

He looked startled when he saw me, nervous almost.

"I don't feel so good," he said. "Do you mind going to the store and getting me some medicine?"

"Okay, sure," I replied, "just let me put my stuff down."

"No, I really need medicine right now. Please," he insisted. His voice trembled.

"What's going on?" I asked, my stomach twisting. I stepped further inside, pushing the door open, and there she was.

A woman sat on my bed. My bed.

"Who are you?" I asked, my voice cracking.

"I'm his girlfriend," she said softly, confusion in her eyes.

My world tilted. "No," I said, "I'm his girlfriend. I live here."

I flung open the closet door. My clothes, my things, were gone, moved, hidden. He had tucked my belongings into a corner, out of sight. The pictures of him and me that once lined the shelves were replaced with new ones—him and her.

"How long have you two been together?" I managed to ask.

"Six years," she said.

Six years. The words echoed through my mind, and everything I thought I knew came crashing down. An overwhelming number of questions filled my head.

How could he have lied so deeply? So completely? How had he managed to lead two lives? Was I blind or just naive?

We both left that house heartbroken—two women carrying the weight of one man's deception.

He begged me to stay.

"I'm not in love with her anymore," he said. "I love you."

But my heart was done being deceived.

"No," I told him, "You owe us both an apology, but especially her."

And I walked out the door.

For weeks, I couldn't eat. I woke up reaching for him, then remembered, and it was like falling through ice. I replayed every conversation, every smile, every "I love you," wondering how I could've missed the truth. My intuition tried to warn me, and I didn't listen. That hurt most of all.

The nights were the worst. I lay awake staring at the ceiling, numb, my body heavy with disbelief. I oscillated between rage and despair, shame and grief. My world shattered, and with it, my sense of self. I didn't trust anyone, not even myself. I felt like my inner compass broke.

That's when the real work began. The alchemy of healing always starts with the burning. Everything I thought I was, every illusion, every dream built on falsehood, had to turn to ash.

Healing wasn't linear. Some days I felt strong; others, I felt like I was dissolving. I tried everything: therapy, journaling, yoga, long walks through the woods, anything to find the version of myself I lost. But nothing seemed to reach the ache that lived beneath my ribs.

I noticed how drawn I was to sound. Music, drumming, even the hum of the refrigerator at night—it all felt alive, like it spoke to me in a language older than words. I didn't understand it then, but sound was already calling me home.

One evening, I saw a flyer for a local sound healing group. I didn't know what that meant, but something inside me whispered, *Go.*

The first time I walked into that healing space, the air smelled of lavender and sandalwood. Candles flickered along the walls, and a small fountain murmured in the corner. I rolled out a yoga mat and lay down, arms open, eyes closed, heart weary.

Then the singing bowls began.

The sound started low and deep, as if the Earth itself were exhaling. Each tone shimmered through the room, weaving into my cells. My body tingled, my chest opened, and I felt the tears before I knew I was crying.

The notes didn't just play, they moved through me, washing away the weight of betrayal, grief, and doubt. It felt like the music was rearranging me, piece by piece.

The vibration was alive, ancient, and intelligent. It knew my story better than I did. I saw colors I couldn't name. I felt energy coursing through my bones like rivers. I heard a voice within me say:

You are not broken. You are becoming.

When the session ended, I lay still, floating between worlds. The facilitator knelt beside me, smiling softly.

"Not many people have visions," she said. "That was a rare, magical moment."

From that day forward, I was hooked. I went every week, craving that sound, that stillness, that sense of home. I devoured self-help books, attended retreats, and even traveled alone just to reconnect with my spirit. Each experience was another layer of alchemy purification, dissolution, and rebirth.

At one retreat in the mountains, I lay beside a river as crystal bowls sang under the open sky. The tones mingled with the water's rhythm and the hum of insects in the grass. I felt the Earth breathing beneath me.

Then came the vision.

A massive egg appeared in my mind's eye, luminous and pulsing with light. I heard the crack from within, like thunder rolling across the sky. When it opened, I saw a baby, radiant, chubby, perfect. My heart swelled with a love so pure it made me tremble. I realized it wasn't just a child I was seeing, it was *me*. I witnessed my own rebirth.

I wept with awe and relief. The part of me that died in betrayal was born again, whole, innocent, free.

That night, I knelt by the river and poured my intentions into the current. "I'm ready, Universe," I whispered. "Ready for real love, for truth, for family, for life."

Two weeks later, I received a message from an old friend, a man whose soul always felt like home, even when life pulled us in opposite directions. We shared a quiet connection years before, one of those magnetic bonds that linger long after goodbye.

"Something told me to reach out to you," he said.

The moment I saw his name, my heart skipped. It was as if a door I long forgot creaked open inside me. We talked for hours, laughter spilling easily between the pauses. Time melted away. I felt the years dissolving the pain, doubt, and guardedness, and in their place rose a familiar warmth, something ancient and deeply known.

He told me he had always wanted a family, one built on love, honesty, and trust.

"You'll never believe this," I said, smiling through tears. "I want that now too."

There was a silence on the line, the kind that hums with recognition. It was more than words; it was a matter of remembering. Our souls circled each other for lifetimes, waiting for the right moment to meet again in human form. Twin flames, finally reunited after both walked through the fires of transformation.

From that day forward, love unfolded effortlessly. There were no games, no masks, no guessing, just truth, devotion, and the electric comfort of knowing. He saw me, all of me, and loved the parts I once hid from the world. With him, I didn't have to earn love; I simply *was* love.

We fell in love the way the sun meets the horizon, slowly, then all at once. There were late-night calls that turned into morning light, soft laughter tangled with tears, and quiet moments, where words became unnecessary because our hearts spoke in the same rhythm.

It felt like coming home to a place I'd never been, yet always belonged.

We married surrounded by the people who witnessed our separate journeys, each of us now whole, healed, and ready. We moved across the country, built a new life together, and soon after, welcomed a beautiful baby boy into the world—a child born from love that survived lifetimes of waiting.

Every image I saw in that vision by the river came to life. The egg cracked open, and love, real, grounded, and divine, was born again.

Now, I'm a stay-at-home mother, traveling the world with my husband and son. Every month, I host moon circles and sound healing sessions. This time, I'm the one holding the bowls, guiding others through the same frequencies that once saved me.

During one recent circle, I paused mid-session and looked around at the women sitting in stillness, their faces softened in release. Candles flickered. Tears glistened. The air pulsed with love. I smiled, realizing how far I've come.

The woman who once lay broken on the floor was now a healer, guide, and an alchemist of sound.

That's when I understood: every heartbreak, every tear, every silence had purpose. The betrayal that once destroyed me was the fire that forged my gold.

That's the alchemy of intuition—turning pain into power, loss into light.

It's the moment you realize your intuition was never trying to protect you from pain; it was guiding you through it.

I've come to understand that intuition is the alchemist's fire. It burns through illusion until only truth remains. When I followed that whisper inside me, even when I didn't understand why, it led me home.

Intuition is the quiet language of the soul. It speaks through sensations, dreams, songs, and synchronicities. It's the compass that points us toward transformation, even when the path looks like destruction. Every heartbreak, every ending, every tear was part of my Great Work, the sacred process of becoming who I truly am.

Now, when I sit beneath the moon, surrounded by women releasing their pain, I smile, because I remember that girl who once felt broken and lost, and I whisper to her: *We made it.*

The Medicine

SOUND HEALING MEDITATION

Sound changed my life.

When I first lay down on that mat and felt the vibration of the bowls move through me, I realized healing doesn't always come through words; it often comes through frequency. Those tones reached the parts of me I didn't know how to touch with my mind. The vibrations reawakened my intuition—the part of me that has always known how to heal.

Now, I get to share that same medicine with others.

Sound healing works through resonance, the universal language of vibration. Every cell in your body hums with its own frequency. When that frequency falls out of tune from trauma, grief, or stress, sound becomes the tuning fork that brings you back into harmony.

Intuition, too, is a vibration felt that hums quietly beneath the noise of daily life. When we slow down and listen, we can hear it. We can *feel* the truth.

A PRACTICE FOR YOU

If you're reading this and your heart is hurting, if you're somewhere between endings and beginnings, I invite you to take a few minutes to experience sound medicine for yourself.

1. **Find a quiet place.**
   Light a candle or place a hand on your heart.

2. **Close your eyes.**
   Take a deep breath. Set an intention to release what no longer belongs to you.

3. **Listen to the sound.**
   Imagine the vibrations flowing through your chest, clearing old pain, grief, and self-doubt. Let them fill you with light. Let yourself be held.

4. **When the sound fades, pause.**
   Notice what's shifted. Maybe it's small. Maybe it's everything.

You can listen to my guided meditation here:

https://www.themysticmuse.org/soundhealings

Then, take a few minutes to write in your journal. Ask yourself:

• What sensations did I notice in my body?

• What emotions rose up to be released?

• What message did my intuition whisper through the sound?

Let whatever comes be enough.

May this practice remind you, as it once reminded me, that healing isn't about fixing what's broken; it's about remembering what was never lost.

Every sound, every vibration, every breath is a doorway back to yourself.

May the sound carry you home to your own intuition, your own gold, your own sacred alchemy.

You are already whole.

Vanessa Pacheco is a gifted sound healer, artist, and community builder whose presence radiates love, authenticity, and joy. Guided by intuition and inspired by the moon's rhythms, she uses the frequencies of crystal singing bowls to help others access deep states of peace, clarity, and emotional release. Her sound sessions are more than music; they're medicine, inviting the body, mind, and spirit back into harmony.

As a stay-at-home mother and devoted wife, Vanessa finds magic in the simple, sacred moments of daily life. Her greatest joy comes from nurturing her family, dancing in the kitchen with her son, and sharing laughter with loved ones. She brings that same nurturing energy into every circle she holds, creating spaces where people feel safe, seen, and celebrated.

Vanessa leads monthly moon circles that weave sound healing, ritual, and intention-setting into powerful gatherings of community and transformation. She has a passion for bringing people together, whether through themed parties that spark joy, painting sessions that awaken creativity, or outdoor concerts that remind her of the pure freedom of music.

Her life's work centers on the belief that healing occurs through connection—connection to sound, to oneself, and to one another. Vanessa partners with Dr. Tiffany McBride to co-host community sound circles and sacred gatherings that blend spirituality, embodiment, and creative expression. Together, they hold space for healing, growth, and the remembrance that every vibration, every voice, and every heart contributes to the symphony of wholeness.

CONNECT WITH VANESSA:

Sound Healings: https://www.themysticmuse.org/soundhealings

Living Now Soul Care: https://www.themysticmuse.org/livingnowsoulcare

Chapter 19

Into the Flow: Synchronicity and Intuition
Honor Your Intuitive Voice and Its Home in Your Body
BECKY WHEELER, INTUITION RESEARCHER AND GUIDESS

My Story

THERE

"Congratulations!" I beamed at my daughter as we sat in the coffee shop and she clicked the final button to accept her enrollment offer at Oregon State University. It was late April 2025. Digital confetti and streamers flooded her screen as her excited face, touched with trepidation, turned to look at me.

"I'm moving to Oregon," she declared. We both felt the hot sting of tears and the genetic reddening of our noses as we realized what it meant— her living 2,052 miles away.

This person, this being, who happened to be born to me as my daughter—and for good reason—is one of my closest and dearest friends. Over the years, the boundaries of mother/daughter have been explored, tested, and ultimately respected through communication, vulnerability, love, and compassion. Our relationship teaches me about lineage healing, self-love, and dedication to growth. And, I realized through the priceless journey spent driving her to Oregon and driving back all alone, letting go of your children, and the version of yourself as their sole provider and caregiver, is something meant to be shed, even amidst the sense of loss and grief it brings. But that wasn't even my journey's biggest lesson.

After the obligatory photos of her smiling broadly next to the confetti-screen, I thought to ask, "Okay, when are we driving out there?" wondering if it would coincide with my birthday in August. "When do you have to move in?"

Her reply initiated one of the deepest opportunities for trusting in my intuition I have ever gotten to knowingly and consciously engage in, once I remembered to let it in. As an intuition researcher, even I forget to involve its wise counsel in my life. But as I teach in my classes, remembering to remember is the first step.

"Move-in is September 18-20th," she replied. My heart stopped.

"For this year?" I asked, hoping there was a mistake.

There was no mistake. OSU operates on a three-term system. The fall term begins at the end of September instead of starting in August like a traditional two-semester college. Her move-in date fell directly *in the middle* of *The Alchemy of Intuition* journey through Ireland, which I spent the past year planning and creating for the incredible participants in this very book, at the inspiration of Dr. Tiffany McBride.

What was happening?

For the following months, I did what I could to find a way to do both. I couldn't imagine choosing. But nothing felt right. It was a snake sacrificing its life on my mother's front lawn that provided me with guidance.

The snake died after becoming caught in some mesh left to help grass regrow in a recently excavated area. My brother found it while doing yard work, and my intuition said: *This snake is here for you. Take it, and honor it.*

I trusted, and successfully persuaded my annoyed brother to leave the snake with me. I buried it in a nearby forest and honored its life. This being the year of the snake, and having worked with its energy multiple times, this was very symbolic and felt every bit sacred. But I couldn't quite grasp the meaning.

During a conversation with a friend the next day, while still struggling with how to navigate my daughter's move and the Ireland journey, I shared what happened with the snake, and the lesson became apparent:

The best-intentioned placement of the mesh to help the grass grow became the trap that ensnared and killed the snake. It was a lesson about how we can become caught in our own best intentions, to the detriment of ourselves and our life's path.

Trying to do both the journey and my daughter's move 2,052 miles away from home, even with the best intentions, would ensnare me somehow and not allow me to show up fully for either. And as a single parent, I knew there was only one option.

* * *

I'm grateful to Tiffany for her understanding through this whole process. I'm grateful to Ruthie for stepping in and agreeing to assist Tiffany on the Journey, and for pulling me a card the first night of it—The River, whose meaning you'll see unfold soon. I'm grateful I was able to show Tiffany Ireland in March, and call in the energy of the group at the places they'd be connecting with in September. And I'm grateful to everyone who went on the journey for their support, and especially their toast while dining in County Wicklow, where I lived with my children a decade earlier.

But most of all, I'm grateful to Snake and my intuition for guiding me to the lessons that helped me know I made the right decision then, and again when I came back from Oregon.

I never could've imagined crafting a journey I wouldn't be able to share with those for whom it was created. But here I was. Having to let go of it. Just to go and let go of something even more precious, my daughter.

AND BACK AGAIN

Snake medicine is about healing, shedding, and being grounded—all requirements for such an intense life change. My intuition once again guided me to connect with its medicine on my return trip from Oregon.

All through the summer, I focused on finalizing preparations for the Ireland journey and my daughter's looming move. My deflective response to any question about my return trip was, "All I know is I'm going to need a lot of Kleenex!"

The full burden of its task was absent until I was standing in my daughter's unpacked and arranged dorm room, and it collided with my reality like a tsunami. You can't fight a tsunami. It roared over me, leaving its trail of debris and detritus in the form of sudden worry, self-judgement, anxiety, and doubt.

What were you thinking? You have to drive all alone, grieving, 2,052 miles home. This was so stupid. Why didn't you take a U-Haul and fly back? Why the hell did you want to drive back?!

I didn't know why, but it was always the plan. It was intuitive. So be it.

I trusted again, asking for its guidance, and in a much different-sounding inner voice, asked: *What do I do? What's the plan? Here I am. What do I do?*

I became still and listened, and the loose plan revealed itself over the following week, fed by snake medicine and synchronicities.

For example, on our drive from Wyoming to Idaho to Oregon, my daughter and I crossed the Snake River many times, greeting it each time, "Hello, Snake River!" In Victor, Idaho, I had a long, moving, and powerful conversation with a mother working in a coffee kiosk, where my intuition told me to stop.

As we were ready to pull off, she asked where we were going next.

"Twin Falls," I said, and to my delight, she answered,

"That's where I'm from! You have to go on the Snake River just under Shoshone Falls. It's beautiful."

The synchronicity of our conversation and us staying that night in her distant hometown was affirming and stuck with me. From her suggestion unfolded an intuitive journey, making my way back along the Snake River, not remembering my card from Ruthie, or even remembering the unfortunate snake that sacrificed its life in the summer. Yet, synchronicity and snake were again showing up to intuitively guide my return trip. There became three parts:

1. The tail/root – at the confluence of the waters, where the Columbia River (with the waters of the Snake nestled in its flow) meets the Pacific Ocean, on the lands of the indigenous Chinook people in Washington. Here, I learned about my foundation, constructed of my own ongoing sacred learning, the energy I carry, and working to live in right relationship with all beings. I learned how solidly anchored my root is in my authenticity, and that my foundation is much stronger and supported than I knew. Thank you, Ancestors.

2. The body/heart and spine – paddle boarding on the Snake River in Twin Falls, Idaho. Here, I wedged my paddle at the edge of the wide river and lay back on my board, surrendering to the flow that streamed beneath me, cleansing, energizing, and opening my heart, and strengthening my spine, encouraging me to stand tall. I was reminded of the connection of all things by their middles, in some ways, the most important part of the journey. Thank you, Middle.

3. The head/crown – near the headwaters of the Snake River in Yellowstone National Park in Wyoming. Here, I claimed a new sovereignty over my life by changing my plans coming from a place of autonomy, respect, and alignment, rather than of resignation and defeat, with the lesson arriving courtesy of a bear. Alongside the banks of the Snake, I felt my crown shine and recognized the responsibility it requests. Thank you, Bear.

Each part delivered a profoundly deep and meaningful experience, sometimes mirroring the alchemy journey in Ireland. Sacred and intentional, I showed up, having no clue what I was doing, trusting my intuitive guidance, until, invariably, at each part, I knew **exactly** what I was doing. And I was shown, taught, and gifted with lessons for my soul's growth and the empowerment of my authentic self.

AWARENESS IS KEY

A snake sheds its skin backwards, beginning at the tail and ending up at its head, with its eyes briefly covered, rendering it blind for a time. As humans, our process of change and growth can unfold in much the same way. Having intuition to rely upon in these moments of change, shedding, and blindness, is a window into seeing our lives maintain an even course, a steadiness through the chaos, a grounding through a destabilization. Snakes aren't taught how to shed. They just do it.

We can just intuit, though it takes self-awareness. We each experience intuition in our own way. This was fully shown to me in 2021 during an online conference where I presented my findings on the use of mental simulation (visualization) in the decision-making process.

A participant asked me, "What about people who can't visualize? Are you saying they can't make good decisions?" They had aphantasia, a condition where no mental imagery is possible, depending on its severity. Shame flooded me for not having known about it. Now, I want to thank that person and tell them, "Of course you can! *You* are the only one who can identify your intuitive voice, and it doesn't need to involve visualization."

So, I began asking in my research: How do you *sense* intuition? Rather than just: What is intuition to you? And I got incredible answers. And I learned. Only you can discern your intuition's voice within you. And the only surefire way to learn about it is to engage with it more. Practice, play, and develop that relationship with your intuition. Bear in mind, you'll be dealing with all the other voices in the inner chorus, along with resistances to its guidance, and many other components, but the first step is to learn where it lives in your body. I've included a meditation in the Medicine section for this purpose.

Using awareness to live in the flow of intuition, the world opens up with synchronicities, gifts, and lessons to help you align with your authentic self.

The self that is steeped in love, compassion, and divinity, and radiates these into the world. Following your intuition sees you uncover your light to shine in our world. Shine bright, lightworker. Shine on.

The Medicine

INTUITIVE VOICE

While the Ireland journeyers moved through their transformational journey in September, guided and held by Tiffany, Ruth, and all the magical energies of that sacred land, I stumbled around the Pacific Northwest, until I let go and allowed myself to experience my own transformative, synchronistic journey, gifted to me through my daughter's courageous following of her own intuitive guidance, and my connection to and *following of* my own.

My intuition of wanting that dead snake, while my inner voice interjected: *What are you doing? What are you going to do with a dead snake? You're probably just going to end up throwing it away anyway.*

My intuition of burying it in the forest, while my inner voice interjected: *What are you doing? You can't just dig a hole here. You can't just randomly bury a snake here. What will you say if someone walks up?*

My intuition of deciding I wouldn't be on the Ireland journey, while my inner voice interjected: *You can't not go. The journey needs you. You did all this work to just walk away? You're abandoning the people who signed up for this journey.*

My intuition of traveling back along the Snake River, while my inner voice interjected: *You can't just stop at random places on your way back. What will people think of you? You're just looking for an excuse to visit the Tetons again.*

Our inner dialogue is as powerful as we let it be. And often hidden by an all-too-cruel chorus is the authentic voice of our intuition giving us guidance. Only you can discern your intuitive voice's tone, cadence, resonance, and home in your body through stillness and awareness.

HALLMARKS

Being aware of the hallmarks, or common characteristics, of intuition can make it easier to discern between the differing voices populating our inner world. It's important to allow a space for intuition to live within our crowded inner landscape full of anxiety, our inner critic, enthusiasm, ego, archetypes, opinions, beliefs, fears, and desires.

Intuition ignores them all and provides us with clear, unadulterated, judgment-free offerings. Suggestions, or subtle options to take or ignore, with no retaliation either way. Intuition gifts us the opportunity to align with a different energy—an energy that supports the evolution of our soul's authentic growth. We just have to honor it.

Hallmarks of intuition and intuitive guidance:

Clear

Direct

Non-judgmental

Unattached to your following of it

Can come with audio, visual, or other sensation-based clues

Oftentimes subtle

SYNCHRONICITY

Even with these helpful hallmarks, with so much inner noise, it can still be difficult to discern our intuitive voice. Luckily, we're also given hints to tune into. Noticing where synchronicities appear in our lives can help identify and strengthen our intuition's guidance. Experiences that seem to magically align are signposts to guide us and help us recognize when we're listening to our intuition. Awareness is key.

Looking back through photos from the journey, I was shocked to realize many synchronicities I had forgotten. For example, twice pulling a bear card, at different times, from different oracle decks on the drive out; putting my hands in and connecting to the Snake River in the Tetons before

I even knew the name of it, and two separate experiences of a mother and baby deer, once before and once after, dropping off my daughter.

Many years ago, I learned to ask the universe to help me see the signs that were showing up rather than asking for signs to appear. They're all around us. We just have to be open to seeing them.

Guiding questions to ask yourself:

How does my intuitive voice communicate with me?

Where does it live in my body?

Am I open to my intuition's guidance?

What synchronicities are appearing in my life?

We don't have to know the specific reason we're intuitively guided to do something, but we can know the overall guiding principle. We're being shown and guided by an energy that only wants to see us transform into our most authentic, highest selves, operating our lives through and with love. We are loved, and that's how we are guided.

MEDITATION
DISCERNING WHERE INTUITION LIVES IN YOUR BODY

Sit or lie down in a quiet place where you can get comfortable and will not be disturbed. Begin by taking a few deep breaths, gently sending your breath down into your belly on each inhale, and softening your body on each exhale.

Relax your body and invite in a sense of calm and centeredness. Taking one more deep breath, send a grounding cord however it feels comfortable, down into Mother Earth, asking her permission. Sending it all the way down through the layers of dirt, clay, rock, magma, until you reach the iron crystal core of the earth.

Connect to this stabilizing and nourishing source in whatever way feels comfortable. Perhaps gently wrapping your cord around the core. Perhaps plugging it in. Perhaps something else. However you feel to connect, trust that.

Begin slowly bringing this grounding energy back up your cord and up into your body. Feel it filling your field with light. Invite it up into your heart, allowing your heart space to expand however it feels comfortable. Breathe into this.

Now, in this connected and nourished state, set the intention to discover where in your body your intuitive voice lives. Ask. And just notice what comes up without judgment or doubt.

Where does my intuitive voice live in my body? Just notice.

Breathe into this space. Allow it to inform you. It may have a message for you. It may have a color or shape, or a sensation. It may just be a felt sense. Breathe into it. And when you feel you have connected, rest in this space. Then, when you're ready, say a word of thanks or give gratitude in any way that feels right to you.

Begin to bring yourself back to the room you're sitting or lying in, and the chair, sofa, or bed you're on. Come back fully into your own body. You may want to journal about your experience.

* * *

Be courageous and test this out. Practice tuning into this space when deciding what to have for dinner, where to get an item you need, or what shirt to wear today. Have fun with it, and just notice what happens. Keep an intuition journal to log your progress. And always practice self-compassion. We're all learning here.

Becky Wheeler is the founder of Beltany Wellness, offering self-discovery and intuition growth through online classes and offerings, and synchronistic journeys through Ireland's powerful and magical landscape, incorporating shamanic and energetic practices. She is an award winning intuition researcher, writer, traveler, mystic, artist, graphic and web designer, and proud mother of two fantastic adult children.

Becky's calling is to deepen her understanding of intuition and its role in her life. Expanding that understanding into her growing curriculum, she helps others strengthen their intuition into a significant and accurate guide through learning to identify and trust their own intuitive voice. Intuition is a powerful tool needed to help humanity evolve into higher levels of consciousness and transform our lives and the world we live in.

After graduating from the Art of Receiving and Transforming Energy Academy (ARTE) and the two-year Shamanic Multidimensional Mystery School, both in 2019, Becky continued her journey with Shamanic Breathwork in 2020, becoming an Ordained Shamanic Minister, and graduating from the Shamanic Healing Initiatory Process (SHIP) through Aahara Spiritual Community. In 2021, she graduated as a licensed Shamanic Breathwork facilitator from Venus Rising Association of Transformation, and in 2022, as a Master SHIP Graduate from Aahara. She facilitated her first Intuitive Ireland Journey in 2024 and, in April of 2025, became the first Master Graduate of the Shamanic Warriorship Path, Aahara's revolutionary signature leadership program. In 2025, she became a Shamanic, Usui, and Tibetan Reiki Master.

Becky has also explored the academic side of intuition, researching as an undergraduate student at the University of Illinois at Springfield (UIS). Graduating summa cum laude as the 2021 Psychology Department Outstanding Student Scholar, she enjoyed conducting her award-winning research on intuition in the decision-making process in 2020 and 2021.

CONNECT WITH BECKY:

Website: https://www.beltanywellness.org/

Instagram: https://www.instagram.com/beltany_wellness/

Email: beltanywellness@gmail.com

Chapter 20

How to Know for Sure
A Basic Guide to Your Intuition Superpower
LAURA DI FRANCO, MPT, PUBLISHER

My Story

I scratched the spot between my eyebrows, expecting a mosquito bite, and thought: *Maybe the fairies opened up my third eye.*

"They will appear in human form, as big as you or me," said our guide Pat, as he stood on top of the grass-covered burial mound and lit another cigarette.

"Mmm, that smells good," I said to Mom. "Yeah, like pipe tobacco," she replied.

"Nothing like gross American cigarettes."

"No, not at all."

Weeks before the author's journey to Ireland, the Universe had her way with me, bringing stressful moments that were later released during breathwork, the cacao ceremony, ecstatic dance, our writing workshops, and now on Pat Noone's farm. I felt happy to be in the magic of the bright green of Ireland, in the middle of a place known for healing (and where fairies live).

It's time to really see what I'm made of.

But even as my third eye lit up and started to itch like some allergic reaction to the farm animals, I doubted it all.

This is stupid. None of this is real. We're all crazy.

On the two-hour bus ride back to Killeen Castle (our third of four amazing accommodations in Ireland), I ran the barbs of my newly found crow feather between my left thumb and forefinger, smoothing out the little split parts back into one, working my way from the base to the tip. I watched the ombre-like pattern meld from black to grey to grey-white and remembered Tiffany saying, "That's a hooded crow."

Every feeling in my body was a "yes" in that moment. It's how I know I'm not crazy. That "yes" feeling is how I know for sure.

I still kept a secret about the moment I first got off the bus at the farm, and my eyesight was altered. Everything had a slightly fuzzy but crystal-clear look to it.

Hmm, that's weird. Maybe I'm getting another ocular migraine.

Mom's going to think something's wrong and try to fix it. Better keep it to myself.

At this point on the trip, I've spent many minutes pondering what my healer friends think about my alien ass, knowing many are experiencing similar versions of that inner critic sabotage. I'm not always drawn to the rituals. I need my alone time, introvert through and through. And there's nothing like travel to bring out the "real" in people.

The fellow travelers in Ireland are all highly intuitive, empathic, sensitive versions of healers, shamans, and witches. We're a rookery of alien badasses, and coming out in the world as an intuitive alien badass is scary. Not everyone feels or is willing to talk about their intuitive superpowers, let alone fairies.

This group? It's what we live with every day, in one way or another. And if some didn't realize it before the trip, I'd say by day two or three, we all felt the witch feckery in our souls. That's a good thing, by the way.

We own our intuitive superpowers and look forward to enhancing them every day. We know what we know. We understand the language of our souls and the Universe. We use that knowing as a decision-making tool, and we know living by this inner compass means we're aligned with what we were born to be and do.

"OMG," my bus-mate Jayme said, taking off her headphones to look at me. "This book is talking about all the stupid decisions made by men at the top of skyscrapers. They aren't connected to the land or to themselves."

"Did everyone draw a card?" asks Tiffany. Tarot became one of the group's favorite activities on this trip, and we're invited to draw a card during our bus ride. "Ooh, me, me!" I exclaim, as I let that thing inside me choose a card from the fanned-out spread before me. I drew *The Land*. And I think back to Jayme's audiobook comment. Tiffany later says, "You can also think of the land as your body."

"Oh, yes!" I answer. And something clicked, big time. This year (2025) was my "get my health back" year, an effort to honor my body, this sacred vessel (land) that carries me as I live my purpose every day. I'm grateful for this body. I haven't been so careful with (or nice to) her all the time. When we toured Tara Hill that day, I picked up a couple of candy wrappers off the grass surrounding the Destiny Stone.

Clearing and cleaning your body is the same as honoring the land. It's time to honor yourself and your body every day.

Fast-forward to a Zoom meeting weeks later. The host says, "Imagine you're only given one car that has to last you your entire life. You'd take really good care of that car, wouldn't you?" How did he know I'd instantly resonate with a car metaphor?

Okay, I may be late to this party, but from now on, my self-care will be a bit more radical.

Following your intuition is a fun (and challenging) way to live. Whether it's a magical blast or uncomfortable depends on who you're hanging with on a particular day. These moments in Ireland were a magical blast.

In Ireland, we challenged ourselves to experience the next levels of these superpowers. We dove into the discomfort, busted up outdated, old beliefs, and experienced what was possible when we opened our hearts to what we feel.

What heaven that was!

What's possible *starts* with feeling.

"We're going to do embodiment practices that help us connect," said Tiffany, to the group.

Yes! This is the trip I've been waiting for!

"I think I just channeled that" was something I wondered back in 2014, just at the beginning of opening up to my intuition and superpowers. Before that day, I would've never used the words "I" and "channeled" in the same sentence. I would've always referred (with envy) to someone else with that ability.

Today, I'm here to tell anyone interested: You have intuitive superpowers, even if you don't have any idea about them or how to discover them. I can't promise you'll ever see fairies, but understand how to make every decision from a place of sure knowing? I can help you start that journey with confidence. It's life-changing.

"Did you ever find that horn you were talking about?" asked one of my friends as we gathered for our evening circle after the day at the farm.

"Wait, I think you're growing a unicorn horn!"

Oh, shit. That's the horn!

"Doesn't the little creature on your card have a unicorn horn?"

"Yes!"

It was the IV card—*The Emperor*—that I drew that day. He had wings and a winged companion with a unicorn horn.

When "horn" came to me in one of our first guided meditations, I drew it in the shape of a banana, but the word *horn* was very clear. I can't complain about growing a unicorn horn.

Should I tell them that next to my computer is a unicorn horn headband for our Best Hat Contest days with my authors?

Then I noticed something even better.

Oh wow, all the anxiety is gone.

I shared with the group.

"Before I came to Ireland, I had daily, relentless anxiety. I chalked it up to menopause. Now I know it wasn't that. All the anxiety disappeared a couple of days into the trip."

The trip was a daily practice of listening to the messages and noticing the miracles. The biggest of the ten days for me was the night after an Irish nomad god named Daryl came to the Rockfield House to share a tea and breathwork ceremony with us.

We lined up yoga mats in a half circle facing the fireplace, where Daryl and his partner sat. They unpacked Chinese tea cups from a wicker basket and set them out on the carpet. Daryl poured from a stainless-steel thermos and talked to us about connecting with the land by making tea from native plants. "This tea has meadowsweet and a couple of other plants in it."

Daryl's monarch butterfly tattoo spanned the entire width of the front of his neck, and sat on top of what looked like a lion, two eyes peering from the opening of the shirt he had unbuttoned just enough to see them.

I wonder if he would take his shirt off so we can see the rest of that!

What inspired the poem below was a conversation I had with another author friend, Christine, about the breathwork, Daryl, and the sound of the people of Ireland.

[Note to reader: See Christine's chapter and scene about Daryl for more awesome details]

"Ever since I got here and have heard the Irish people speak, I fell in love. And when Daryl guided us through that breathwork—OMG, that voice, it was like this feeling of being home," I told Christine.

"I felt it as we got off the plane and the workers in the airport shooed us through the line, but something else clicked today."

Once I expressed that to her, I felt a huge urge to write. Something deep and fierce walked me to my journal. I started the poem that night and finished it the next day (a first because I usually rush to finish). I re-wrote it three times (another first because I usually don't obsess).

The Sound of Ireland

You can say anything.
and I'll melt.
Your brogue is the road
to a piece of my soul
long forgotten.

Your voice is a primal origin story.
All the love that exists
pours from between your lips
to my ears
and it's perfectly clear.

Here is where my heart sings
plumps, beats,
swoons, and spins,
and is best kept. . .
. . . here in the sound of Ireland.

Your words form bliss vibrations
meadowsweet resonations
gently, neatly aligned
a deep rhyme medicine
following me into my dreams.

They weave their way in

skillfully connecting the silver string
mending gaps
answering questions I've had
my whole life.

Here is where my heart sings
plumps, beats
swoons, and spins,
and is best kept. . .
. . . here in the sound of Ireland.

Every tone, every hello,
each joyful greeting,
it's like you're secretly seeing
the whole of me
so carefully.

It feels like coming home
into that final light
only way more alive
and only the beginning
an infinite chance at ecstasy.

Here is where my heart sings
plumps, beats
swoons, and spins,
and is best kept. . .
. . . here in the sound of Ireland.

I stand grounded and sure
connected through to the core.
As you share your story
every cell shakes and integrates
in recognition.

Like a giant magic magnet
I float, hopefully pulled in
your frequency an anchor
keeping me so here
I'm finally free to flow.

Here is where my heart sings
plumps, beats
swoons, and spins,
and is best kept. . .
. . . here in the sound of Ireland.

Whisper-speak your spell
bring me in again
help me remember the love
that I am
and the power resting within.

Wake me for good
I'll breathe your melody in
slowly sip the gift
the one that feels like God
and a hymn of sunrise light.

Here is where my heart sings
plumps, beats
swoons, and spins,
and is best, forever, kept. . .
. . . here in the sound of Ireland.

Here in the sound of Ireland.

Dear reader, it's time to listen to the sound of your soul and practice the awareness that'll help you do that. Awareness is how you connect with and enhance your intuition. Awareness is noticing what you feel (hear, see, think, taste, smell, etc.). And feeling is healing. Feeling is a superpower, and the key to your intuition.

To my highly sensitive people (HSPs), empaths, intuitives, witches, and anyone else who feels everything and wonders if they can go on another day with that burden. What else is possible? Grab hands with this community. You're not a freak. You're not alone.

To my friends waking up to feeling, unlearning what you've been taught, and learning to walk to the beat of your own heart and soul:

congratulations—you're about to claim your superpowers. The following medicine will help you get a step closer, maybe even to seeing fairies or channeling whole poems.

With awareness, you have a choice. Choose the magic—choose love.

The Medicine

When I learned how to know for sure, I learned to feel what aligned with my soul (felt joyful) and what didn't. This is so simple. Many of us, however, weren't taught to connect and feel. Instead, we were taught to do as we're told or be seen but not heard.

If you're recovering from some kind of good girl syndrome, or twisted, conditioned version of people pleasing (maybe go read my mom, Susan Ernst's, Chapter 5 about that), you can begin with this very simple way to know if something is right for you and your soul, or not.

It's about feeling the "Yes!" and the "No!" in your body. Once you have this basic awareness, the rest is about honoring it and practicing discernment. You can fine-tune your intuition to the point of feeling like a magical badass.

What you'll need: A piece of paper (normal spiral notebook size), a pen, and some time without distractions. Put your phone on *Do Not Disturb.*

Draw a line down the center of your paper to create two columns. Label the top on the left "YES!" Label the top on the right "NO!"

Start on the right with the "NO" column.

Think about when something feels bad, uncertain, or not for you. Think about when it's a "no." Think about people, places, or circumstances that feel like they go against what you stand for or make you feel sad, fearful, cloudy, confused, or bad.

What do those things feel like in your body?

Begin to describe them by making a list of those descriptive words in the "NO!" column on the right side of your page.

For example:

Tight
Contracted
Cold
Shriveled
Closed or small

Give yourself a couple of minutes to write down as many descriptive words as you can think of. If you write words like "bad" or "confused," think about where "bad" or "confused" is located in your body and describe how that feels instead.

The "NO" has a feeling. See if you can connect with what happens in your body with a "NO."

Now, go over to the "YES" column on the left.

Think about what something fully aligned with your heart and soul feels like in your body. Think about the things and circumstances in your life that you love. Think of what you were born for: things, people, places, or circumstances aligned with your purpose that turn you on and that help you feel happy, uplifted, and joyful. What does that feel like in your body?

Begin to describe them by making a list of those descriptive words in the "YES" column on the left side of your page.

For example:

Flexible
Chest open
Light
Warm
Spacious

Give yourself a couple of minutes to write down as many descriptive words as you can think of. If you write words like "happy" or "energized," think about where "happy" or "energized" is showing up in your body and describe how that feels instead. The "YES" has a feeling, posture, and body language. See if you can connect with what happens in your body with a "YES."

At the end of this exercise, you'll have a pretty badass cheat sheet to refer to any time you're wondering if something you're considering is a "yes" or a "no."

A FINAL STORY ABOUT CONFUSION

"Robin, I'm confused. I don't know what to do."

I said this to my very talented and wise healer friend during a session one day.

"It's easier to be confused," she said. "It's harder to make a decision and take action about what you already know you need to do."

I had one of the biggest aha moments of my life that day.

I realized that when you're trying to make a decision and it feels like it's in a grey area—confusing, foggy, unclear, or uncertain—guess what? **It's a no.**

Because *confusing, foggy, unclear,* and *uncertain* all have a feeling in the body, and they certainly aren't a "YES!" Those feelings are not joyful.

Now, whenever I find myself wanting to say, "I'm not sure this is right for me; I'll think about it and get back to you," I immediately catch myself in that very clear moment. It's not a yes, so it's a no. It can also be a "Not right now."

Being clear about that helps me take action that's aligned, authentic, and straightforward, serving me and everyone I'm involved with.

This is a ninja move of awareness and discernment. My body is the place to listen for the answers. I love being bodyful instead of mindful.

When I founded my publishing company, Brave Healer Productions, I made certain our authors knew that writing, publishing, launching, and promoting their brave words is a healing process and journey. I call that Brave Story Medicine™. When we take responsibility for sharing words from this connected and aware place, we change the world in wonderful ways. I'm honored to be doing that here in *The Alchemy of Intuition* and in every book we share with the world.

What if that thing you're a little afraid to share is exactly what someone needs to hear to change (or even save) their life?

It's time to be brave.

A special note of thanks:

To Dr. Tiffany McBride for saying yes, not only to this book (and rookery), but to taking us on this journey to Ireland, which quickly became my favorite place in the world. Many of my fellow authors and I have said, "It feels like home." Tiffany, in our closing circle, you said to me, "I'd follow you anywhere." My feeling about you, crow goddess, is the same. Thank you for the magic, love, and support you bring to the world.

To Ruth Souther, whether we identify as a bog hag, sacred hussy, or fairy fecker, I will forever be grateful to you for helping to bring out the soul of our writers, both in Ireland and here on the pages of our books. You are a magical love-alien.

You can read more stories from Tiffany, Ruth, and several of the other authors in other Brave Healer Productions books. We're changing the world, one brave word at a time. And this, I know for sure.

Laura Di Franco is the CEO of Brave Healer Productions (including Brave Business Books and Brave Kids Books), an award-winning publisher for holistic health, wellness, and business professionals who want to become bestselling authors, build their community and business, and leave their legacy in a more conscious way. She created Brave Story Medicine™, a proprietary storytelling and collaborative publishing method.

She has a master's and 30 years of expertise in holistic physical therapy, is a third-degree black belt in Taekwondo, and is the author of 14 of her own books. Brave Healer Productions has published over 100 Amazon bestselling books with a mission to help the world experience what's possible.

Laura is a divorced mom (of two adult kids and one dog), a lover of the sunrise and dark chocolate, a spoken-word poet, an inspirational speaker, and convinced she was a race car driver in a past life. She has a contagious passion for helping you share brave words that build your business and leave your legacy.

Come Write with Us!

Want to write in our next expert collaboration? Find our projects here: https://lauradifranco.com/expert-book-collaborations/

Get access to The Brave Healer Resources Vault with thousands of dollars' worth of training, master classes, and workshops for author-entrepreneurs:

https://lauradifranco.com/resources-vault/

CONNECT WITH LAURA:

Website: https://BraveHealer.com

LinkedIn: https://www.linkedin.com/in/thelauradifranco/

YouTube:
https://www.youtube.com/c/BraveHealerProductionswithLauraDiFranco

Closing Chapter

When this journey began, *The Alchemy of Intuition* was just a spark, a whisper that asked: *What if we listened to our inner voice and followed where it led?*

I had no roadmap. Only a vision, and a deep knowing that this book was meant to exist.

What followed was both initiation and transformation, years of creating, planning, holding, guiding, and surrendering. I poured my time, heart, and resources into this work. There were moments of loss and disappointment, times when doors closed, when plans shifted, and when I questioned if I had the strength to keep going. I had emotional meltdowns, moments of doubt, and times when it all felt impossibly heavy. And yet, I kept moving. I kept believing because I knew in my bones that this vision was sacred.

And now, standing at the end of this journey, I can see that every challenge was part of the alchemy.

This book, these stories, are proof that transformation is never clean or convenient. It is messy, humbling, and holy work. It asks everything of you. It burns away who you thought you were so that what remains is true.

To my incredible co-authors, I see you.

You answered the call. You wrote from your wounds, your wonder, and your wisdom.

You turned your fears into medicine and your vulnerability into power.

You have created something luminous, alive, and real—a collective voice that speaks to the human soul.

Each story in this book is its own initiation.

Together, they form a map—from silence to song, from confusion to clarity, from fear to faith.

What began as a book has become a living ceremony: a space where intuition meets courage, where healing becomes art, and where every one of us is changed.

To those who read these pages:

May you feel the pulse of our journey within your own.

May you remember that intuition is not a whisper you must chase; it is the voice already inside you, waiting to be trusted.

May our stories remind you that even in your darkest moments, the light is never gone, only hidden, waiting for your courage to call it back.

This book is not the end. It is the beginning of something greater, a movement, a remembering, a return.

May these words be wings.

May our voices rise together like rooks at dawn, calling one another home to truth, to intuition, to love.

Love,

Mama Crow

(Dr. Tiffany McBride)

About the Author
Dr. Tiffany McBride

Dr. Tiffany McBride is a Doctor of Shamanic Psycho-Spiritual Studies, Healing Arts Minister, and Creative Coach devoted to the alchemy of healing, artistry, and soul embodiment. A clinical psychotherapist turned mystic, Tiffany bridges the worlds of science and spirit, shadow and light, trauma and transformation.

With over two decades of professional experience, she holds advanced training in somatic psychotherapy, expressive arts, EMDR, Internal Family Systems, Reiki, and trauma recovery. Tiffany has served as a therapist for youth in crisis, a grief and death doula, a music leader, and a guide for countless clients and communities navigating birth, death, and rebirth.

After burning out in traditional mental health systems, Tiffany followed her dreams. Guided by visions and synchronicities, she answered a shamanic calling that led her through initiations in the mountains, temples, and sacred sites of the world. Her lived experience has become the foundation of her business: teaching others to reclaim their intuitive voice, integrate shadow with compassion, and live in embodied sovereignty.

Through her sacred brands, Holistic Vibrations, LLC, and The Mystic Muse, Tiffany offers trauma-informed healing, intuitive mentorship, and creative direction. She believes in amplifying the voices of those who carry medicine through their stories, helping bring their visions to life through design, ceremony, and Spirit-led collaboration.

Tiffany's body of work includes *Mama Crow's Magic,* a shamanic healing program offering ritual, tarot, and energy medicine, and *The Wild Muse Healing Arts Studio,* a creative sanctuary for expressive embodiment through voice, movement, and art.

She is also the creator of *The Lotus: Healing from the Root Up,* a trauma recovery program that integrates expressive arts, chakra work, ancestral healing, and nervous system regulation. This program weaves body, emotion, spirit, and story into one path of embodied wholeness.

She is a seven-time bestselling author whose offerings weave trauma recovery, expressive arts, ceremony, and intuitive spirituality into one integrated path of transformation.

Tiffany holds a Doctorate in Shamanic Psycho-Spiritual Studies from the Venus Rising Institute for Shamanic Healing Arts, a Master's in Counseling, is Licensed as a Clinical Psychotherapist, and is an Ordained Priestess, Shamanic Minister, and Healing Arts Minister.

Her medicine lives at the crossroads of psychology and mysticism, where every story becomes sacred, every breath a spell, and every act of creation an offering of remembrance.

Acknowledgments and Gratitude

To my teachers, **Carley, John, Ruth, Stephanie, Jeremy, and Teri: thank you for modeling what authentic leadership looks like**—rooted in compassion, guided by wisdom, and sustained by Spirit. You have each taught me how to walk as a leader and way-shower, to guide not from ego, but from love, integrity, and humility.

To my dearest friends, **Mary, Vanessa, Natalie, and Zakk,** you are the heart of my circle.

Mary, you have been there through every storm and sunrise. You adopted me as your own and have loved and supported me through the hardest and holiest moments of my life.

Vanessa, you are both my best friend and business partner, my grounded sister in creation. Your support, strength, and fierce loyalty have helped me build this dream with joy and courage.

Natalie, you are my go-to person, my steady truth-teller, and my sacred mirror. You have held me when I needed to fall apart and spoken clarity when I needed to rise again.

Zakk, you've seen me at my lowest and witnessed my becoming, never judging me, always reminding me that I'm not crazy for being who I am, and continually encouraging me to follow my dreams. You've shown me that love can be both free and kind. You've been a teacher, an anchor, and an inspiration to my growth.

To **Becky,** thank you for your heart and vision in helping to design and guide the pilgrimage that inspired this book. You charted the map, wove the details, and created the structure that allowed our co-authors' journey to unfold with beauty, grace, and alignment. Your devotion helped turn an idea into a living experience.

To my extraordinary **co-authors,** thank you for saying yes to the call of your intuition and for sharing your wisdom, your medicine, and your hearts. Together, we have created something truly alive—a living testament to the power of intuition, embodiment, and courage. I love you and honor your artistry.

To **Laura Di Franco** and the team at **Brave Healer Productions,** thank you for holding this sacred container with vision, trust, and authenticity. You empower healers and truth-tellers to share their medicine with the world, and this book reflects that beautiful mission.

To the **land of Ireland,** thank you for your magic, for the stones that remember, the rivers that cleanse, the winds that speak, and the rooks who fly between worlds carrying messages of transformation.

To my **ancestors,** thank you for walking beside me, for your strength, your songs, your unfinished prayers that now move through my words.

To **The Great Mystery,** the invisible collaborator at every step of this journey, thank you for the whispers, the visions, and the courage to trust them.

And finally, to **you, the reader,** thank you for answering the invitation to journey inward. May these words remind you that your intuition is sacred, your story matters, and your voice is the key that unlocks your own alchemy.

Your Path to Healing Begins Here

If you're longing to heal, awaken, or come home to yourself, I invite you to explore my offerings through *Holistic Vibrations* and *The Mystic Muse,* two sacred branches of one vision devoted to personal transformation, intuitive embodiment, and creative remembrance.

My work integrates trauma-informed psychology, shamanic wisdom, expressive arts, and spiritual guidance to help people recover from trauma, awaken their intuition, and embody their wholeness. I offer private sessions, circles, and retreats that invite deep healing, gentle restoration, and reconnection to spirit.

Under these umbrellas live my signature programs:

Mama Crow's Magic, energy healing, tarot, and ceremony for spiritual guidance and intuitive awakening

The Wild Muse Healing Arts Studio, expressive arts, movement, and voice practices for creative embodiment and sensual liberation

The Lotus: Healing from the Root Up, a trauma recovery and soul-integration program blending somatic healing, expressive arts, and ancestral work

Each program is rooted in the same truth: healing is an act of remembrance, a return to the voice, body, and spirit that already knows the way home.

To learn more, schedule a session, or explore upcoming circles and events, visit www.tiffany-mcbride.org or www.themysticmuse.org

Your healing is sacred. Your intuition is your compass.

And your life is your medicine.

"Intuition is the quiet compass that never lies; it will burn away what isn't true until only the soul remains."
~Dr. Tiffany McBride